'These thoughtful, poignant reflections bring forth vividly some of the human dimensions of one of the great tragedies of current history, the forced dispossession of Palestinians from their homeland. They bring to mind experiences in a miserable refugee camp in Lebanon, where I was invited to the "home" − a room − of a family expelled from the Galilee, who showed me their treasures − a photograph, the key to their destroyed home, other cherished mementos of a life stolen from them for which they yearn.'

Noam Chomsky

'Diaspora is linked to displacement but is not synonymous with it, not least because displaced people may re-root themselves in new places. In this volume, Diaspora comes into being in the maintenance of personal and collective roots to an Original place of return. This handsome collection of essays speaks in a multiplicity of voices and textures that capture the enduring presence of the homeland in every Diasporic home. Palestinians and non-Palestinians will be moved by it in equal measure.'

Azmi Bishara, Arab Centre for Research
and Policy Studies, Doha

'This combination of haunting and elegant prose, gifted metaphor for unutterable loss, the rhythm of dispossession and dislocation, and triumphant love of life can only be Palestinian. What a remarkable collection of luminous essays: these stories inform and attach the reader to Palestine and her people more than a shelf of books on the "Arab–Israeli conflict".'

Karma Nabulsi, University of Oxford

'In diaspora, in Shatat, at home in exile, in historic Palestine, in refugee camps, scattered in every continent on the globe, gathered around their common cause, Palestinians are the masters of their own destiny, authors of their own lives, a nation by virtue of not just their ancestral homeland but also by a sustained history of struggle against the occupation and theft of their country. Yasir Suleiman's magnificent volume, *Being Palestinian*, gathers a number of brilliant essays reflecting on what it means to be a Palestinian. The result is an uncommon constellation of insights by some of the brightest Palestinian minds on the open-ended nature of identities and alterities we inhabit and invent as we go through a life dignified by a noble cause. A tour de force and a must read!'

Hamid Dabashi, Hagop Kevorkian Professor of Iranian Studies
and Comparative Literature, Columbia University

BEING
PALESTINIAN

Personal Reflections on Palestinian Identity
in the Diaspora

Edited by Yasir Suleiman

University of Cambridge
The Doha Institute for Graduate Studies

EDINBURGH
University Press

Edinburgh University Press Ltd
The Tun – Holyrood Road
12 (2f) Jackson's Entry
Edinburgh EH8 8PJ
www.euppublishing.com

Typeset in Baskerville by
Servis Filmsetting Ltd, Stockport, Cheshire,
and printed and bound by CPI Group (UK) Ltd,
Croydon, CR0 4YY

A CIP record for this book is available from the British Library

ISBN 978 0 7486 3402 6 (hardback)
ISBN 978 1 4744 0539 3 (paperback)
ISBN 978 0 7486 3403 3 (webready PDF)
ISBN 978 1 4744 0540 9 (epub)

Published with the support of the Edinburgh University Scholarly
Publishing Initiatives Fund and the Centre of Islamic Studies,
University of Cambridge.

In memory of Edward Said, 1935–2003

Edward Said (right) with the Editor picking up his Honorary Doctorate from the University of Edinburgh, 2000.

Contents

Yasir Suleiman   Prologue 1

Samer Abdelnour   Becoming Palestinian 15

Leila Abdul Razzaq   Beyond Recitation and Ritual 19

Danah Abdulla   Only Icons 22

Ishaq Abu-Arafeh   Resident of Both, National of None 25

Nuha Abudabbeh   Without my Jaffa: Other Seas 28

Lila Abu-Lughod   Buffeted By How Others See You 31

Lama Abu-Odeh   Disrupting the Peace of Others 34

Mahdi Abu-Omar   Fate: A Blessing 37

Salman Abu Sitta   The Invisible Face of the Occupier 40

Leena Al-Arian   A Palestinian State of Mind 44

Sami Al-Arian   No Land's Man Determined to Return to Palestine 48

Najwa Al-Qattan   An Ornithologist from Iceland 54

Samer Al-Saber   A Recurring Sound. A Familiar Image 56

Atef Alshaer   A Journey in Progress 60

Hala Alyan   In Dust 63

Kholoud Amr   Citizen of the World 66

Anonymous   Being Nobody 69

Iman Arab   Embracing Uncertainty 72

Sa'ed Atshan   'Our Country Lives in Us' 75

Abdel Bari Atwan   Forever Gazan 78

Ida Audeh   Ties that Bind, Ties that Sustain 88

Omar Aysha   Pal.I.Am 91

Ibtisam Azem   Things We Carry With Us 94

Fuad Bahou   The Sadness Continues 98
Aida Bamia   Childhood Curtailed 102
Ibtisam Barakat   Forty Days of Mourning 105
Ramzy Baroud   Seeking 'Home' 109
Sahera Bleibleh   Voices from Within 112
Reja-e Busailah   The Tree 115
Selma Dabbagh   A Road Taken 119
Taysir Dabbagh   Living in a World of Double Standards 122
Souad Dajani   Walking in Her Years 125
Susan Muaddi Darraj   Claiming Citizenship 128
Izzat Darwazeh   Breathing Politics 131
Dawoud El-Alami   Motherland 135
Najat El-Taji El-Khairy   Painting my Way Back Home One Stitch
   at a Time 137
Sharif Elmusa   A Demon of Hope 140
Doaa Elnakhala   Contradictory Worlds 145
Amal Eqeiq   *Bint Liblaad* on the Road 148
Randa Farah   Darker Shades of Exile 151
Rawan Hadid   Present in Absence 161
John Halaka   Inside as an Outsider 164
Anwar Hamed   Caught Between the Taste of Sunshine and Chopin
   Nocturnes 168
Sousan Hammad   I See Palestine in my Rear-View Mirror 171
Laila Hamzi   I Am, and I Am Always Becoming 174
Nathalie Handal   Guide to Being Palestinian 177
Jean Hanna   Memories that Live 180
Marwan Hassan   A Boy from Mash-had 183
Ghazi Hassoun   Reconciling Araby and America 186
Johnny Hazboun   When Will it be Vacant? 189
Khaled Hroub   Living in Letters or the Arrogance of a Cityless Man ... 192
Sarah Ihmoud   Palestine in the *Nepantla* 195
Mohamad Issa   Enduring Ties 199
Asma Jaber   The Pain and Beauty of Dispossession 202
Salma Khadra Jayyusi   The Durable Cords of Memory 206
Salwa Affara Jones   *Mujaddara* – Arabian Haggis! 210
Fady Joudah   Still Life 213
Khalid Kamhawi   Subversive Abstraction 215

Ghada Kanafani   Where to Now? 218

Ghada Karmi   Fitting Nowhere 221

Victor Kattan   Home is Where the Heart is. But Where is Home? 230

Tanya Keilani   A Vision Affirmed 233

Reem Kelani   Bridge to Palestine 236

Basem Khader   Badge of Honour 239

Lisa Suhair Majaj   Homemaking 241

Jean Said Makdisi   Stranger to my Own Story 244

George Makhlouf   No Room in my Luggage 247

Bashir Makhoul   Labyrinth of Memories 250

Sinan Suleiman Malley   Palestine the Brave 253

Khalil Marrar   From Ajjur to America: Rootedness in Diaspora 257

Dina Matar   In, but not Of 259

Nabil Matar   Lurching at Jericho 262

Alaa Milbes   Rolling Grape Leaves on a Map of the World 264

Fouad Moughrabi   An Act of Resistance 267

Michel Moushabeck   The *Mukhtar* and I: A Day with my Grandfather
   in the Old City 270

Ibrahim Muhawi   Parsley, *Miryamiyah*, Rosemary and *Za'tar* 274

Nadia Naser-Najjab   In Search of a Common Language 277

Sharif Hikmat Nashashibi   Fostering Palestine 280

Jamal Nassar   Seeds of Justice 284

Maha Nassar   My Resilient Flag 287

Naomi Shihab Nye   Written on his Forehead: My Father, Aziz Shihab ..296

Bashier Oudeh   Aiming High 299

Yousif Qasmiyeh   My Mother's Heels 303

Loubna Qutami   Images from a Shattered Mirror 306

Najat Rahman   Be/longing 310

Hanan Ramahi   Eating Forbidden Palestine 313

Omar Ramahi   Palestinian-Something 316

Aftim Saba   No Paradise to Recreate 319

Karl Sabbagh   A Mission to Explain 323

Najla Said   A Heavy, Unwieldy Bag 326

Mohammad Sakhnini   Lost to Geography 330

Saliba Sarsar   Transcending Blind Allegiance 333

Suha Shakkour   Still a Palestinian 336

Abbas Shiblak   Homing Instincts 339

Ghadir Siyam   Born(e) in the Heart 342

Linda Tabar   Bodily Wounds and the Journey Home 345

Simine Tepper   Holding Palestine Close to my Heart 348

Omar Tesdell   When All is Not What it Seems 351

Lena Khalaf Tuffaha   The Weight of Our Blessings 354

Nadia Yaqub   A Sometime Palestinian 358

Munther Younes   Entry Denied 361

Jameel Zayed   Barricaded 364

Glossary 367

Prologue

The year is 2006. In the Palestinian national consciousness, 1948, the year of the *Nakba* (Catastrophe), and 1967, the year of the *Naksa* (Setback), are traumatic watersheds that mark the loss of Palestine. These two dates are flanked on both sides by other dates that are etched deep in Palestinian national consciousness: 1917, the year Arthur Balfour, British Foreign Secretary, promised Palestine to the second Baron Rothschild (Lionel Walter Rothschild, 1868–1937) as a 'national home' for the Jewish people; 1936, the year of the Palestinian Revolt against British rule in Palestine and Zionist immigration to the country; 1982, the year of the Israeli invasion of Lebanon and the massacre of Palestinians in the refugee camps of Sabra and Shatila in Beirut; 1987, the year of the First Palestinian Intifada, and 2000, the year of the Second Palestinian Intifada; 2002, the year of the massacre at Jenin Camp on the West Bank; 2009, the year of Operation Cast Lead, in which many Palestinians in Gaza were killed in a massive air, sea and land attack by Israeli forces; and 2014, the year of Operation Protective Edge, in which thousands of Palestinians in Gaza perished in another massive attack by the same forces. Judging by the disastrous logic of the past, the list is bound to grow.

In this context, 'Prologue' is, sadly, a fitting name for this preface. It signals a beginning without a foreseeable end. There is no 'Epilogue' here, in spite of the fact that a 'Prologue' seems to demand its 'Epilogue'.

The year is 2006. This is when the idea of working on this book came to me. I had been living and working in Scotland for more than a quarter of a century at the time when I decided to uproot myself and my family and move to England for a professorship at the University of Cambridge. For a Palestinian who was desperately trying to put down roots, the decision to dismantle his 'temporary abode' and move it elsewhere was a personal trauma: not 1948 or 1967, but still a small tremor on the Palestinian Richter scale for one Palestinian and his family. I thought then that I had settled down comfortably in Scotland with my Palestinian wife and two Palestinian-Scottish children, where I worked happily as a professor at the University of Edinburgh, but the decision to move south gave the lie to this feeling of settled-ness. As a Palestinian in the diaspora, I reasoned to myself, life must be lived on the move, as a state of being in search of a resolution that is unlikely to be achieved in my lifetime ('home is carried home in one's bones', as one contributor tells us). It was at that muddled moment of soul-searching that, as a form of personal therapy, I decided to look into the possibility of asking other Palestinians to reflect on their personal identity in the diaspora; hence the title of this book – *Being Palestinian: Personal Reflections on Palestinian Identity in the Diaspora.*

'Diaspora' is a generic term which encompasses the diversity of Palestinian lived experience. It comes in different forms and intensities that are full of 'palestinian moments' (the lower case of Palestinian is intentional). Even for Palestinians who stayed put when Israel was established in 1948, the earth violently rocked and moved from under their feet, diasporising them in situ. Palestinians in the Palestinian Administered Territories, East Jerusalem and Gaza are stranded in a space between two oppressive regimes: the quixotic banality of Palestinian rule, where 'Administered' acts as a surrogate term for 'Occupied', and the oppressive reality of Israeli hegemony that transforms 'Occupation' into 'Administration'. Palestinians in Lebanon are outcasts across the border of their ancestral homeland, so near yet so impossibly and excruciatingly far. Palestinians elsewhere in the Arab world are in a state of limbo waiting for that self-same Godot that all Palestinians, Samuel Beckett-style, are waiting for. Will Godot ever come? No one knows! But wait the Palestinians must!

The term 'diaspora' in the title of this book was problematic for some contributors. While all contributors agreed that they are not immigrants in their countries of abode, they do not all agree on the use of 'diaspora' to describe their situation. Some prefer 'exile' to diaspora, as a few of the contributions reveal. This is not an academic book, so I will eschew my instinctual clamour for precision in favour of discursive ambiguity. The Palestinians are in the

diaspora, whatever this means, not out of choice but because of bitter necessity. As exiles, they dream of returning home one day or having their home
back, but they are not allowed to exercise this right of return. Some contributors prefer the term *Shatat*, meaning 'dispersal' in Arabic, to refer to their situation of being forcibly uprooted from their native land, painfully separated
from family, agonisingly scattered around the world and illegally denied their
right of return – all within living memory.

Diaspora is *Shatat* in this book. Initially, I wanted to use this term in the
title of the book to inscribe the Palestinian experience in Palestinian idiom.
At one stage in the process of compiling the contributions to the book, I even
played with the idea of implanting this term in the title as *Shat-at* rather than
Shatat to signal aspects of the Palestinian experience in 'metaphorical' terms,
but was dissuaded from doing so because of the vulgarity of the hyphenated
term and the offence it may cause the readers, especially Palestinians. In the
end, I decided against using the Arabic term *Shatat*, hyphenated or not, lest it
stands as a barrier between the book and its readership, most of whom I hope
will be of non-Palestinian descent. This is a book by people of Palestinian
descent for, mostly, people of non-Palestinian descent who may be curious to
learn (more) about Palestine and Palestinians. For these readers the book is
about 'diaspora'. Readers of Palestinian descent can gloss diaspora as *Shatat*
if they prefer this term.

One contributor describes diaspora like this:

> Diaspora is an endless absence, time-lapse photography in reverse. It is the
> desire to become an archaeologist or preservationist, to become the keeper
> of memories belonging to others. To remember names of villages long
> buried in dust. Diaspora is reminding yourself, in the bleakest moments –
> another war, another smattering of bombs – that as long as you have
> lungs, and air to fill them, you, and those that come after you, will be the
> memento, the living memory of place.

Diaspora? *Shatat*? 'What's in a name?' The reality is the same. There are no
roses here and the experiential scent is not so sweet.

Identity comes to the fore at times of collective stress, conflict or moments
of great national joy and celebration, of which there is a dearth in Palestinian
life. Considering the kind of conditions Palestinians live under and their
transnational connectivities, Palestinian identity exists in a state of constant

alert, waiting to come to the fore at every pulling of a trigger, destruction of a home, uprooting of an olive tree, burning of a field, crossing of a checkpoint, building of a settlement and at every border crossing, even when a diasporic Palestinian travels on a passport of his or her acquired citizenship. Border crossing as a site of anxiety and identity negotiation is mentioned by several contributors in the volume. Being American, British or Canadian does not shield a diasporic Palestinian from being Palestinian. In some cases, a name can act as a sign of earlier belonging for border officials. In other cases, a place of birth in Palestine has the same effect. At borders, this identification ignites a host of feelings in Palestinians that range from fear and insecurity through discomfort and victimisation to feelings of pride and resentment. I am therefore not surprised that one contributor glosses being Palestinian as a 'preference of closeness over distance [and] the choice of domestic comforts over adventures abroad'.

Being Palestinian may act like a burden at border crossings, as it does for some in everyday life, but it serves to remind a Palestinian that she or he can never take who they are for granted. Being Palestinian is a destiny within which one can negotiate a space of one's own but from which one cannot escape. Having amassed more than 1,500,000 British Airways air miles in less than a decade, I have had experience with these feelings. At some Arab airports I get asked if I am Israeli because of my place of birth, Jerusalem, in spite of my name. At non-Arab airports, I am simply assumed to be Israeli. When I answer that I am not, it initiates a conversation in which I declare that my part of Jerusalem was occupied by Israel in 1967, but this does not make me Israeli. 'Who I am' is not, as the contributions in this volume reveal, a quotidian part of life for Palestinians as it is for most people: it imprints itself as a marked state of being which hovers close to the surface during encounters with border officials. Being Palestinian reminds you of your statelessness in spite of the fact that you have a mark of citizenship in your possession. You are absent-present and, as one contributor puts it, you must 'occupy your absence with cheerful presence'.

This is not a book of memoirs. It is a book of personal reflections. The contributors were asked to avoid formal politics as much as possible and to focus on what it means for each one of them to be Palestinian in the diaspora. They were also asked to speak from the heart without the overly obtrusive intervention of the intellect. This is an unrealistic constraint to place on any piece of writing, but it was flagged to draw contributors away from the public to the private domain of 'being Palestinian' as much as possible. The final judgement on whether this has worked or not will be left to the reader. From my perspective as editor, I was surprised by how successful this 'formula' was.

On reading and rereading the contributions over the course of preparing the book for publication, I was drawn again and again into private worlds that differed from mine in their materiality but resonated with me on an emotional level. That being said, it was not possible in all cases to wean contributors off the 'overt' or 'high' politics of Palestine. Every time I pressed this point the response was one of incredulity: how can the editor, a Palestinian, divorce Palestine from its politics? Can the personal be divorced from the collective? Why can't a spade be called a spade? In every case, I retorted that Palestine needed to be narrated through reflections, however short, that can give readers a glimpse of what it means to be Palestinian for those who are considered to be lucky enough to live in the diaspora. In every case, the comforts and privileges of the diaspora, whatever these may be or are imagined to be, could not erase engagement with Palestine as a location and object of belonging that is inseparable from injustice, bewilderment, disbelief, denial, grief, vulnerability, loss, pain, suffering, struggle, adaptation, survival, resilience, resistance, hope, anger, friendship, marginality, oppression, transgression, occupation, bombardment, siege, brutality, rupture, displacement, temporariness, statelessness, restlessness (as one contributor expresses it: 'I am a Palestinian rock that is still rolling to its final resting place') and a myriad of other emotions which the reader will easily identify, directly or indirectly, in the contributions that follow.

In a memorable formulation of what being Palestinian means, one contributor tells us: 'Being Palestinian, I learnt from a young age, means being hammered on an anvil . . . [It] is waking up to displacement, lunching with diaspora and going to bed with dispossession.' Another contributor couches being Palestinian in the idiom of love: 'In some ways, [it] is like being young and in love, feeling a passion and a tenderness that never fades even if the beloved departs.' Another contributor writes that 'being Palestinian is a pain in the neck'. No wonder one contributor says: 'Sometimes, often, I wish I could forget Palestine', before she tells us that she couldn't. Another contributor arrives at the same point from a different angle: 'I don't know what kinds of birds make Iceland their home, but it has become my custom to conclude many of my rants regarding events in Palestine with a refrain, according to which, in my next life, I want to be an ornithologist from Iceland. Being Icelandic might not necessarily protect my name from universal butchery, but who hates Icelanders and who doesn't love birds?' This feeling is reiterated, with a twist, in another contribution: 'Being Palestinian, in the end, might actually be worth its cumbersome, unwieldy, often torturous, weight'.

It would be impossible to cover all the reflective strands in this book. I have referred to border crossing above as a site of encounter and identity in these reflections. I have also highlighted the view of Palestine as a burden that can't be shed. Another strand of identity and belonging consists of material culture, including the binding force of food (*knafeh, labaneh, malfouf, maqloubeh, mujaddara, molokhiyeh, musakhan, tabbouleh, zait* and *za'tar*), with its textures and aromas; trees (olive, lemon, fig, orange, plum, grape, vine, cactus); embroidery and landscapes (fields, hills and the sea). To this strand may be added such cultural forms as music, poetry and dance, especially *dabke* (a ceremonial dance at weddings and other occasions). These items recur in many reflections. Out of all of them *dabke* surprised me the most, but the more I thought about this site of belonging the more I understood its importance in articulating Palestinian identity. Dance is a celebratory public activity that is associated with joy, an emotion in short supply in Palestinian national life. *Dabke* is also a collective form of dance where the exuberance of youth is expressed through feelings of national pride and bonds of togetherness that cut across the gender divide. It affords the dancers the opportunity to display the sounds and sights of Palestine, the former through music and song and the latter, emblematically, through the traditional embroidered dresses of Palestine. *Dabke* therefore emerges as a form of tactile encounter with Palestine as point of reference. It engages the eyes and the ears, in the same way as food engages the taste buds and spring blossom engages our sense of smell. In spite of all the pain and suffering that are an integral part of being Palestinian, Palestine remains an object of love.

And as a scholar of language in the social world, I was delighted to note how, for some contributors, the special cadences and flavour of Palestinian Arabic act as an anchor in weaving Palestinian identity.

Another strand of being Palestinian is connectedness to family. Mothers, fathers, grandparents, children and grandchildren connect the present to the past and the future. In various forms of familial commemoration, Palestine continues to be re-enacted as a story of loss and hope, mourning and delayed recuperation; a legacy that is passed down the generations with re-energised and renewed meanings with every passing. Whether a half English, quarter American and quarter Palestinian grandchild playing for the Palestinian national women's football team, a daughter on a visit to Palestine remembering her dying father in the diaspora, or a father pondering whether it is right to inflict Palestine on his children, Palestine continues to be a locus of self-definition even when the erasure of that identity is contemplated. It is interesting to note that even when active efforts are taken to deny Palestinianness, they often don't succeed. Some of the contributions in this volume bear witness to that. The grandson will always try to recover what the grandfather wanted his son to forget. Forgetfulness is easier when the object of the heart is there to have, but is harder to achieve when this object is absent-present as Palestine is.

I have always been aware of the role of family as a conduit for sustaining Palestine as a site of memory and identity. My father imprinted this on me through stories of his exploits as a recruit in the Ottoman Army in Palestine, especially of how he escaped from Ramle (between Jerusalem and Jaffa) and trekked back to Jerusalem to find his elder brother on the other side of the trench, armed with no more than a Palestinian-style Irish shillelagh, bluffing to shoot him for trespassing, not knowing that he was threatening to shoot his own brother. Another exploit was my father's love affair, an 'innocent' one I am sure, with a Greek Orthodox girl from Bethlehem. Her family threatened to dispose of him, a Muslim boy, for transgressing the faith divide. A plucky young man, he sought protection from a rival Greek Orthodox family from Ramallah who changed his family name from Ma'ālī to Dibā'ī, producing a faith hybrid, helped him to obtain a Palestinian passport with his newly acquired identity and then sent him to Tiberias to work for a Palestinian Jew of some independent means.

The young Ibrahim, a handsome man (to that I can testify), bought the Jew off, acquired wealth and married Aziza, a Damascene woman of Kurdish origin. Aziza's family had left Damascus for Tiberias when their only son was shot dead by a Senegalese soldier, at the time of the French occupation of Syria, for breaking a city-wide curfew. Lurking behind this story of wealth and romance lies a story of unrequited love. Prior to his marriage to Aziza, the crafty Ibrahim had led the Tiberian Jew to think that he would marry his daughter who had fallen for him, but he didn't. As a little boy I would ask my father if he turned her down because she was a Jew. 'No,' he would answer,

'I just couldn't bring myself to marry one of the ugliest women in Tiberias!' My elder brother from my father's first marriage remembered the woman in question well. He always backed our father up every time I asked him the same question on my visits to Graz, Austria where he lived most of his life until his death in 2001.

I relate this story here as an act of remembrance to paint a picture of communal life before and immediately after the death sentence that Arthur Balfour issued against Palestine in November 1917: Christians, Jews, Muslims, Kurds, Jerusalemites, Tiberians and Damascenes in a melting pot of love, rivalry and feuding, coalescing in the life of one Palestinian. It is this image of Palestine that I nostalgically yearn for, aware of the fact that my nostalgia is a hopeless form of romanticism that will never be realised.

The reflections in this book follow different formats, styles and stances. The majority are in prose of different degrees of evocativeness. A small number are in poetry. Others combine poetry with prose. Some are sure of what they say. Others are more tentative. Some are forward in their assertions. Others are more subtle. Some are allegorical. Others narrate from the hip. Some scream. Others whisper. Some think of Palestine as a gift from the gods. Others think of it as a burden they cannot shed no matter how hard they try. This raises the question of what Palestine is for Palestinians in the diaspora. It is a hard question to answer because of the many inflections and variations Palestine receives in this book. Perhaps the answer should be that Palestine means different things to different people, but these different meanings resonate with all Palestinians in the diaspora even when they hold different views of the 'one and the same' Palestine. Don't worry if you are confused. I am too.

As used in this book, 'reflection' is not the mirroring of experience but a refraction of it. It involves distortion, fracture and (re)construction without, however, totally losing the connection with its source. The refraction of a stick in a glass of water will be perceived as refraction of that stick and not of some other object. The cover page of this book provides an illustration of this notion of reflection as refraction. It is a constructed representation of aspects of my diasporic Palestinian-ness. In the middle stands my younger son, Sinan, a kilted Scottish-Palestinian who has his own reflection in the book, with his back to the gazer but with his gaze fixed on a constructed image of two cities: the Old City of Jerusalem to the left and Edinburgh, Scotland to the right. Our between-ness as father and son is bounded, in different inflections, by these two places with all the feelings they evoke in us.

However, the image of Jerusalem on the front cover inverts a dominant gaze of the city among Palestinians whereby the Dome of the Rock, or some other Islamic monument, tends to be the central object of the gazer. Here I chose to put the church before the mosque to reflect my belief that Jerusalem's strong ties with Christianity constitute a Palestinian strand of identity that transcends the narrow confines of faith. In that sense, Jerusalem belongs to non-Christian Palestinians as umbilically as it does to Christian Palestinians. By framing the image in this interpretative gaze, Jerusalem begins to go beyond narrow or blinkered interpretations of Palestinian-ness that privilege its links to Islam in contemporary Palestinian discourse. In fact, I wanted to include an image of the Wailing Wall in the same snapshot to press the point that there was a time before the intervention of Zionism in Palestine towards the end of the nineteenth century when Jerusalem belonged to Jewish Palestinians as much as it did to their Christian and Muslim compatriots, but, regrettably, I was unable to find such an image. I am therefore inviting the reader to use his or her mind's eye to rectify this deficit in order to restore to Palestine its native Jewishness that Balfour, a Scot, helped cause it to lose.

Would my son in the cover picture have been born in Edinburgh, capital of Balfour's country, had it not been for his promise to Baron Rothschild to dispossess the Palestinians of their land? I think not. In spite of this, Scotland was kind to me and my family, a kindness my mother refuses to acknowledge even to this day. At the age of eighty-eight, she continues to remind me that my father, who was born in Palestine in 1889 under Ottoman rule, would, until the end of time, never forgive me for coming to think of Scotland as a 'home' from home. Maybe it was a mistake to take her to visit the grounds of Balfour's stately home, outside Edinburgh, when she came to visit in 1993. She stood there in total disgust and prayed to God Almighty that one day I would inherit Balfour's estate and that, to appease my father's soul, I would raise the Palestinian flag over his home as if to claim a share of my Palestine in my Scotland.

My mother is a strong believer in God. Her prayers remain unfulfilled. She is an old woman and she hasn't forgiven me. I doubt if she ever will.

There are many books on Palestine and the Palestinians, mainly in Palestine itself and in the Arabic-speaking world, that tell the story of the place and its people. As noted above, this volume is not a collection of personal memoirs, but a book of reflections from afar. The contributors to this book are drawn from the English-speaking world, mainly Canada, the United Kingdom and the United States. The restriction to parts of the English-speaking world was a pragmatic one. It would have been difficult to include contributors from diverse linguistic backgrounds. If it is true that people live their lives in language, different languages are bound to refract our experience of life differently. Also, a book in English by and about Palestinians in the English-speaking diaspora may take advantage of the global reach of the language. It is therefore hoped that the book will find its way into the Arab world and beyond, and that it will be emulated and bettered to help build a more comprehensive picture of what it means to be Palestinian in the diaspora.

I have said above that this is not an academic book. There was therefore no strict method in choosing the contributors to the volume. What we have here therefore is not a representative sample of Palestinians. The guiding principle for inviting people to contribute was 'variety'. I wanted to include Palestinian men and women of different faith or no faith background, different ages and different educational and professional achievements from Canada, the UK and USA. Following this, I prepared a two-page statement of the purpose and format of the proposed volume to include in the invitation to contributors, with two sample contributions from *Being Scottish: Personal Reflections on Scottish Identity Today* (Edinburgh University Press, 2002). I sent this statement with the samples (in spite of the fact that the book from which these samples were drawn had a different focus) to a few friends for comments, and asked them to send me names, with short biographical notes, of people who they thought would be willing to contribute and able to write. This process yielded a set of names which, through snowballing, expanded with every invitation. Needless to say, not everyone who was invited agreed to contribute. Some turned the invitation down for lack of time. Others thought that the strict format of allocating circa 1,000 words for each contribution was too restrictive and declined to take part. Most, however, agreed to write. Some contributors veered from the purpose of the book and offered overt political reflections, which I had to turn down. The majority took the project to heart. In some cases a reflection was accepted in the form it was submitted. In other cases contributors were offered comments to help them produce a new version. Most interventions of this kind touched on matters of style and sequencing, with no attempt to interfere with content.

Originally there was no intention to include titles with the contributions, but this changed in the later stages of the project. Contributors were therefore asked to provide titles which, while being informative and tempting, could also serve as heuristic devices that would enable the reader to capture the content in a memorable way. The suggestion to incorporate photographs came later too, the intention being to add a visual element to the reflections. Contributors were therefore invited to submit images which in some way reflected the content of their contributions or are of special meaning to them. This was not an easy task for all. Nadia Naser-Najjab and her daughter trawled through the archives of their local library to get a scan of the newspaper article about their husband and father caught in Palestine during the Second Intifada; Aftim Saba took on the bruising Arizona sun in the height of summer to take pictures of a variety of trees in his 'Palestinian' garden; and Victor Kattan coordinated with his parents in the UK from Singapore to dig through their archive of family photos. I hope the reader will find the images in the book of some interest. In this context, I should declare that I am guilty of including more than one image of my father, my defence being that they link well with what I said above.

I have edited several academic books in my lifetime but none proved harder and, I am glad to say, more rewarding than this one. To my surprise, I discovered that it was not easy to find one hundred or so Palestinian contributors to write. It was also hard to keep track of all the contributions. Turning a contribution down was always heart-breaking. Asking for revisions was at times very tricky. However, the vast majority of contributors realised the value of the project, took it to heart and cooperated fully. To each and every one of them a heartfelt thank you! I was, however, sad that Basem Khader passed away before we were able to publish this book. May the Lord bless him and may his soul rest in peace.

A project of this kind is a big undertaking. I thought of it and 'took the plunge' before I realised that it would be impossible for me to continue without editorial help. Dr Saeko Yazaki, now of the University of Glasgow, helped in the initial stages. I am grateful for the help she gave me. However, I owe a huge thank you to Philip Rushworth, who stepped in halfway through and got the project going again when I feared it would never be finished. Philip kept an impeccable record of all contributions and all correspondence. He immersed himself in reading every contribution, offered editorial suggestions and ensured that contributors did not lose patience with the editor. Philip and I used to meet at Café Nero on King's Parade, Cambridge to discuss the project. Over cups of espresso in what Philip christened my 'Alternative Office', we discussed every step of the project. When we realised that an image of the grave of Abbas Shiblak's mother was an important image to have, Philip travelled to Oxford – the 'Other Place', as we call it in Cambridge – to take the picture we included in the volume. I am therefore happy to record my personal thanks, in spades and in one hundred and three bottles of extra-virgin Palestinian olive oil – one on behalf of each contributor plus one from me personally – to Philip for his stalwart support, perseverance and insatiable sense of humour.

In the process of helping me edit this book Philip came as close as possible to becoming a Palestinian. Such was his dedication he visited Palestine at his own expense for a month to immerse himself in what it means to be Palestinian. Because of this and everything else I am happy to declare Philip an 'Honorary Palestinian'. I hope he will find satisfaction in knowing that the book has, at long last, seen the light of day.

This book is dedicated to the memory of Edward Said. I am not sure if Edward would have agreed with the idea or the title of the book, or with this Prologue. Nor am I sure he would have written for it had he been invited, although I am delighted that Najla Said and Jean Said Makdisi, his daughter and sister respectively, are among the contributors. I had the good luck to host Edward in Edinburgh, Scotland on three occasions: twice as a keynote speaker at conferences held at the university and the third when I proposed him for an Honorary Doctorate, which the university happily conferred on him in 2000, a year ahead of the 250th anniversary of the teaching of Arabic at the university. The last occasion gave me and my friend Ibrahim Muhawi, a contributor to this volume, the opportunity to travel with Edward in and around Edinburgh to visit places that interested him, including the Scottish Borders, Sir Walter Scott's country and Rosslyn Chapel, with its connections to the Holy Grail and the one hundred and ten Green Men which Ibrahim connected to our homeland, in an act of great erudition, through the figure of St George, the Patron Saint of Palestine, who is called Al-Khader by Muslim Palestinians. Observing the generous man behind the public persona over two days was sufficient to convince me that his international standing was rooted in 'palestinian moments' of the kind in this volume. Edward was our guest, but he often insisted on paying, and he often won.

The reflections in the book are arranged alphabetically. I originally intended to organise the reflections thematically, but this proved impossible.

Such was the rich and multifarious content of the reflections that any thematic arrangement would have proved to be arbitrary and unconvincing. That being said, this is not a book that needs to be read sequentially from beginning to end. The reader may start from any reflection and go back and forth as he or she wishes.

It is a formality for an author to take responsibility for all errors and mistakes in a publication that appears under his or her name, whether it is a monograph or an edited volume such as this one. I do so here not as a formality but in a genuine acceptance that all mistakes and errors are mine. However, I cannot take responsibility for the content of the contributions. The responsibility here remains with each contributor.

Finally, I would like to thank Nicola Ramsey and Ellie Bush of Edinburgh University Press for their patience and for keeping faith with me and the project. I am grateful to them for not giving up (others might have done so). I also wish to record my thanks to Rebecca Mackenzie who worked very closely with me to produce the book cover, and to Sinan Malley who accepted being in it, taking time out of his studies to be photographed in different locations in Edinburgh. Wearing his kilt, Sinan cut a handsome figure. Tourists thought he was a celebrity and posed for pictures with him, not knowing that inside the kilted Scot there was a Palestinian. At the risk of being smug as a parent, Sinan's image gives this volume an exquisitely special meaning that I will cherish and treasure until the end.

Yasir Suleiman
Cambridge
May 2015

Samer Abdelnour

Samer Abdelnour is an academic, activist, and founding board member of Al-Shabaka: the Palestinian Policy Network. Born in Canada to Palestinian parents, he now lives in Europe. His family is from Nablus / Salfit and Nazareth.

Becoming Palestinian

As a child, Palestine was omnipresent, manifested in stories of dispossession, long-distance phone calls to Ramallah shouted over bad connections, photos of my young parents and our baptism, visitors from abroad, shouting at the evening news (which almost always equated being Palestinian with terrorism). My parents were working hard to make a life for us in Canada, yet Palestine was very much part of their lives: political talks between my father and uncle, mom calling family on holidays, our traditions, food. I did not know Palestine but she was somehow there.

When enquiring about a job (at around twelve or thirteen years old), I recall a clerk asking me my name. With my response followed another question: 'Where are you from?'

'Here', I responded.

Unsatisfied, the clerk asked, 'Are you Arabian?' I was confused. 'Where is your family from?'

I somehow sensed the essence of the question: 'Oh, Palestine!'

Growing up in a culturally diverse immigrant working/middle-class environment, everyone was both Canadian and from somewhere else. Yet my parents were not simply from somewhere else, they were from Palestine. And Palestine was like the moon: beautiful, mysterious, present on most evenings, something to talk and dream of, faraway and out of reach; a place we never visited.

This notion of Palestine began to change (also around thirteen) with new-found political consciousness. In a very short time Palestine morphed from background-mundanity to grotesque-abnormality. I came to understand my parents' frustrations and the family situation 'back home' as part of a wider system. What was this Palestine, then? A theatre of occupation, displacement, injustice and oppression, humiliation, fears for family, state violence, vilification. Palestine was a struggle and my personal *Nakba* a product of her narrative – a history of violence. Like many youth at that critical age, I found political hip hop. The lyrics of Public Enemy reached into me, deeply. They spoke an angry, sophisticated education of undercurrents in the world around me. Palestine was at once a Black struggle, a fight against institutional discrimination and violence, olive steel in an era of chaos. Palestine became an indigenous struggle for self-determination, a stand against ethnic cleansing; I could be idle no more. South Africa's Bantustans, Biko,[1] defiance at Oka;[2] I began to understand. By the time of the Gulf War I had no choice but to make sense of my own politics, my difference. I refused the labels others spoke our way: 'fucking Arab', 'Iraqi Paki'. No – I am Palestinian!

As an undergraduate student I first met other Palestinians outside of family and church; from different places we came together to explore shared politics and culture. I was ashamed at my inability to command our language, and envious of the others who knew my family and places of origin back home. Yet these anxieties faded, to be replaced by a powerful unspoken connection. Together we celebrated being Palestinian. We reached for the moon. Palestine: duty and pleasure, love and burden.

Of course, the elation of being Palestinian does not come without pain, frustration and cynicism. No, we in the diaspora do not suffer the same violence and humiliation as our people back home, but I tell you, there are times we suffocate and break under the impossible weight of our own helplessness.

Gutted empty soul shattered heart. Tortured among the dead, I will not rest in peace. Broken, I no longer feel pain.

Demon! You displace families, rewrite history, bulldoze villages and cover them with alien trees and smiles. In 1982 you lit the skies for your henchmen to cut open the wombs of mothers. You birthed me that day, demon. Traumatised with bombs and sonic booms; those insane days, months we did not sleep and went insane. Broke my little fingers for throwing stones at tanks, crippled my hands. I ate prison over curfew for wanting milk and bread. Our leaders poisoned, universities destroyed, to kill dreams. You treat dogs better than us. You crush aspirations, but I remember.

I can't breathe from the weight of destroyed buildings; collapsing chest prevents my drowning in your river of our blood. My body is broken, soul dead. My heart is void of love, hope. Buried. Do you not know that I am here?

From this living tomb I hear sounds of massacre. In Gaza I survive your genocide project. Drink from the pool of this pain so it doesn't drown us. Maggots and roaches crawl into mouths, nourish broken bodies, heal bones. I wait for strength to shed the dead weight of this broken spirit. I resist by throwing shards of my shattered heart into your eyes. I survive this holocaust inheritance. I reclaim all that you've taken from me.[3]

Landed, an alien at home. Family, soil, history, all strangely familiar. At once I knew the family in Palestine better than those I was raised with in Canada. How is it possible that in Palestine I am both whole and invisible? Not anonymous, but an imposter: too soft with childish Arabic, a tourist with family. Lineage displaced by violence. Olive trees from before the time of Christ – powerfully inconsequential.

> dark clouds crown *Jerusalem*
> the *ithan* battles the wind
> each wants to be heard
>
> God and man's interpretation
> demanding i submit
> my insignificance[4]

Going through boxes of photographs at my late grandfather's flat, I found pictures and holiday letters, many from us and of us. Imagine! All these years we were there in a drawer, or perhaps on display, with Sido, in the heart of Ramallah.

A plot of grass, the unmarked grave of my grandparents.[5]

The journey continues. We work to connect ourselves in Palestine and the world over through spaces of dialogue, disagreement, strategy and shared vision. Each generation more sophisticated, with new tools and initiatives to ensure our voices travel. Our ideals and aspirations must continue to shape the path to rights, freedom and return. Many wonderful people join our struggle and we embrace them. Some may fall out of our favour and we theirs (and that is fine). We must be cautious of those who use our cause for psychological and financial gain (and there are many).

What does the future hold? We live the catastrophe; dark times which demand vision and honesty. We work to shed egos, turn our pockets inside out. To me, the materialisation of Palestinian ideals requires the preservation of history, a celebration of shared cultures, institutional equality and economic resistance. But we should not be fooled. Like South Africa, a Palestine free from apartheid's poisons will be a place of immense social inequality. In freedom, Palestine will find herself in disarray, disoriented, fragile; in subtle, serious decline. We are nearing the midpoint of a long journey and struggle. 'Institutions' do not confer rights. Citizenship alone will not sustain life. Statehood does not equate freedom. Land and return are but a pretext; we must prepare now – for health, happiness and wellbeing.

Notes

1. Steve Biko was an anti-apartheid activist who died in prison in Pretoria on 12 September 1977 after being interrogated for twenty-two hours in Port Elizabeth police headquarters.
2. The Oka Crisis was a land dispute between the Mohawk people and the town of Oka in Quebec, Canada from 11 July to 26 September 1990.
3. Poem titled 'Gaza (reflections from a living tomb)', January 2009.
4. 'Calling', March 2013.
5. 'Nablus', February 2014.

Leila Abdul Razzaq

Leila Abdul Razzaq is half Arab, half white, and entirely Palestinian. Born in Chicago, she spent seven years of her childhood in Seoul, South Korea. She is an undergraduate at DePaul University, organises with Students for Justice in Palestine (SJP) locally and nationally, and is the author and illustrator of Baddawi, *a graphic novel about her father's life.*

Beyond Recitation and Ritual

In the beginning, being Palestinian was nothing more than a recitation. When asked, the six-year-old's stock reply was, 'My dad's Palestinian but he's from Lebanon.' When questioned further by adults who knew more about the history of her people than she did, she came up empty-handed. Still, she knew the difference between ethnicity and nationality at an early age, and better than most of her peers – except for maybe those others whose parents' tongues were laced with other languages, and whose dinner tables featured inordinate amounts of chickpeas-and-other-strange-foods.

It was at some point in middle school when things started to shift. Suddenly her friend said something bad about Arabs. 'But I'm Arab,' she said. 'You're not really Arab,' was her friend's reply.

What was 'really Arab'? Was it like *Teyta* praying in the guest room, performing an unknowable ritual? Like *Jiddo*'s hairline she didn't have, sweet tea she didn't drink, or the way her father sang off-key in the car along to lyrics she couldn't comprehend? Her favourite pastries were the fingers – was it something in all the nutty squares and triangles she had been missing out on? Or maybe it was related to the way her father made her recite those words as she fell asleep: '*bismallah al rahman al rahim*' (In the name of God, the Compassionate, the Merciful), and almost half the *sura*. He said 'repeat after me' until she had committed it to memory, and that was the extent of her religious education – syllables sans understanding. Maybe that was the problem.

At any rate, when she returned home from school and reported what her friend had said about people from the Middle East, the American mother was angrier than her Arab daughter.

Often as people get older and begin to learn things, the world starts to make more sense. Eventually, you realise most people's parents did not grow up in a civil war. Eventually, your mom tells you that your grandparents survived a massacre – a hidden piece of history you had unknowingly carried around comes to light, and you're not sure what to do with it. Eventually, the question, 'What's the West Bank?' You can find Lebanon on a map, but locating Palestine is harder because it's unlabelled, peeking through something named 'Israel'. Eventually, you catch a glimpse of just how far your father came from the refugee camp – a distance that can't be measured in miles travelled or hours spent in the sky or years whisked away by work. And eventually, the realisation that you'd always imagined your stillborn sister would have been blonde like your mom, even though you and your brother are all dark curly hair and big brown eyes.

This is probably when the totality of the situation descends upon you: you are Palestinian. Your father is from Lebanon. And suddenly you find yourself entrenched in something that you didn't know was there, but that was always around you. So you realise that even though you're older, stuff doesn't make more sense. In fact, everything is kind of falling apart. And this is when we in the *Shatat* find ourselves at a crossroads; we have the option to embrace our identity or disown it.

So suddenly you wish you knew how to speak Arabic. So suddenly life is all frantic reading and you are the student that keeps arguing with her teachers, and you are the angry fifteen-year-old posting naïve political tirades on Facebook. So suddenly that difference between nationality and ethnicity is really important. So when you reach the crossroads what can you do but set aside official forms of identification? You forget foreign passports and state IDs and say, 'I am Palestinian.' You say, 'My mother is white, my father is Arab, I grew up in Chicago and Seoul, and all of these things are precisely what make me Palestinian.'

This is the realisation that it's because of diaspora, not in spite of it, that you are Palestinian. This is the realisation that gives you peace when at last you see that just because others are confused by your identity, doesn't mean you have to be confused about it too. This is the realisation that often being Palestinian is a multinational, multiracial and transcontinental experience that spans miles, moments and years but cannot be measured in any of those ways.

So this is what we use to measure the unique experience of being Palestinian: the names and ages of our loved ones. Their birthdays. How many cups of coffee did we drink today? What is the name of our family's village? And what is the name of our favourite fruit? And what shall we put on the grocery list? It's pretty mundane stuff and I guess that's what being Palestinian is too – mundane. But it's a beautiful kind of mundane that makes you want to live forever, just so you can see the freedom of your people as the wall is smashed to smithereens, and the looks on everyone's faces as they flood through the gates of the Old City, just so you can witness in reality the elaborate fantasy of return that you've spent a lifetime composing in your head, even though you know it will probably be far messier than you imagine because nothing in our history has been clean, or simple, or devoid of blood, but hey we can dream, can't we?

So once again, we find ourselves at recitation. 'I am Palestinian,' we say, always waiting for the response, because there always is one. Sometimes it's surprise, like they've never met one before. They may ask about our political views. Sometimes sympathy, pity, confusion or fear. Sometimes fetishisation. Sometimes a blank stare, or 'Do you speak Palestinian?', or 'That's next to India, right?' And occasionally enthusiasm, usually from other Arabs or Palestinians in diaspora who recognise the choice you've made at the crossroads.

Danah Abdulla

Danah Abdulla is a designer, writer, researcher and editor. She is the Founder, Creative Director and Editor of Kalimat Magazine, *an independent, non-profit media production company about Arab thought and culture which also functions as a collaborative design studio. She obtained an MA in Social Design from the Maryland Institute College of Art, and a BA (Honours) in Communications from the University of Ottawa.*

Only Icons

I often get asked where I am from, and I deliberately attempt to avoid answering because, frankly, I dislike the question. 'On Mondays I'm Mediterranean, Tuesdays I'm Arab, Wednesdays I'm Levantine, Thursdays I'm Palestinian, Fridays I'm Canadian, and on the weekend I take a break from the identity gods', is the answer I provide. My purpose is not to confuse, because I am in fact a hybrid. But not a hybrid in the sense that I grew up in one place and absorbed different cultures through my travels. After all, before I became Canadian at a very young age, I was Jordanian (and still am), but I was never really Jordanian – just on paper. I do not feel Jordanian, despite engaging in elements of a Jordanian experience. I feel Canadian because I grew up there and associate with it, and most of my friends are Canadians. I feel Palestinian because I was raised to be. But in reality I feel Arab, I identify with the Arab peoples, and Palestine is an Arab cause – it always will be in my opinion.

Being a hybrid is not the only reason why I deliberately choose not to emphasise my Palestinian-ness. Another is because I am Editor and Creative Director of *Kalimat,* an open platform that invites Arabs worldwide to share their work and ideas. With this responsibility comes certain expectations about my views as a Palestinian, which could lead to a measure of self-censorship on the part of the contributors – defeats the purpose of an open platform then, doesn't it?

I have a third reason for choosing not to emphasise my Palestinian-ness. You may think I'm going off on a tangent, but bear with me, it's all related.

I have many Palestines, or many experiences of Palestine. My uncle was a martyr, and I grew up looking at an A6 photo of him with a black band hanging on one side, representing someone who has passed away. I often wondered who he was and, in the days of Alta Vista and Yahoo! (Google's search predecessors), I looked up any information I could about him and scoured the library for books that contained even a brief mention of his name. As I grew older, I soon realised being Palestinian was not a choice; it was forced down my throat. I began to grow more and more uneasy with the idea. Whatever I read, whatever I watched, and whatever I was interested in had to be related to it. After all, I was told that if I let go of Palestine it would no longer exist.

It was as if being Palestinian consisted of an abundance of patriotic colours (decorated in gradients, stencil and script typefaces), and symbols like the *tatreez* pattern, the romanticised idea of the strong female fighter, *keffiyeh*, villagers, olive trees, slingshots . . . I don't believe that sticking to these stereotypical symbols makes you more Palestinian. Even in my PhD studies, people are taken aback by the fact that my study is not based in Palestine, but in Jordan.

I have been fortunate enough to visit Palestine three times. I don't think I've ever felt so un-Palestinian. I could not relate to their experience, nor most of their ideas and thinking. Sure, some things were similar – mainly our accent – but even then mine was obviously different.

As a teenager and well into my early twenties I was very involved in the activist community. Quickly though I realised the hypocrisy in the community. Activism has become trendy, and I'm not talking about Urban Outfitters and Freshjive taking hold of symbols to design controversial T-shirts and scarves. I'm talking about the number of people who have gone to Palestine, fought a few soldiers, made a necklace from bullets, stayed in a refugee camp, befriended a few kids, posted pictures with said kids and then spent a nice weekend in Tel Aviv. I'm talking about the academics, journalists and others who have made their careers on Palestine. The authors who after one visit are sudden experts, flying first class on speaking engagements and book tours, tweeting every five minutes about Palestine and how they wish they were there now. Palestine is no longer about educating, but rather about ego. And there I was, not Palestinian enough because I had no 'real' Palestinian experience. I was fighting to be Palestinian but I couldn't be without being a victim, so I put myself into a sort of self-exile from my community. I even experienced people lying about what they lived through in order to gain acceptance.

What I came to realise was that being Palestinian in Palestine and being Palestinian in the diaspora – or being Turkish, Armenian, Portuguese, French or any community that has a diaspora – are not the same. Palestinians in the diaspora are, in my opinion, obsessed with the idea of being authentically Palestinian through cuisine, music, dress, dialect, cities, villages and so on. It is all about difference and distinction which I felt many people I met in Palestine were not as concerned with. The movement of people and ideas in the era of globalisation calls on people to define and demonstrate their identity, and debates on issues such as national cuisine are more common in diaspora communities.

Okay, I'll admit, sometimes I am guilty of defending my identity when it is under attack (defending claims on the origins of *knafeh*, for example), and this is where the problem lies. We have generations of Palestinians who are extremely proud to be Palestinian, but only know the patriotic symbols and not the reasons for our continued exile. My Palestinian-ness is not signified through wearing a *keffiyeh*, a solidarity T-shirt, practising *dabke* on the weekends, or regularly attending rallies. I believe that being Palestinian comes with greater responsibility, one that is about educating and understanding. Being Palestinian is not about preaching and defensiveness, nor imagined patriotic symbols, but through a sustained and constantly developing knowledge of facts and history (or histories), understanding the Palestinian cause and having your own opinion on it. But most of all, it is knowing that being Palestinian does not tie you down to imaginary boundaries. As someone who has grown up in the diaspora, I must acknowledge all the places, ideas and forces that have influenced me and that define all that I am as a person.

Ishaq Abu-Arafeh

Ishaq Abu-Arafeh – MBChB (Jordan), MD (Aberdeen), MRCP, FRCPCH, DCH – is a consultant in paediatrics and paediatric neurology in Scotland. His main professional and research interest is in childhood headache. He has served on the councils of several national and international professional organisations and chaired the Central Scotland Regional Equality Council.

Resident of Both, National of None

Conflict of identity may seem a strange idea for many people, but not for a Palestinian. My grandparents were born in Palestine under the Ottoman Empire and my parents were born in Palestine under the British Mandate. I was born in Jerusalem under Jordanian rule and I grew up in Palestine under Israeli military occupation. Ahmad, my eldest son, was born in England and Hashem, my second son, was born in Scotland. This is a typical story for most, if not all, Palestinians of my generation.

Living in Jerusalem before the 1967 war, I completed six years of primary school education as a 'Jordanian', reciting the Jordanian national anthem every morning and singing 'God Save the King'. After the 1967 war, I completed another six years of secondary school education under the Israeli military occupation as an 'Arab' and my Israeli Identity Card, that accompanied me wherever I went like a shadow, said so. At university in Amman, I was 'Jordanian', but an 'Arab' during the summer holidays that I spent with my family in occupied Jerusalem.

Being a qualified doctor meant a lot to my parents, so I moved back to Jerusalem and took a junior hospital post there and later in Bethlehem. It felt great to be close to family, but opportunities for progress in my career were severely limited, so when I had the opportunity to train in the UK I grabbed it with both hands. However, travelling to the UK from Palestine meant a new document was needed. The Israelis called it a 'Travel Document', but it was really a small blue booklet with exit and re-entry visas with stringent timelines and expiry dates. Presenting the 'Travel Document' to the British immigration officer at Heathrow was an interesting encounter.

'Are you an Israeli?' he asked.

'No, I am not,' I replied.

'This document says you are a resident of Israel and your British visa says you are a resident of the UK, so which country are you a national of?' he exclaimed.

'Sir, the papers say I am a resident of both, but a national of none.'

'You must be a Palestinian,' he said, shaking his head.

Being Palestinian in the UK means I have to be tactful in the way I introduce myself to avoid disadvantaging myself and my family. To my friends I am Palestinian. At job interviews I come from Jerusalem. On the birth register I am Jordanian at the birth of my first child and Palestinian at the birth of my second (as the political atmosphere changed), and at airports I am definitely Jordanian and lately British, for obvious reasons.

The conflict of identity was very confusing to me as a child, but the emergence of the Palestinian resistance movement in the early seventies and the growing sense of belonging helped to crystallise my identity, and that of many young people of my generation. It helped me identify my relevance to this world. My greatest fear, however, is about the effects of my identity conflict on my children, who have witnessed how unjust the world has been to their parents.

Being Palestinian means that I have to accept the most humiliating injustice in order to live as a second-class citizen in my own country under Israeli occupation. Palestinians are expected to live in refugee camps hoping for justice and a return to their homes and villages. Palestinians have to seek the kindness of foreign nations for grants to obtain a university education and possibly employment.

Being deprived of living in my own country and watching foreign settlers digging my parents' land gives me a feeling of great loss. The emotions go through stages of denial, anger, outrage, sadness, acceptance and, finally, rational reasoning and the desire to succeed. However, these emotions are not separate and they may all be felt at the same time, producing a very distressing feeling that I cannot find the words to describe in full. At times of reason I can be less confused and I am able to feel the pain of so many people from different backgrounds who have suffered, just like me, different forms of discrimination and injustice. I can feel how bad it must have been for the persecuted Jews of World War II, the Black population in apartheid South Africa and the Bosnians in 1992–5. I try to explain my emotions towards the Zionists of Israel but I can only find one word to describe them: racists.

Being Palestinian allows me to see the big picture of all people who suffer at the hands of racists, wherever they are. I feel, sorely, the plight of minorities, the dispossessed and those who have been forced out of their homes anywhere in the world. 'Being Palestinian' has taught me to appreciate the impact of prolonged human suffering and has guided me into wider issues of social justice, civic responsibilities and human rights.

Nuha Abudabbeh

Nuha Abudabbeh was born in Jaffa, Palestine, but her parents moved to Mersin, Turkey, when she was one month old. She completed high school at a Quaker boarding school in Ramallah, Palestine. She received a bachelor's degree and a master's degree from the American University of Beirut, Lebanon, and her PhD from the University of Maryland. She has been practising as a clinical and forensic psychologist in Washington, DC since 1972 and has held consulting jobs with the United Nations as well as the World Bank. Presently she is associate professor at George Washington University and a consultant with the Court Services.

Without my Jaffa: Other Seas

My entire life has been a journey of non-belonging, an outsider: homeless and adjusting. The feeling of non-belonging has its roots early for me because for the first thirteen years of my life I was an Arab and a Palestinian in Turkey. Although I grew up in Turkey, my identity as a Palestinian was nurtured by committed parents, but it was neither obtrusive nor a noticeable part of my daily struggle. However, as I grew older and my grandparents, uncles, aunts and parents passed away, the meaning of being Palestinian began to feel more and more painful. As I approach my own demise I am more aware of the tragedy of having been denied a homeland, especially when I face the strong possibility, if not certainty, that I will die very far away from where I was born. As I review my life, I am impressed by how disjointed it has been. In its multicultural exposure it feels rich, like a delicately embroidered quilt, but in this multiplicity of experiences it feels like multiple lives unfulfilled.

I was born in Jaffa, a beautiful city full of laughter and wonderful lovely people who are no more around. I was born in a city referred to by Palestinians as 'the bride of the sea'. My connection to this city, which has been yanked from my life and where I have never had the privilege to live, is probably why I love the sea so much. My happiest days as a Palestinian were always when I was near the sea. I loved the sea in Beirut and in Tripoli, Libya, and I was so happy when I visited Rabat and Tangiers and enjoyed the beaches – as if I were back in Jaffa. I loved being in Algeria, where I was serenaded by the village children when they found out I was Palestinian. I eventually went back to visit my Jaffa and saw how it has lost its charm and beauty as it has become a haven for tourists in Israel. All the more reason why other seas had to fulfil my need to smell Jaffa.

I came to Washington, DC and I was two hours away from any sea. This was the beginning of a journey where I have been forced to face the most painful part of having been born and raised with a Palestinian identity. Being Palestinian in the United States meant that I belonged to a people who were demonised. I had to constantly fight my way and my status in society. As time went by, and as the Palestinian situation got worse, and my family and what bonds I had to Palestine unravelled, my pain became more and more palpable. What was most unbearable was the fact that the country I lived in, that I supported with my hard-earned money, was one of the architects of the demolition of my own people.

As I live probably the last decade of my life, I cannot help but lament the fact that I will have to spend that decade in a country that has squashed the Palestinian dream. This is the most painful fact that I must endure as I give up for good the idea of ever seeing an independent Palestinian state. But the thought of seeing such a state does not give me solace. It will never make up for all the tragedies so many Palestinians have suffered. It will never make up for the discrimination Palestinians have had to endure all over the world. I carry the pain of all of my people. I am a psychologist and I take care of people.

I began the journey to caretaking in childhood as I was the oldest of three siblings. I must have always been the strongest health-wise because my younger sister, as I recollect, was always sick. She was the stronger of the two of us when it came to reality, however, but her health issues got the better of her and she succumbed to breast cancer at the age of fifty-one. She was the true Palestinian who gave a lot of her life to the struggle.

The loss of my sister was a triple tragedy as she was indeed a caretaker in a different way to me. She was the pragmatist and the economist who was in charge of what really matters in this day and age. She looked out for our financial survival, along with Mother who was quite smart on these matters. By the time we lost my sister, only I and Mother were left to manage the family, or what was left of it – we had lost my father when he was killed in a hit-and-run accident in Libya. The loss of my sister left me in charge of Mother as well as my only brother, who was born with a cognitive disability. Because I was a psychologist I took a special interest in Nedi and he remains my responsibility to date. Nedi is another reason why the Palestinian tragedy is multiplied, as we struggle to provide services for someone with special needs. My brother Nedi was born in Palestine, and my mother, the perfectionist, never gave up looking for a resolution and services for him. Our homelessness thus contributed to the tragic impact of this situation.

Today I am alone with Nedi with my memories of a family unfulfilled. My father died a very unhappy man who was so disillusioned not only with the United States he loved, but with his own people as well. His son was disabled, his dreams were shattered but his idealism never forsaken. I follow in his steps as I complete my own sad journey through life. I carry my father's unhappiness, my sister's pragmatism and my mother's ability to endure. I carry on so I can take care of those who need me. I continue to see my patients, and I continue to see those who need others as society discards them. The Palestinians are at the top of the list of the discarded, followed by a litany of groups of people who have become a burden on a world that has shifted its priorities.

Lila Abu-Lughod

Lila Abu-Lughod, the Joseph L. Buttenwieser Professor of Social Science at Columbia University, teaches Anthropology and Women's and Gender Studies. She has authored or edited Veiled Sentiments: Honor and Poetry in a Bedouin Society; Writing Women's Worlds; Dramas of Nationhood: The Politics of Television in Egypt; Nakba: Palestine, 1948, and the Claims of Memory; *and* Do Muslim Women Need Saving?

Buffeted By How Others See You

To be Palestinian is to be at once rooted – in family, community, memory and history – and to be buffeted, often violently, by the ways others see you. For me, the rooting has never been fully secure because I am not fully Palestinian; an American mother and only brief periods of living with Palestinian relatives balancing the pull of a father who deeply identified with Palestine. And the buffeting – because I move so regularly between the US and Egypt – lurches me between humiliation and special status, anger and gratitude, helplessness and determination.

For someone like me, the daughter of a 1948 refugee who never herself experienced expulsion, the most intimate sense of belonging to Palestine consists in the embodied closeness to relatives who share my name and who gave me a childhood taste for special foods like wild thyme (*za'tar*) and fragrant olive oil, and an ear for a familiar dialect. The limits of belonging come in finding out, only after my father had died, that the language that filled my young life as he talked affectionately to friends or argued political points was a dialect specific to Jaffa, the city of his birth and dreams of return.

Even if I had not had these childhood tastes and memories of family, there would still have been no way not to be drafted into being Palestinian. You see the news of terrible events affecting other Palestinians and know that they are connected to you, somehow. You carry a name that raises eyebrows. But more than anything, you experience the different ways Palestinians are viewed, constantly seeing yourself through the eyes of others.

In Egypt, where I lived happily as a child and now do research, I like to identify myself as Palestinian so as not to be taken for American. Being Arab, being Muslim, make a difference. But to be Palestinian is distinctive. When I lived with Bedouin in Egypt's Western Desert, they told me about the Palestinian refugees from Gaza they had seen close-up when a few pathetic families made their way out west. Like everyone in the Arab world, they knew the basic history of what had happened to Palestine in 1948 and thought it wrong. But in the 1980s, when the Egyptian government began confiscating Bedouin land, they began composing poems they thought I'd like. These described what was happening to them as their being turned into Palestinians.

Later, when I began to spend my time in a village in Upper Egypt instead of the northwest coast, television was everywhere. In the 1990s and beyond, whenever I visited I saw people watching the news. They saw the daily violence, the incursions, the Second Intifada. They recognised the icons – Muhammad al-Durra, the innocent boy shielded by his father, shot dead; Shaykh Yassin, the elderly founder of Hamas and spiritual figure, blown out of his wheelchair, blood everywhere. They saw Palestinian boys throwing stones at well-armed Israeli soldiers. They saw tanks and bulldozers crushing Palestinian homes. They saw women wailing. How many women looked into my eyes in sympathy. How many confided that they wept as they watched. When they exclaimed, 'May God give them victory', I would bathe in their support and solidarity.

How different from the experience of being Palestinian in America, where the lies one reads lash the flesh and where one is stunned by what people believe about Israel. How can they be blind to the everyday violence of checkpoints, imprisonment, racism and death? How can they be complicit in the rhetoric of retaliation and security? How can they be silent about the primal injustice of 1948 even when, in the best case, they are righteous about opposition to 'the occupation' or 'the settlements'? Argument only makes you feel more helpless. How small you feel when a UN investigation of what happened in Gaza in late 2008, when more than a thousand Palestinians were killed in two weeks under enormous firepower, is dismissed out of hand by a vote in the US Congress of 344 to 36!

Because I live in the US, I too sometimes watch other Palestinians with ambivalence, forced to see them through the eyes of others. I take my children to demonstrations in New York and Washington, DC when there is a crisis. I feel gratified that there are people walking side-by-side with Palestinians. But

I have moments of discomfort when I'm overtaken by unshaven young men with green headbands waving Palestinian flags and shouting angry slogans about spirit and blood. I know they have relatives who are being killed and maimed. I know they may have grown up in refugee camps. I admire their passion. But I know that I don't have to live, as they or my father did, as a 'full time Palestinian', even if my attachments are real (and if my daughter's attachment is strong enough to have made her want to play for the Palestinian national women's soccer team when she turned eighteen).

Even in Egypt I can be ambivalent about being Palestinian. A bright village girl in fifth grade tells me proudly that she has memorised a poem about Palestine. I ask where she learnt it. She takes me to YouTube where she plays two highly melodramatic clips for me. One shows a fourteen-year-old reciting a poem, her voice rising to a pitch as tears stream down her face. The other is a short film in soft focus that tells the story of a pious patriot who sacrifices herself for Palestine. The closing scene is a close-up of her abandoned wedding dress lying sadly in her young brother's lap. We know his future.

This ambivalence doesn't mean I don't feel illicit pleasure when I seek out, again on YouTube, a music video of a Palestinian hip hop group from the ghettoes of Lydda, whose lyrics 'Who's the terrorist?!' are repeated as Israeli fighter jets rain bombs on Palestinian camps. But I also long for a presentation of the truth of our story that can convince the kinds of people I know in the US who do not know what we know. A representation that works with a different aesthetic or structure of feeling.

I was overcome by a calm determination when I finally had a chance to work on Palestine as a scholar. With a colleague from '48 Palestine who I met at my father's funeral, I worked on a book, poignant and truthful, about the event that has defined Palestinians as a people who cannot feel rooted, because they cannot be at home. Called *Nakba: Palestine, 1948, and the Claims of Memory*, this book was a labour of love, rooted in the way I want to be Palestinian.

Lama Abu-Odeh

Lama Abu-Odeh is a law professor at Georgetown University Law Center. She teaches and writes on women and the law, the law of the market and legal issues related to the Palestinian/Israeli conflict.

Disrupting the Peace of Others

It is a peculiar thing to be a Palestinian in the US. Our people are visible in a way other migrants would envy. Our people are, to quote the title of a section in *The New Yorker*, the 'talk of the town'. Our tunnels, walls, rockets and 'hardliners' are delicious food for the American reader-eye; 'our' Hamas and the Palestinian Authority and their internecine conflict a mass-mediated meal one could never refuse; our endless, sometimes-on/sometimes-off talks with Israelis is where, in case you ever wondered, we are to be found. We *are* the forever failing Middle East peace process.

We are visible in a unique kind of way, so unique I have come to call it a 'Palestinian' kind of way. For our plight is made visible only to show that it is 'deserved'; no sooner has our victimhood been identified than it is justi-fied as our own fault. The military barriers that are erected in Palestinian neighbourhoods, the olive trees that are uprooted, the identity cards that are withdrawn, the land that is confiscated, the limit on the number of calories that are allowed to be consumed – all of this we Palestinians have 'earned'. It is our terrorists, militants, suicide bombers and hardliners – all the 'bad stuff we're always up to' – that is the reason for these 'punitive measures'. It is all so rational: how else can Israel defend its 'national security'? As for those poor Palestinians? Well it is just too bad!

The tease of visibility/invisibility of our people is the fate of the Palestinian in exile. No other international victim group has consumed so much ink, alphabet, paper or cyber entry. No other group has been so crushed by the weight of the words purporting to describe it. In the face of the overwhelming will to misrepresent, one wishes one's people to be ignored, to vanish in the mass of nameless third world 'others' . . .

To be a Palestinian in exile in the US is to be the particular on whom the judgement of the universal is never bestowed. It is to cause liberalism to discover its limit at Zionism; it is to have Human Rights Watch 'ignore' your right of return; and it is to be the only victim who is always compelled to 'understand' their victimiser. To be a Palestinian in the US is to never really be a victim.

To be a Palestinian in the US is to confront an adversary that has universalised its interests and turned them into common sense. It too has acquired the qualities of visibility/invisibility, but whereas for us Palestinians this serves as a punishing fate, for the adversary it is a way of waging the war. It hits us with the spear of ethnic conflict before it vanishes behind the lines of the universal 'White'. It attacks, and before we can decipher its particular face, it quickly retreats into the nondescript 'American'. It marshals the resources of the US state to its aid to assert that we are the enemy of all Americans, not just them – the supporters of Israel. It forces to the background the theft of our land (the news that is non-news) and foregrounds our own badness (our 'terrorism' *is* the news). It posits supporting us or our cause to be abetting terrorism. It is the 'common sense' behind which its interests, as an ethnic nationalist minority, are generalised.

Paradoxically, to resist one's plight as a Palestinian in America is to discover the authoritarian nature of US government and society. It is to be on the 'terrorist list', or an 'unintended co-conspirator', or a 'Hamas sympathiser'. It is to circulate one's syllabus on the 'Israel-Palestine: Legal issues seminar' to every Jewish colleague one has ever heard mention the word 'Israel' to seek approval. It is to barge into the Dean's office (the same person who had told you during the Gaza assault that his 'friends in Tel Aviv support the invasion') to demand he gives you protection in the event that a Jewish student in class screams foul and mobilises the school's rabbi, the alumni and the media if you teach the class in a way he or she deems 'offensive', read: if one teaches it to register the victimhood of the Palestinians.

Our adversary has pre-empted us already. Anything you say – 'Palestine my homeland', 'Palestinian', '*my* Jerusalem' – sounds shrill, atonal, outside language, unintelligible.

It is in 'bad taste' to be a Palestinian in the US. You risk hurting the feelings of your Jewish host, or embarrassing your non-Jewish co-hosts into taking a 'position'. To be a Palestinian in the US is to be a party pooper; asserting your right is spitting in the main dish and poisoning dessert; expressing the hurt you feel from the ethnic war waged against you is threatening the ethnic peace of others.

To be a *good* Palestinian in America is to occupy your absence with a cheerful presence.

Mahdi Abu-Omar

Mahdi Abu-Omar, PhD, completed his secondary school education in Jerusalem. He held academic appointments at California Institute of Technology and University of California, Los Angeles before joining Purdue University, where he is currently R. B. Wetherill Professor of Chemistry and Professor of Chemical Engineering. His research is in sustainable chemistry and renewable energy. His hobbies include golf, soccer and travel.

Fate: A Blessing

I am an American, a Palestinian and a monotheist Submitter, a follower of the religion instituted by Abraham and culminated in Muhammad through the delivery of the Quran. Out of these identities, and despite the connotations associated with being a Submitter (*Muslim* in Arabic) in America, it is being Palestinian which is most difficult to describe to friends in the US and Europe. I am Palestinian by birth and American by choice – although there wasn't another choice. It was fate.

Even though I was born in Jerusalem after the Six-Day War and under Israeli rule, I was never given Israeli citizenship. As a child I did not have the freedom to express my national identity; raising or even possessing the Palestinian flag was unlawful. I left Jerusalem at the age of seventeen, just months after the First Intifada when the Israeli authorities closed Birzeit University where I was a freshman and it was not clear when, or if, the university would be reopened. I took a leap of faith and left the country for the United States, and with God's blessings I was fortunate to be awarded a merit scholarship to attend Hampden-Sydney College in Virginia and found a generous and welcoming land. America took me in with open arms. She adopted me and I eventually became a fully fledged American citizen. Many of my fellow countrymen and women are not so fortunate. They live their daily lives with the inequalities of an Israeli rule that favours Jews in an apartheid state.

Kindness and generosity are the two prevailing traits of being Palestinian that have shaped my experience in diaspora the most. I was raised in a culture where much emphasis is placed on hospitality, in which, as my dad would say, 'Making the guest feel at home is to show one's Palestinian attribute.' I am reminded of the exemplary hospitality Abraham sets in the Quran [11:69]: 'When our messengers went to Abraham with good news, they said, "Peace". He said, "Peace", and soon brought a roasted calf.'[1] He didn't ask the strangers of their purpose before sharing a meal. My family and I in the US cherish the opportunities we have had to host relatives from back home as well as exchange students from other countries. Hosting parties with food from the Middle East for my students and friends is a staple at our household which keeps us connected to Palestine.

But my identity is a constant internal struggle. While I am very proud of everything Palestinian, from traditional embroidery to the Nabulsi *knafeh*, I am quickly discouraged and disheartened by all the blame the media places on the shoulders of the Palestinians, from being held collectively responsible for the acts of 'terror' perpetrated by radical groups, as if we, as a nation, are supposed to be ashamed, to the failure of the peace process. I remember in the summer of 2008, during the blockade of Gaza, whenever I was asked about my origins I would say that I am from Jerusalem and people would assume I was Jewish, which would lead them to express their sympathy and how horrible it must be to contend with 'Palestinian troublemakers'. The conversation would end abruptly once I clarified that I was actually Palestinian.

My story and experiences are similar to many Palestinians in the diaspora. I have two national identities: I am an American, and this is where my loyalty lies, but I can never forget the motherland, Palestine. Her history, people and culture have shaped who I am today. My children are Palestinian-Americans who are proud of their heritage, with strong ties to their family members in Palestine. They love visiting family in Palestine, touring historic sites, bathing in the Dead Sea and indulging in the cuisine, which they share at school functions that highlight the cultural diversity of our community.

Now, when I travel with my family back to Palestine, the country of my birth, the country of my ancestors and their ancestors, I travel as an American tourist. But unlike most American tourists, my passport declares that Jerusalem is my place of birth, and this declaration is sufficient for the Israeli authorities to take me out of the passenger line and hold me for hours at the airport before they allow me in. On one trip a while back when my children were still very young, I was held for several hours. My wife and three children waited with me patiently through several sessions of questioning. My youngest turned to me and said, 'Daddy, what did you do that they are taking so long?' It was very hard to explain to a child that I had done nothing but was treated differently because of my ethnicity. But despite these conflicts, I live with the conviction that being Palestinian is a blessing because God rewards those who emigrate: 'As for those who emigrate because of persecution, then continue to strive and steadfastly persevere, your Lord, because of all of this, is Forgiver, Most Merciful' [Quran 16:110].

As a Palestinian in the diaspora, I am filled with optimism, despite the feeling that my original identity is wounded by uncertainties about the present, and future, of Palestine. The resolve to look outward and think globally have become the defining characteristic of my Palestinian identity.

Note

1. Rashad Khalifa, *Quran: The Final Testament*, Islamic Productions, Tucson, AZ, 1989.

Salman Abu Sitta

Salman Abu Sitta was born in Beer Sheba. He is an engineer by profession. He is the Founder and President of Palestine Land Society and is the author of The Atlas of Palestine *and* The Return Journey. *He is a frequent writer on Palestinian refugees and the Right of Return.*

The Invisible Face of the Occupier

I discovered I am 'Palestinian' the first time I stepped out of Palestine. Not because I lacked identity but because I did not need to prove that to my family, neighbours or countrymen.

My biggest shock came when I was studying for my PhD at University College London. One day I went to renew my Aliens Card in the early 1960s at the Home Office. I looked at the renewed card and saw next to my nationality: 'Uncertain'. I looked at the clerk in disbelief: 'But I am Palestinian, my father is Palestinian, so is my grandfather. You British should know that.'

'It is only a formality,' he said gently.

This challenge to my identity – indeed to my being – was devastating.

During and after our *Nakba*, we went through a traumatic experience of a different kind. I experienced being a refugee from the age of ten. In 1948 and 1949, I saw the mass of humanity driven from their homes in 250 villages in southern Palestine to take shelter under trees, in schools, in mosques and with relatives or friends. They were huddled in the one per cent of Palestine that was left unoccupied in the south, in what is famously known now as Gaza Strip.

We were all engulfed in the whirlwind of the *Nakba* which befell us. The villages, places and lands we came from were crystal clear in our minds. We knew every feature of them. In earnest hope of swift return, people sold their field crops, and mortgaged or exchanged plots of land with each other in territory now occupied by the enemy.

We knew the enemy in name as 'the vagabonds of the world'. Although the enemy spoke a babel of languages and wore a wild variety of semi-uniforms, it had a secret tongue, known as Hebrew, which nobody knew. We knew nothing about the invaders' structure, strength or their plans other than that they attack, conquer, kill and expel people from their homes. Some of us, with knowledge of history, recalled Hulagu, the leader of the Mongols, or the princes and kings of the Franks, aka the Crusaders. Some, with a religious inclination, professed that this plague was visited upon us because we did not obey God's word.

In all this, we never felt that our 'Palestinian-ness' was challenged in any way. We spoke of *al watan*, 'the land you tread on', in our colloquial language, or the homeland. Nobody doubted who a Palestinian was or what his country was.

Young men I knew, relatives and neighbours, returned to attack the occupiers. They scored great successes as the enemy could not at first control the vast land it had conquered. Later these young men formed *fedayeen* groups and their leaders became members of the PLO.

The traumatic experience in London of having the word 'Palestine' erased, and its people forgotten, was aggravated by the great celebration in Britain, and the West generally, of our demise. The Israeli conquest was seen as a victory for civilisation and the fulfilment of divine will.

While doing part-time essays for BBC Arabic, I had to enter into desperate arguments with supposedly well-informed BBC reporters to say we exist, that there is Palestine. I saw with great sadness prestigious institutions like the British Library and the Royal Geographical Society cross out the word 'Palestine' in their directories and replace it with the word 'Israel'.

So am I not Palestinian after all? I went to libraries, exhibitions and searched the archives of institutions in London to copy and acquire any documents I might find, first about my family and birthplace, then Gaza and Beer Sheba and, later, all of Palestine.

The findings were impressive, which was not surprising: it was the colonial West, the source of the original sin, which had been mapping and researching Palestine since the nineteenth century.

The journey into the depositories of information on Palestine extended to other sources in the UK, then to Paris, Berlin, Leipzig, Munich, New York and Washington. This journey took forty years but finally gave birth to *The Atlas of Palestine*, which documents every kilometre of Palestine.

While looking at tens of thousands of place names I marvelled at how Palestinians carved their history in these names. They recorded it in their happy and sad days. Place names such as 'the Wedding of the Beauty', 'the White Spring', 'Haj Ali Gardens' or 'the Death of the Hero' compose the alphabet of Palestinian history.

This history is more ancient than many believe. Most of the village names date back at least two thousand years. I say 'at least' because we have a record of these villages from the Bishop of Caesarea, Eusebius, in the year AD 313. They are older than London, Paris and probably Rome. The oral history of the *Nakba* collected sparingly from the survivors is another record of the destroyed landscape, confirming what Eusebius saw seventeen centuries ago.

The huge amount of data I collected and analysed on every spot in our Palestine was compared with the situation today after Israel's occupation in 1948. With available technology it was possible to monitor changes in our homes and landscape, and see what the Israelis did with them, which Jewish immigrants lived there, where they came from, what they built on it and what they destroyed. It was therefore possible to chart a realistic scenario of how our return could be implemented.

This led to a surprising result which has been concealed for decades by Zionist misinformation. I found our dispossessed land is largely empty. The Jews still live in the coastal region and western Jerusalem as they did during the British Mandate, admittedly with the necessary expansion that comes with an eight-fold increase in the population. I found that 90 per cent of the village sites are still vacant. The vast, confiscated land of the refugees has been allotted to kibbutzim, which constitute only 2 per cent of Israelis, and to the Israeli army.

It was therefore possible to devise a Return Plan for the refugees outlining the demography and geography of the landscape, and the applicable law of return. Another atlas was published, *The Return Journey*, showing the possible routes of return.

Talking about return has been deemed 'impossible' in Western and Israeli eyes. Not anymore. At a dozen conferences in the last two years and with the rise of the Boycott, Divestment and Sanctions Movement, this is being seriously discussed as the only way for permanent peace. Earlier this month (May 2014) a small Israeli NGO, Zochrot, released an Apple application called iNakba, which guides you from any point in Israel to the depopulated villages and gives information about them. This is a small step on the road to return.

For some Palestinians, to be Palestinian is to appreciate an olive tree, to enjoy a *za'tar* breakfast, to hang a map of your hometown in your house or to marry a girl who would have been your neighbour before exile.

But that is just to keep the memory alive.

To be Palestinian is not to forget, nor to surrender this great heritage, not to kneel and resign to the tragedy of the *Nakba*. To be Palestinian is to resist the ravages of evil deeds, to insist on the restoration of rights and to plan for their restoration. To be Palestinian is to be stubborn in adherence to the principles of justice which can only be achieved by return home.

To be Palestinian is to be a refugee in a camp with a street called 'Lydda Street' and a grocery called 'Ramle Store'. To be Palestinian is to be a fourth-generation Palestinian born in New York who refers to Bayt Daras as his or her hometown. To be Palestinian is to say to the Home Office clerk, or his successors: 'No, I am not "uncertain". I was Palestinian, I am Palestinian and I will forever be Palestinian', in any language, in any city, in any year.

Leena Al-Arian

Leena Al-Arian is a Palestinian American living in Boston, MA. She holds a master's degree in Middle Eastern Studies from the University of Chicago. She has worked at the Middle East Children's Alliance and the National Coalition to Protect Civil Freedoms, and interned with Human Rights Watch. At the time of writing, her father, Dr Sami Al-Arian, was a political prisoner in the US awaiting deportation. Despite living there for nearly forty years, he remains a stateless Palestinian in search of a country.

A Palestinian State of Mind

Throughout my life people have often observed that I have a bit of a 'defensive' personality. While I am inclined to dismiss such comments as totally ridiculous and unfair assessments of my otherwise affable character, I guess there could be *some* truth to it. Well, fine, if I am being completely honest, perhaps I have shuffled a few steps past the neutral zone, embracing a slightly more critical, nay 'judicious', and cynical – I prefer 'savvy' – attitude than most others. But what can be expected of someone who was thrust into the spotlight when her father, a nationally recognised activist and professor, was arrested in a major terrorism conspiracy case, charged with horrific (and purely imaginary) crimes such as 'plotting to murder and maim Israelis', and tried on a national stage? When you live in a city where almost everyone, it seems, has formed an opinion about him? Or when your friend's random cable guy – who you have *obviously* never met – claims to have been to your house and found flight manuals during a routine installation? (*As if we would leave them scattered about the TV stand! Have you seen a Palestinian mother's home?*) Or when news cameras follow you to school on your first day of college? Or when your professor asks you in front of your entire class if you are the daughter of the 'notorious Sami Al-Arian'? Or when you are innocently watching the Olympics one night only to be visually assaulted by a prime-time television ad smearing your father by a US candidate for Senate who, incidentally, goes on to win the election? Or when you discover that probably every phone conversation you have ever had in your life was recorded and listened to by God-knows-who? Worse yet, that your father might come across some of them in preparing his defence?

As one might imagine, these experiences have left me somewhat pessimistic (if not outright paranoid), with a latent expectation of being at best misunderstood and at worst loathed and cast out by mainstream society. But it also ignites in those who are afflicted the inexorable drive to challenge the dominant narrative, dispel common misconceptions, and uphold principles of justice and equal rights above all else. And that is not just because I happen to be the exact middle child of five siblings. For me, this ideal is mostly what *being* Palestinian represents.

Growing up in the United States South as a Palestinian-American-Muslim-hijab-clad female, and in Tampa, Florida no less – known for its scenic parks, zoo, world-famous strip clubs and for serving as the main headquarters of US Central Command – I have in many ways *literally* embodied the very political causes and issues that polarise families, terminate friendships and ruin Christmases. *By the way, the hijab part was totally my choice. Hand to God. Did I mention that wearing hijab was* my *choice? Just wanted to make sure y'all knew that! Not that the words 'women' and 'choice' carry much weight with this crowd.* In other words, my mere existence has given cause to offend, with powerful fringe groups investing millions in this country to perpetuate the fear and hatred of any, or all, of the categories to which I belong.

Yet, the sad paradox lies in the fact that for me, the US, despite having made a political prisoner of my father for over a decade, is the only place I have to call 'home'. You would think that being raised in a sizeable Palestinian community in Florida would give one a strong sense of, well, *community*, but more often than not the environment intensified my feelings of alienation. From an early age, I realised that there are roughly two kinds of Palestinians living in the diaspora: those who enjoy a direct relationship with 'back home', frequently travelling to visit their *teytas* and *jiddos*, reconnecting with cousins and traversing familiar streets in the West Bank while bonding with other diaspora friends; then there are people like me who can never relate.

As a child of Kuwaiti and Saudi Arabian-born Palestinian refugees who spent their formative years in Egypt before emigrating here nearly forty years ago, I have always been denied this clear-cut dual Palestinian-American identity – *and not for a lack of hyphening!* (I concede that some may insist this duality is not remotely clear-cut, but it is at the very least based on a marked engagement with both cultures.) Aside from inheriting basic religious and cultural practices – *though I tragically admit to having once been kicked out of a* dabke *line* – and linguistic idiosyncrasies that one might only develop from parents whose intractable statelessness forced them to relocate and adapt to strange milieus, I cannot speak fully to *knowing* exactly what it is like to *be* Palestinian. This is particularly true for those of us whose ties extend to *Yafa*, i.e. who originally hail from cities and villages within the '48 territories of historic Palestine and who, for many years, were left out of whichever insidious numerical equation (two-state, three-state) was being contemplated in solving for p.

Still, for what those of us non-*hawiyya*[1] holders lack in summer holidays spent in the *blaad*, or a tangible connection that allows for a more nuanced understanding of what *being* Palestinian entails, we compensate by clinging on to more abstract notions of belonging. Belonging to Palestine means replacing the physical with the political, and it is to recognise this cause as one of the most defining issues of our lifetime. It means viewing the resilience of the Palestinian people who have survived and prevailed over seemingly insurmountable challenges as an ideal to uphold. Moreover, it is maintaining the conviction that we are all one in the struggle, with each of us having to shoulder some of the responsibility in attaining freedom and self-determination. And it is my personal commitment to such principles that has long nurtured my identity and fuelled me with a deep sense of purpose.

Indeed, it was this perceived unity in struggle that helped me endure the most difficult time of my life, when my father was held in solitary confinement for years and my family and I fearfully wondered if he would ever again see the light of day. But because he was widely known for being an outspoken *Palestinian* advocate for Palestinian rights, it did not actually come as a big surprise that he would be targeted. After all, thousands of Palestinians continue to linger in Israeli jails, falling victim to a racist, apartheid regime that punishes any form of dissent. Thus, framing one's individual struggles as part of a collective resistance has always been, I believe, an essential component of what it is to be Palestinian.

But while I may never have a complete understanding of what *being* Palestinian comprises – and, admittedly, a part of my 'defensiveness' growing up can be attributed to insecurities that I was not Palestinian *enough* – I have learnt over the years that one's identity need not be so rigidly defined. For many Palestinians in the diaspora our identity is firmly rooted in the political, in the fight for liberation and in our unshakable commitment to preserve the land's culture and people – even for those of us whose Jewish therapists have pegged as 'thoroughly American'.

Note

1. A *hawiyya* is an ID card issued to Palestinians from Gaza and the West Bank and refugees to these territories from 1948. It is denied to exiled Palestinians. In many ways it creates problems for Palestinians within the Green Line by denying them access anywhere outside their designated area. However, for Palestinians living in the diaspora it is sometimes the only document they have to prove their national identity. Therefore, my four siblings and I technically have no documented 'proof' that we are Palestinian.

Sami Al-Arian

Sami Al-Arian was born in 1958 in Kuwait to Palestinian refugees from Jaffa, and grew up in Egypt. Since his arrival to America in 1975, Dr Al-Arian has been an active community leader and organiser. As a result of his effectiveness on many fronts, the US government pursued him for over ten years and charged him in 2003 with multiple-count indictments over which he eventually prevailed after ten years in detention, solitary confinement and under house arrest. After winning his latest case in 2014, he is facing deportation from the US and, as a stateless Palestinian, is looking for a country. Between 1986 and 2003 he was a tenured professor of computer science and engineering at the University of South Florida where he received many academic and teaching awards. He is married and has five children and four grandchildren.

No Land's Man Determined to Return to Palestine

Being Palestinian in the diaspora is to be fully conscious of the historical struggle and grave injustices our people have endured for a century – a history I have absorbed since childhood from my father, mother and grandparents. Despite tracing her family's historical roots in Palestine to the seventh century, my mother, along with her parents and siblings, was forced to leave Jaffa, the 'bride of the Mediterranean', in May 1948 at the barrel of Zionist guns. They walked miles just for the opportunity to sail to the Gaza Strip in a small boat.

> My mother was ten when she left her home
> Hungry, terrified and away from the dome
>
> Her mother has worn the house key around her neck
> But in a hurry she forgot her ring on the deck
>
> She thought she'd be back in a week, why the tears?
> The weeks became months and the months became years . . .

> . . . My son was two when my mother called me
> Grandmother's died, around her neck was the key[1]

At age twenty-two, my father, who had already lost his younger brother in battle, barely survived after he was shot in the back several times while defending his home and his family's soap factory in Jaffa from Zionist gangs. Most Palestinians have similarly tragic stories that capture the enormity of the *Nakba*, which our people have experienced for decades, whether at home under Israeli occupation, in squalid refugee camps, or in the diaspora. This wounded yet determined generation imbued their children, grandchildren and great-grandchildren with the *Nakba*'s graphic details. Each story was unique, vivid, painful and personal.

For decades, Palestinians have been the victims of oppression, transgression, occupation, brutality, violence and abuse. Unfortunately, such moral degradation has not only taken place under Israeli occupation, but in many other societies Palestinians happen to live in, especially across the Arab world. Though my father served faithfully as an employee of the Kuwaiti government for ten years, he lost his job and was summarily expelled from the country in 1966 because he refused to become an informant against other Palestinians. After moving to Egypt at the age of eight, I witnessed a year later the terrible defeat of the Six-Day War, and saw my father's tears upon hearing of Jerusalem's fall on that dreadful day in June 1967.

Another part of my identity as a Palestinian refugee has been to exist in a permanent state of homelessness, statelessness and separation from my siblings and extended family. Being denied the basic right to citizenship, as the son of Palestinian refugees, is one of the most dreadful experiences one might suffer. Despite living in America as an academic for decades, I remain a stateless Palestinian after being refused naturalisation because of my Palestinian activism. Even as a youth in Egypt I was denied access to higher education due to my heritage, despite graduating among the top of my high school class. Like many Palestinian parents in the diaspora, my father sacrificed his life savings so that his son could receive a quality education in America. To that generation, education became their primary defence against dispossession, powerlessness and international indifference.

Being Palestinian is to be profoundly sensitive to the ugliness of racism and institutional discrimination, to the suffering of others, as well as any injustice inflicted on human beings individually or collectively. As with most

Palestinians, it was natural for me to identify with the massacres perpetrated against Native Americans, the African-American Civil Rights Movement, the struggle against apartheid in South Africa, or imperialist policies in Latin America, Asia or Africa. I made common cause with activists in these struggles, and understood and worked within the political system to affect real change in policy and attitudes in government and the media. Living in America, one of my main goals was to serve my Palestinian brethren by making a difference in a country that has contributed greatly to their misery in its blind support of incessant Israeli aggression and occupation. Throughout my studies and beyond I was active in lecturing, debating and writing on many college campuses around the country. My efforts more than a decade ago with a wide coalition of civil rights groups to repeal the use of secret evidence – employed against Palestinians, Arabs and Muslims in American courts – prompted actual legislation by congressional committees, even though it was vigorously opposed by major Zionist organisations.

For me, being Palestinian in the West has always necessitated challenging the dominant narrative, and to be active speaking, debating, writing, composing poetry, marching, organising, networking, mobilising our community, or joining civil liberties, peace and anti-war groups. It was my form of resistance to injustice and oppression, to occupation and the sins of Zionism, and I consider it a modest contribution to pay our debt towards the great sacrifices of our people. Consequently, I had to endure ceaseless efforts to dismiss me from my tenured academic position at university, to silence me and smear my reputation. This eventually culminated in a politically motivated criminal indictment in 2003 that took advantage of the hysteria that engulfed the US after the attacks of 11 September 2001.

During my 2005 trial, US government prosecutors tried to portray me to the jury as an extremist, a radical, a violent terrorist, an anti-Semite, and even an elitist, for being a university professor. In essence, I was on trial for being a Palestinian activist. Yet, one of the most profound ironies a stateless Palestinian could ever encounter came in the form of one of the criminal charges that the government levelled at me: 'Conspiring to extort land from the State of Israel.'

While the government presented eighty witnesses, including twenty-one who were flown in from Israel, my attorneys rested the case without calling a single witness, basing our defence on the US constitutional principle of freedom of speech and association. Indeed, much of the government's evidence presented to the jury during the six-month trial were speeches I delivered, lectures I presented, articles I wrote, magazines I edited, books I owned, conferences I organised, rallies I attended, interviews I gave, people I knew, news I heard and websites that I had never even accessed. It was no surprise that the jury did not return a single guilty verdict on any of the more than one hundred charges facing me and my three co-defendants. It was a testament to the fairness and integrity of the American jurors that they looked at the facts and were unperturbed by media bias or the intimidation of the government's underhand tactics.

The zealotry of the US government in its prosecution of me, and by extension my family, is a microcosm of the challenges faced by Palestinian activists in the US and indeed in many Western countries. By choosing to defend Palestinian rights in a society dominated by the Israeli narrative and infested with Zionist institutional support, one must be ready to face the consequences: job loss, a ruined career, a smeared reputation, deportation and another forced exile, after ten years in solitary confinement and house arrest, and over five years in prison under harsh conditions.

> Get used to it
> You're livin' in the SHU[2]
>
> Let's establish some rules
> Until you get your next review
>
> In solitary 'round the clock
> Enjoy the shielded view
>
> Your hands cuffed behind you
> They may turn black and blue[3]

In another poem, titled 'Shakedown', I describe another aspect of my experience in solitary confinement:

> They came Monday morning
> In front of my door
> Five COs and one LT[4]
> At six-foot and four

Come up shut up,
Cough up they said
Turn around back up
Hold down your head

They joked and laughed
It's time for shakedown
Control, Destroy,
And don't you dare frown

But all this is still insignificant compared to the tremendous sacrifices of the Palestinian people. Throughout my activism and ordeal, I was blessed with a loving and supportive spouse and devoted and resilient children. My wife, Nahla, was a full partner in many of our achievements. She was the bedrock of our family, particularly during the most critical phase of our lives, as many friends abandoned my family because of fear or intimidation. It is a great example and tribute to the role Palestinian women play in maintaining the spirit of resistance and determination.

She had a vision
He was carrying her
On a white knight
Ever since they took him
From her arms
In the middle of the night
He's never really
Been away or
Out of her sight
Because he's always been
Inside her soul
As a guiding light[5]

In life, people make momentous decisions that drastically affect their lives, which they might regret in due course. But I cannot in good conscience regret the central theme of my life. Palestine is the noblest struggle of our time, and standing for principle and serving in that struggle is an honour and privilege. We Palestinians are not only deeply tied to the physical land, its sea, hills and sky, its history and geography, but also to its depressing fate, tragic present and unrealised future. We might be forcefully uprooted from our ancestors' land, made stateless and scattered around the world, but the land, its orange groves and olive trees, its grassy plains and fertile earth, its sacred and resilient character, its determined and proud people, its robust and unfolding history, are etched in our memories and implanted in every fibre of our being. No cost is too great and no burden too large to contribute some small part in the great effort to free our country from the yoke of oppression and occupation and to return our people from exile to their rightful home.

Notes

1. 'My Mom & The Key', 2003.
2. Special Housing Unit.
3. 'Livin' in the SHU', 2003.
4. CO: Correctional Officer; LT: Lieutenant.
5. 'Enduring Love', 2003.

Najwa Al-Qattan

Najwa Al-Qattan is associate professor of history at Loyola Marymount University in Los Angeles. She holds a BA in philosophy from the American University of Beirut, a MA in philosophy from Georgetown University and a PhD in history from Harvard University.

An Ornithologist from Iceland

As every refugee, exile and immigrant knows, who you are in your adopted home is in large measure who you are not. But there is something else, the question of who you'd rather be in a different world – a fanciful game born of home-envy. Being Palestinian, who I am not and who I'd rather be has shifted over time. I used to envy the Lebanese-ness of my Lebanese friends. I still do.

I am a Palestinian who is American and wants to be something else next time around. I am also an historian of the Middle East. I don't know what kinds of birds make Iceland their home, but it has become my custom to conclude many of my rants regarding events in Palestine with a refrain, according to which, in my next life, I want to be an ornithologist from Iceland. Being Icelandic might not necessarily protect my name from universal butchery (let's face it, al-Qattan has become a conspicuous name in America thanks to al-Qaeda), but who hates Icelanders and who doesn't love birds?

Palestine burned brightly in our beautiful home in Beirut in the 1960s and '70s. Its light got rather dim as soon as I stepped on to the school bus. At school, Palestine was an important marker and barrier. At home it was also a burden of scorched memory, shame (after 1967) and guilt, because my parents were wealthy and we did not live in the camps.

Palestine leached into the fabric of our lives: resplendent oranges within sight of the sea at Jaffa when my father was a boy. The year 1948: a very ugly year. The relentless politics and heaps of newspapers. But our deprivation was never material, unless you were my sister, Lina, whose birthday (6 June) was never celebrated after 1967. But Palestine was also Tata's Balfour.

My grandmother had Balfour on her mind most of her life after 1948. She had long fingers that she liked to link together in her lap, leaving the thumbs free to twirl round and round in calm agitation. In loud whispers and with a quivering lower lip, she often interrupted herself to release a tirade or two. Invariably Israelis topped the list but, no matter what the issue at hand, Balfour was sure to follow. My father was once stopped at Heathrow Airport because his place of birth as it appeared on his passport is Palestine. The English passport official had not heard of Mr Balfour. I used to tell Tata to forget Balfour; to redirect her wrath towards more distant shores.

I was in Washington, DC at the time of the Iranian hostage crisis. I experienced a new sentiment: gratitude that I was not an Iranian in America. It was safer for a few years to be Palestinian, at least among those who knew there was a difference. Today, even with all the unspeakable violence that has been visited on them over the course of many decades, I would still opt to be Iranian.

More recently, in crowded airports at summer time, I watch with undisguised envy as Greek and Turkish American mothers pack off their American children to visit family back home. This is an envy of old family homes still standing and high schools that are still possible to visit. I used to take my children to London. It was in my parents' huge house that, over the summers, they got to know their cousins, some English-born, some half-Norwegian. But that was London and the house has long been sold and torn down.

In the early years of my American life in the late 1970s, my long answer to 'Where are you from?' was 'I am Palestinian, but I was born in Kuwait and raised in Lebanon.' Perhaps I felt the need to qualify the Palestinian in me in order to pre-empt the question that invariably followed about when I had left Palestine. Many times the question was: 'Do you still have family in Pakistan?'

As a matter of fact, I don't. Not in Palestine, at any rate. Never had. I am not from the West Bank or Gaza. If I had my choice, I'd be an Israeli Arab. I am a Palestinian from nowhere. Though shielded, I might add, by a career and material comfort, higher education and a US passport.

Today, volcanoes and the economy have made a mockery of my dreams of an Icelandic national identity. And politics has made the conflation of Palestine with Pakistan acceptable. Perhaps I should rethink my future options.

Samer Al-Saber

Samer Al-Saber is a Palestinian theatre director, writer, actor and scholar. He researches the intersection of cultural production and political conflict in the Middle East. He completed a PhD in Theatre History, Theory and Criticism at the University of Washington (2013) and held an Andrew W. Mellon Postdoctoral Fellowship at Davidson College (2013–15).

A Recurring Sound. A Familiar Image.

Noise.

Time passes.

I pick up the phone. I listen to the dial tone.

Time passes.

I call the travel agent.

'Yes. Seattle–Tel Aviv. No, I've never been, but I don't need a visa. I'm Canadian. Yes. My dates are flexible . . . No, I don't need the insurance. I never buy it . . . I'll give you my credit card number. Oh, hold on a second. Put the insurance on there anyway.'

Time passes.

I tell very few people about this trip. My brother is the only family member I tell.

Time passes.

On the aeroplane, I am asked to give up my seat so a family can sit closer together. It all happens so fast. I'm not thinking clearly. I am paralysed by the quickness of it all. When I settle in my new seat, I look at the seat from a distance. I wonder whether I had a choice. My seat is gone, not by choice. I flip through the TV channels until I fall asleep.

Time passes.

I step off the aeroplane. I see words written in Arabic: 'Welcome to Israel'. I can't understand the Hebrew version. I am on autopilot. The mantra I practised plays in my head: 'I am an academic here on research. I am an academic. I am an academic . . .'

Time passes.

I offer my passport.

A long time passes.

I am leaving the airport in a friend's car. I look outside the window. My friend is driving. A greeting committee of three little kids sits in the back. I see the Hebrew letters everywhere. Suddenly, I am slapped by the reality: Israel is a real country with a system of highways, buses, aeroplanes, buildings and institutions. Israel is real.

Time passes.

In the car, I am mentally in and out of the conversation until my friend says: '. . . and those lights over there are Tulkarem. You see Qalqilya in the distance?' I am suddenly slapped back in place by the other reality: we're still here.

A long time passes.

I am on the bus, on my way to Haifa. A soldier boards. He has a gun.

Time passes.

I am lost in a shopping mall. An old man speaks to me in Hebrew.

'I don't understand,' I reply in English.

'What are you doing here?'

'I'm shopping.'

'Where are you from? What other languages do you speak?'

'I only speak English. Is there a problem?'

'Me? I have no problem. It is you who has a problem.'

The old man walks away. I quickly find my way out.

Time passes.

Haifa. I am in the Hadar. It's a busy day in the market. I am exhausted. I feel the heat on my skin. I see an oncoming figure, a woman. She is blonde. She is middle-aged. I stop, mesmerised by the image. Her body sways right and left as her heavy shopping bags create an intricate rhythm. She looks directly at me, first with anger. I am paralysed. Then her eyes soften, and she smiles knowingly. I smile inexplicably. Right before she passes me, I see her necklace, bearing a cross.

Time passes.

I am hungry. I walk into a *shawarma* shop, exhibiting the familiar atmosphere. I feel uncomfortable. I don't know why. I walk out.

Time passes.

I am hungry. I walk into a *shawarma* shop. I stay and eat.

Time passes.

I am hungry. I walk into a restaurant. I see a sticker: right of return. I sit. I eat. I pay.

'Around the corner, down that way, there are a lot of empty old buildings, like houses. What are they?' I ask as I walk out.

Knowingly, the man replies: 'These are your homes.'

Time passes.

I take a taxi. I speak in English. The driver replies in English. I buy my ticket. I sit close to the front. The taxi moves. The taxi stops. A passenger boards. She speaks Arabic. The driver replies in Arabic. She sits. I speak to her in Arabic.

'How did you know to speak Arabic?'

She looks at me, amused.

'Why do you ask?'

'I got on. I spoke in English. I didn't know to speak Arabic.'

She looks at me, this time clearly intending to make eye contact.

'There is something called those Palestinian eyes.'

A long time passes.

Jerusalem. Old City. I am lost and can't find my way out. I arrive at a small gate. Soldiers. They are checking IDs. I stand and watch. One person is admitted through a crack in the gate. In the thin opening, I quickly glimpse the beautifully decorated building inside with the golden curvature of a familiar dome, the blue sky is its backdrop. Time stops. My heart stops. I can't. I can't see it yet. I walk away.

Time passes.

Jaffa. Old city. Awaiting an old lady as she slowly climbs narrow stairs. She addresses me with a distinctly East European accent.

'I have been going up and down those stairs for forty years. I am much slower now.'

'You are doing very well.'

She smiles knowingly.

'Where are you from?'

Pause.

'Canada.'

Time passes.

I am lost again. It's the early morning. A few men are in a corner chatting, drinking coffee and smoking cigarettes.

'Where is El-Haram El-Sharif?' I ask.

'Where are you from?' he asked back.

'Where am I from?' I dared him to know.

'The coast.'

'Yafa.'

'Yafa.' Pause. 'Inside or outside?'

'Outside.'

'Left, right, then left', he pours half his cup of coffee into a plastic cup, offers it to me and says, 'Welcome home.'

A long time passes.

Silence.

Atef Alshaer

Atef Alshaer was the Leverhulme Post-Doctoral Research Fellow in Political Communication and a senior research fellow and a senior teaching fellow in the Faculty of Languages and Cultures at the School of Oriental and African Studies, University of London. Recently he was appointed a lecturer in Arabic Studies at the University of Westminster. He has several publications, including his forthcoming book, Poetry and Politics in the Modern Arab World.

A Journey in Progress

For the ten years I have been outside Palestine I have never ceased to think about it and its occupation. For me, the occupation of Palestine and its daily humiliation are what wound me most.

When I was in Palestine, I saw the world with Palestinian eyes, but when I left to live in cosmopolitan London, Palestine became like all the other countries of the world, except for the fact that it was occupied. As I see it with worldly eyes, I despair at its ever-deteriorating condition, but at the same time marvel at its greatness in giving rise to world-class intellectuals and poets such as Edward Said and Mahmoud Darwish. I find it inspiring, creatively stubborn, open and beautiful. It promises, in the eyes of people who have seen and laboured for Palestine, a tolerant, diverse, open and secular space on the map of the world. Palestine for me is secular and liberated in its spirits, while keen about its rights. It is this spirit that I remember and wish to see in the future.

It is hard to write who I am in relation to Palestine, for I read a lot about other countries and peoples. I have come to love every patch of earth where I have felt love and humanity. I have come to adore people who hardly know Palestine, but who by their sheer sense of common humanity and respect have won my heart, broadened my mind and expanded the scope of my senses. But yes, Palestine remains my reference point. I love Palestine in the world and its historical significance as a place of coexistence for people from different faiths for millennia. It is not exclusively for anyone, but special to all those who hold it dear without the ardent sense of exceptionalism that has plagued it for so long.

I remember when I was in Gaza, where I grew up with my family during the First Intifada, feeling overwhelmed by the frequent and intrusive presence of Israeli soldiers imposing their will on us as a civilian Palestinian community aware of its history and its political rights. We experienced the violation of our homes and our intimate social space in such a random manner that it reduced our sovereignty and normality as individual human beings and as a community. The sheer military power of Israel conveyed a vulgar practice of superiority and exclusivism. Ultimately, it remains to be said that for me the dream of an inclusive Palestine is no less important than that of a liberated Palestine.

Being Palestinian, if that has an abiding meaning, imposes for me a sense of obligation, a humane and social one, towards my family in Gaza. I think of them, worry about their well-being, the many children they have, the many women and men that I cannot speak to, the countless incidents that I cannot follow anymore.

Palestine continues to be vividly present in my memory. O Gaza, the love looming as you approach the coast, the beautiful children, young men and women and families having a picnic by the ever-scenic Mediterranean. The beautiful landscape around Birzeit University, where I studied, gives me some of my fondest memories because of its extraordinary students and teachers who were good because of their humanity, not only because of their education. I cannot forget the liberating sense of Birzeit, with students filing in and out of faculties looking forward to a bright future, notwithstanding the occupation and other dark socio-political forces which target and cheapen the spirit of worldly love and replace it with petty ideologies of revenge and extravagant moralisations.

But for me, it's also difficult to think of the unjust conditions of occupation in Palestine without feeling desperate about the parts of the world where there is power, such as the United States and Europe, whose leaders continue to support or turn a blind eye to the oppressive Israeli occupation of my country, making it difficult to talk about worldly love or justice without painful qualifications.

There is Palestine from the outside: the last ten years during which I have studied Palestine and have tried to find out more about its language, literature and culture, the philosophical infrastructure of its soul. Palestine from the outside is one that I found through studying in the library of the School of Oriental and African Studies and other places, and through many fruitful discussions and debates in classes. In the face of nostalgia or negative headlines in the news about Palestine, I often felt relieved when I retreated at night to the poetry of Mahmoud Darwish, or the books of Edward Said and other worldly authors, whose words are well-scented and mindful of finding hope and beauty amid harsh thorns.

And there is Palestine the necessity: the obligation to speak about it to people, to situate it on the map of those who have no knowledge about it, to teach about it, to make poetry of its tears.

Palestine leaves me enough space to be liberated from within because its people, their spirits as I experienced them, have often been liberated and tolerant. I find it unsettling when I hear ill-informed and divisive individuals try to tear the Palestinians apart and make them suspicious of each other. For me, long live Palestine! The secular, bound-to-be-free and hopeful Palestine I have in my heart, not the other Palestine, plagued by occupation and narrow ideologies.

Hala Alyan

Hala Alyan is a Palestinian-American writer currently residing in Manhattan. Her poems have appeared in journals such as Third Coast, Copper Nickel *and* CALYX. *Her first full-length collection of poetry, entitled* Atrium, *was recently awarded the 2013 Arab American Book Award in Poetry.*

In Dust

Diaspora is the sharp longing for that which remains nameless, an echo of some lost music. Often, it is not memory. It is wistfulness.

It is the men of your childhood leaning tensely towards news reports on the television. They curse and smoke and crack pumpkin seeds between their teeth as politicians and armies flicker on the screen.

These men are your family. Father, uncle, cousin. You grow up listening to their talk of wars and refugees, of the houses left behind. They speak of cities across the ocean, and you learn that *el-blaad* is just another way of saying *remember*. Some nights you tiptoe out of your little bed and pause in the doorway. The television light dapples their faces and, unseen, you watch the fires and bombings and bulldozers in another land.

It is the flag that sat on your father's desk. Red, white, green, with a black triangle on the side. As a child you would filch touches of it, the fabric silky between your fingers. Years later, you would watch it unfurl from the hands of young men on the television as they cried out and flung stones, and think it looked like liquid fire, a beautiful thing.

It is the middle of June, hot and dry, as you sit in a courtyard in Ramallah. A woman in an azure veil gives you tea so sugary your teeth ache. She guts a watermelon in swift, precise motions, and arranges the slices on a platter.

'Taste, taste,' she tells you. 'Our watermelon is the most delicious you will ever eat.'

The trail that you like to retrace sometimes, the chain of turns and valleys and choices that scattered your family, that fated you to have a life of America and lipstick and Beirut nightclubs and poetry, instead of the ones your cousins have – an upbringing in Kuwait, a childhood in Wichita. Or even a life in Gaza, some of them never leaving the sea's side, watching the skyline brim with white phosphorous.

It is your name becoming another, an Americanised rendering. A flowering plant with toxic berries. This new name falls easily from your teacher's mouth, from the other children.

There is a blooming relief, when you return to Arab cities, to hear your old name again. Nobody ever complains of the guttural *h*.

Your grandmother, father's mother. She lay on her deathbed in Syria, face creased in pain as she named a Palestinian village.

In the years that follow, you will ask your father to repeat it over and over, will write it down on the corners of notebooks, recite it at parties.

You will admonish yourself when you forget it and tell yourself that if you cannot remember then it becomes mislaid. Vanished.

It is the songs and verses and stories. The landscape you paint in your mind's eye, a place you architect to carry all the things you love in this world – bread with *za'tar* and fig jam, your father's accent, Mediterranean sunrises, *dabke* drums – and keep them safe. This becomes Palestine.

It is a slender grey box in the closet of your Manhattan apartment. Inside there are a dozen keys, small and large. You lose track of which cities they belong to, which doors.

It is how you never leave an apartment without saying goodbye to the walls and windows, as if they were lovers. How, upon returning to Arab soil – and this is what your life feels like, an endless series of departures and returns – you stand quietly at dusk, eyes shut, as the echoing voice of the *muezzin* fills the veins of your cities with a call for prayer.

It is the room in Ben Gurion International Airport that you sit in for hours, outside a sun setting over thistle and a crescent moon rising. It is the letters you write down as you bite your lips.

G, and you wonder what the mint will taste like. A, and your fingers clasp the pen tightly. Z, and you picture the sun setting elsewhere. A, and you are quietly waiting for this land.

Your grandmother, mother's mother. She named her first-born, the one that died within a month, Jaffa. She stretches her legs on a balcony, her face tilted towards the sun as she says, 'I thought it was the most beautiful name.'

It is the fitful, dexterous love affairs with cities. Writing about Jerusalem from a hotel room in Bangkok. Seeing a Beirut sky on New Year's Eve, and remembering a woman in Vienna. It is the wandering, the impatience that you once thought you inherited from your father, but which you now know he inherited from lost soil, a homeland waltzing him into restlessness, leaving him to live a life of cardboard boxes, dots on a map, the endless scent of freshly painted rooms.

Hiraeth.[1] It is the word lighting up your cell phone screen, your brother telling you to look up its definition. And when you do, you sit amazed, hand over throat for minutes, at the precision of it, how it has so perfectly summed up an impossible feeling.

You are enormously grateful there are words such as this one.

It is the seven buses you have to take, the buses that rumble to Nablus and Ramallah. To Akka, where your grandfather took his first breath. To Bethlehem, where you drink water sweetened with honey. To Jaffa, where you sit on sand and touch seawater and cry.

Diaspora is an endless absence, time-lapse photography in reverse. It is the desire to become an archaeologist or preservationist, to become the keeper of memories belonging to others. To remember names of villages long buried in dust. Diaspora is reminding yourself, in the bleakest moments – another war, another smattering of bombs – that as long as you have lungs, and air to fill them, you, and those that come after you, will be the memento, the living memory of place.

Note

1. *Hiraeth* is a Welsh word indicating homesickness tinged with grief and wistfulness over one's lost homeland.

Kholoud Amr

Kholoud Amr has worked as a broadcast journalist for the BBC, Al Jazeera and Al-Arabiya satellite channels covering news and current affairs. She has also worked as a professional translator for a number of newspapers. Currently she is studying for an MA in Film Making and TV, and producing her own documentaries.

Citizen of the World

'Well, you look white enough to me!' the black receptionist at the local surgery answered me back. Filling in the application forms to register at the local surgery upon my arrival in London, I could not identify myself as 'white', 'black', 'Chinese' or 'mixed'; I was simply none of those! Such a question was really confusing for somebody who had never been asked something like this before.

In the years before I came to live in Britain I never really thought much about my identity, or 'colour' for that matter. I was merely one of many: a Palestinian born in Amman, Jordan. As a newcomer to London, though, I was surprised to discover that I could be many other things as well.

What an excitement I felt to live in a cosmopolitan city like London! I was amazed when I walked through its streets by the number of black people, the number of Indian and Pakistani shops, the number of Chinese restaurants! Back in Jordan I could only count three black people, a few Pakistanis and Indians and no Chinese, whom I had never seen in all my life! It was an incredible move for that twenty-year-old Arab girl who had never travelled before, and whose entire knowledge about the world came from books and TV. Now she felt she had the opportunity of meeting the world in person.

As time went by I excitedly embraced the fantastic new environment of ethnic diversity. Not in my wildest dreams had I imagined I would have a circle of friends that included a Crimean, an Amazonian, an Assyrian, a South African, a New Yorker and many more. My new experiences even began to shape the way I felt about myself. I wanted to relate to everybody regardless of their blood or geography. 'Was it possible?' This was the persistent question in my mind but the utopian dream of becoming a member of the big human family was attractive enough that I claimed to be a citizen of the world.

However, the sweetness I was feeling in pursuing the warmth of utopian dreams in London was spoilt by the bitterness of reality, as a consequence of the conflict which I had come from. Two incidents burst the bubble I had briefly been living in, and dragged me down to face the cold ground. The first took place on a train from London to Cambridge. Here I was on my daily journey home from work, tired and sleepy. The man next to me started talking on his mobile. With the little Hebrew I knew I realised he was Israeli. When I opened an Arab newspaper to read, he became curious and decided I was someone he needed to check on. He asked: 'You know Arabic? Where are you from?' I said, smiling: 'I'm Palestinian'.

We had a normal conversation until I mentioned I was born in Jordan, then the man suddenly gave himself the right to decide for me who I was, wondering how I still called myself a Palestinian when in fact I was born in Jordan. I smiled back and said, 'Well, is it not the same as the many Jews who were born around the world but moved to Palestine/Israel and call themselves Israelis?'

Some months afterwards, I received a second slap in the face at Ben Gurion Airport, Tel Aviv, when I was going to Israel for the first time in my capacity as a journalist. I handed the security lady my British passport and press accreditation. She looked in my passport for too long. Perhaps my Arab name and Western appearance did not really 'match' and confused her. Without any explanation she went inside a small room and disappeared for a while before coming back and asking: 'Do you hold other passports?'

'Yes, I hold a Jordanian one as well.'

After bombarding me with what felt like a hundred questions, she unleashed her final question: 'Where were your parents born?'

'They were born in Hebron,' I replied, losing my temper.

She nodded her head with a smirk all over her face. Her body language said it all: 'You thought you could trick us with your British and Jordanian passports. You're a Palestinian!'

These encounters made it clear to me that for some Israelis I cannot be Palestinian, but for others I am, no matter what! Granting me Palestinian identity, or depriving me of it, seemed to depend on their convenience. I found myself rethinking my identity again. Being a citizen of the world, for me, means putting universal human values above territory, nationality and race. However, the same values oblige me to identify with occupied Palestine. Therefore, for me, being Palestinian means putting freedom and liberty before geography or blood. As long as Palestine is occupied and the Palestinians are not free, I choose to be a Palestinian.

Anonymous

Being Nobody

Like any other person, especially Arabs living outside the Arab world, I am a collection of seemingly confusing and contradicting assertions. My mother tongue is Arabic, yet I express myself best in English. I was born and raised a Catholic, yet I am an atheist. I enjoy Fairuz, *zajal* and a *zaffeh* as much as I enjoy opera, rock music and techno. A medium-rare steak with peppercorn sauce will indulge me as much as a good *mansaf*, or *zait* and *za'tar* from our garden. So when I was asked specifically about being Palestinian in diaspora, I paused with confused hesitation and asked: 'Who am I?'

I was born and raised in Jordan to 1948 Palestinian refugees. Through hard work, extensive family support and good luck I ended up at a top university in England. Years later, with a PhD and a lovely non-Arab wife and children, I'm building a life in the UK. When I go back to Jordan, some people lament how the country has 'lost' me (apparently I am part of the 'brain drain'), while others wonder what I will do when I eventually come back (note the implicit assumption) and others give me stern warnings to 'never' come back (again, note the assumption). What no one has ever realised is that me living in the UK is not due to a lack of opportunities in Jordan, but a rejection by me of the society I grew up in.

Living in the UK, I consciously traded social structures that I do not like with those that I like, or at least tolerate. I traded a society that settles serious disputes with a *jaha* and a sip of coffee with one favouring lawsuits and psychiatric therapy. Instead of being defined as a Palestinian or as a Christian or by my family name, I am now an individual, a doctor. I left a very socially conservative society for a significantly more liberal one.

Yet I traded a society the mainstream Western media mocks for having little privacy and personal freedom with a society that is constantly watched by CCTV cameras and whose successive governments, apparently, liberally eavesdrop on all communications and have passed into law the right to detain without trial. Indeed, my replacement for an imperfect Jordan is also imperfect, but it speaks more of my language.

Being an Arab who constantly mingles with non-Arabs, I am, obviously, the go-to authoritative reference for all things relating to people from Morocco to Afghanistan and Muslims; sadly, bad knowledge of geography and religious assumptions define the 'Middle East' for many. Amusingly, Westerners expect anti-Israeli commentary from me, and Arabs simply assume that I dislike Israel. The reality of the situation shocks and annoys both sides. To Westerners, I regularly have to explain that most Arabs, especially Palestinians, are not gun-toting, camel-riding, hummus-eating, bearded maniacs who 'speak funny' but, on the contrary, are mostly nice people who want to live in peace with their families and friends, and that several Israeli policies hurt this harmless majority. To Arabs, I defend the right of Israelis to live peacefully with their families and friends, and I explain that some Arab and Palestinian policies hurt the pursuit of peace.

This is a constant theme in my life as a Palestinian in diaspora. I am a messenger for both sides, preaching to pro-Arab and pro-Israeli people that the other side is not automatically wrong simply because it is unknown or unfamiliar to them. I aggressively defend the Arab way of life that I left behind because Arabs have as much right to live as they wish as British people and others do. There must not be any presumption from anyone that their way is 'better'.

The other theme in my life is where is home. I left Jordan because its ways of doing things are incompatible with mine. I live in the UK, but given the constant political and social bombardment against Arabs, and immigrants in general, I cannot yet safely call it home either. Honestly, right now I do not have a home beyond the homestead where my wife and kids and I reside. There is no place where I have really deep roots, where my local knowledge is greater than what I learnt at university, and where local traditions are unquestioned truths. Even the word 'local', right now, is quite vague.

My parents stumbled out of Palestine and managed to recover and lead relatively good lives. I am stumbling too, and travelling in search of my own home and good life. It is as if I am a refugee from 1948, just decades late. I am a Palestinian rock that is still rolling to its final resting place, having travelled through literally dozens of countries and been shaped by winds from dozens more. I am a melting pot of Palestinian, Arab and Western thoughts, with none dominating.

I have done nothing particularly newsworthy or attention-grabbing. I exercise choice over the things I like, want and dislike. I live in the pursuit of happiness and fulfilment from my social and professional lives. I try to reason as much as I am predictably irrational. I sometimes vote. I am, honestly, an average middle-class nobody.

And so perhaps the best answer to the question of being Palestinian in diaspora is simply being a person, like any other, from anywhere else around the world. As such an abused people, the fact of realising we are, after all, typical human beings, is perhaps the best answer to what it means to be Palestinian, no matter where that may be.

Iman Arab

Iman Arab is a physician who specialises in public health. She worked in the Middle East before emigrating to Canada. She is currently working in the mental health sector while pursuing her passion for advocacy. She is the founder of The Diversity Centre for cultural competency training and diversity research. She lives in Kitchener, ON, with her husband Jamal, her son Bashar and her daughter Rasha.

Embracing Uncertainty

Growing up Palestinian filled me with pride, dreams and hopes for the future: attending the best school, living in beautiful houses, having wonderful vacations, moving around with a total sense of entitlement, being surrounded by successful people, listening to the stories of our family's heritage, legacy and duties, and learning to cherish our land deeds; I thought that was the norm!

I can't remember exactly when I started to see 'being Palestinian' in a different way. It is true there were many wars affecting my family and too much moving around and changing residences all the time, but for me it was all part of the adventure. At the time the only thing I found odd was my extended family: why did other kids have their grandparents around whom they could go and visit when the school day was over while I had to travel to see mine when the school year was over? But again, it was fun to travel to different places to see them!

As part of a family that was very involved in the Palestinian struggle, I had all the uncertainties and fears of not knowing what was happening around me: war times, painting the windows blue to dim the lights, listening to the radio in the dark, waiting for my father to come back home and dancing around when we knew he was safe. They were all part of the adventure. Living away from my family was another part of it. Even hiding in a basement while the building was being bombed did not shatter any of my dreams or scare me. I knew I would be 'out' the next day, out on another adventure.

Growing up, I learnt that not everyone had the same privileges I had, but almost everyone shared the same hopes, dreams and fears. For them it was not a happy adventure, and for many there was no 'out' the next day.

The news of death, misery and poverty among the Palestinians decided my career choice: advocacy or medicine? Could I become one of those doctors with a magic wand that saves people? Why not? I had performed very well at school and I had the support of my family. So I became a doctor, and afterwards I did a public health master's degree learning the art of preventing disease, prolonging life and promoting health, a good combination between medicine and advocacy.

Everything happening in Palestine affects the lives of Palestinians in diaspora, even if our level of involvement or the impact of events are different, but it remains there on a daily basis. Every bride is worried about the dress, the venue and so on, but I had other worries. It was after the First Intifada: would something happen in Palestine that would stop us from having the wedding? Would there be an outrageous Israeli assault? Would someone be arrested and unable to attend? Where should we hold our wedding? In which country do most of our relatives live? Which country are they all allowed to enter, regardless of what passport they carry? I prayed hard for peace.

For me, being Palestinian is always associated with dreams and hopes, goals set and achieved and, most of all, definitions and concepts.

Looking back, I have had two definitions to my life: temporary and permanent. Under the temporary category falls schools, houses, friends and countries: everything that could change in a few hours, everything that would be replaced in the next adventure. This resulted in a sense of freedom and an embracement of uncertainty. However, it also added to my sense of not belonging anywhere. I have no concrete memories or established connections to anywhere I have lived. It is very easy for me either to say, 'I remember that place, I attended school there once! And I think I made some friends there.' Or, just as easily, 'Frankly I cannot remember the name of the high school I graduated from, was it this one or, no, wait that was where I finished grade 10.' While going through these experiences I developed a firm belief that nothing is irreplaceable. A life lived with no attachments and a sense of curiosity and excitement for the next adventure is, I believe, a life that is solely good.

However, I sometimes do envy people who have lived in the same place with all their family and friends around them, and I have tried to give my kids that same sense of belonging. But for me, I cannot change my life – and it was good.

The other category is the permanent category, which includes my family, my homeland and my identity. Sometimes they are so mixed together that I cannot differentiate between them; these are the things that will never change. Moving around, crossing borders and living ten thousand kilometres away from Palestine did not affect these constants. On the contrary, it made them more profound. The constant moving created a strong bond and sense of connectedness to my family. I do not mind spending my nights talking to my sister in Australia, or calling my mother in Jordan on a daily basis.

When it comes to my homeland, I feel that it is my duty to teach people about Palestine: the land, the history, the culture and the cause. I proudly seek and seize every opportunity to do this. I enjoy having a Christmas tree, just to start a dialogue with Canadians about the fact that we Palestinian Muslims lived peacefully with our fellow Christian citizens all the time and that Jesus Christ is Palestinian and, more importantly, he is our first martyr. At Easter I like to tell people that my mother, who was born in Jerusalem, was in fact born in the place that witnessed the Last Supper and that it was her family home. For many generations they lived there, were entrusted to protect it and keep it safe. They were the guardians of that holy place, which they preserved and looked after for hundreds of years till they were forced out by the Israeli occupation. I add, innocently, 'I wonder what happened to my grandparents' house now. Would you please check?'

Without planning, I became an expert in history, political science and human rights. I am always ready with information, evidence, links and photographs to prove what I am discussing or advocating. Always ready to defend something or someone. And I am always attributing my smart moves to being Palestinian, and the not-so-smart ones to any other influence in my long journey. Did I mention advocacy as a career path? Well my wish has been granted.

Being Palestinian means a lot of pride and dreams which I am passing on to my kids with the hope that one day the owners of Palestine will return there.

Sa'ed Atshan

Sa'ed Atshan is a postdoctoral fellow at Brown University's Watson Institute for International Studies. He holds a PhD (2013) and MA (2010) in Anthropology and Middle Eastern Studies from Harvard University, an MPP (2008) from Harvard University, and a BA (2006) from Swarthmore College.

'Our Country Lives in Us'

'Every people live in their country, but for Palestinians, our country lives in us.' This widely known expression among Palestinians around the world has always resonated with me. Based on my experience and that of my family and loved ones, these words are certainly true. I am a Palestinian-American who in twenty-nine years on this planet has been straddling two worlds: that of Palestine and that of the United States. The way I have balanced these disparate spheres has been mediated by educational institutions as well as my identity as a gay man. My love for my ancestral homeland, my passion for social justice and my desire to remain compassionate towards others are by-products of my experiences as a diasporic Palestinian.

You come to understand what it means to be Palestinian when you are part of a refugee family, when you live under Israeli military occupation, or when you are apart from Palestine in the diaspora. Both sets of my grandparents survived the *Nakba*, and they always remind us that the spirits of our ancestors buried beneath the lands we have lost – and from which we were ethnically cleansed – call on us to return.

While growing up to a refugee family in the West Bank, I felt a deep attachment to the rest of historic Palestine, but was physically cut off from other cities outside of Ramallah due to the system of closures and immobility imposed on Palestinians. While we were so close and yet so far from the Mediterranean, dreaming about the day that all Palestinians will have the freedom to swim in the sea helped me cope with the trauma of the Second Intifada.

The Ramallah Friends School was also a haven for me during the Intifada. With a rich history, having been founded in the 1800s by American Quakers in Palestine, the school cultivated my intellect, nurtured my spirit and exemplified the coexistence between Palestinian Christians and Muslims in Ramallah of which we are so proud.

My childhood memories from Palestine have stayed with me ever since. When I matriculated at Swarthmore College in 2002, an institution also founded by the Quakers just outside Philadelphia, I often felt as if my grandparents were beside me. I would daydream about picking olives from the trees in our garden and pressing them to make fresh oil. We would sit on our balcony, the fresh air in our faces, the rolling hills in our midst, sipping mint tea and dipping my grandmother's warm, home-baked bread in our olive oil, along with fresh white cheese and pieces of watermelon. Such daydreams remind me of Palestinian resilience and the beautiful and revolutionary acts of everyday survival. After all, as we always remind ourselves, 'existence is resistance'.

While coming of age in Palestine, I did not have the conceptual toolkit or vocabulary to truly understand that I was gay, but I was conscious that there was a normative masculinity expected in society to which I could aspire but never attain. When I did come out to my family years later, I was largely met with unconditional love and acceptance. But my experience as a gay Palestinian, at the margin of the margins, has shaped my relationship to my second home in the United States. You cannot go from a social milieu of statelessness and brutal military occupation to the most powerful nation-state on earth without being keenly aware of injustice, in all of its forms, wherever it exists. Even in the face of Zionism and homophobia, I will never be silent.

Thus it was an honour for me to complete my doctorate at Harvard University, and retrace the footsteps of the late Palestinian intellectual and political giant Edward Said who was a graduate student on the Harvard campus. In speaking with many diaspora Palestinians about my experience, it is almost as if both Palestine and Harvard are magical places, only accessible to those who are incredibly fortunate. I appreciate how privileged I have been to benefit from the educational opportunities afforded to me, but this is coupled with memories that will always take me back to Palestine. It is with heavy hearts that our days pass without the realisation of the Palestinian 'right of return'. My belief in the responsibility everyone shares to end all forms of oppression, to rectify injustice, and to realise Palestinian freedom motivates all of my pursuits. Palestine is my anchor and the source of my moral compass.

I remember arriving at the John F. Kennedy School of Government at Harvard and entering the Forum where the flags of countries from across the world that represent the student body were prominently displayed. Yet the Palestinian flag was nowhere to be found. It took me months of negotiations with the administration until I was able to convince them to add the Palestinian flag so that I, too, could feel that I belonged and that I was an equal member of the community. Although I do not want to romanticise nationalism or flag-waving, we live in a world where unless we speak LGBTQ activists will continue to be detained for flying the rainbow flag in their countries, and the Israeli military can impose policies on the population it occupies, such as banning displays of the Palestinian flag, as was the case during the First Intifada.

Just as I needed a haven in Palestine, my haven as a graduate student in Cambridge, Massachusetts was Algiers Café. Algiers has been owned since its inception in 1970 by a Palestinian named Emile Durzi, who left Palestine in his youth. This restaurant in the heart of Harvard Square is where I could find Arabic music playing in the background and art from across the Arab world displayed on the walls, including an image of Handala. It is where I could order mint tea and my favourite dish of *mujaddara* with its rice, lentils, sautéed onions and yogurt. In these moments I would be transported to Palestine and feel even more determined to do everything I could to reclaim my own voice and that of the Palestinian people, a people whose spirits can never be crushed.

Abdel Bari Atwan

Abdel Bari Atwan is the Editor-in-Chief of Rai al-Youm, *the Arab world's first online news and comment site. The established author, broadcaster and former editor of* al-Quds al-Arabi *was born in a refugee camp in the Gaza Strip two years after the Nakba. Having fled to Jordan in 1967, he has lived most of his life in exile.*

Forever Gazan

I remember how the year 2009 was ushered in by me with tears as news of the Israeli onslaught on Gaza continued and casualties mounted rapidly.

While I was sitting in my office in London, overseeing the production of the next day's newspaper, my professional life came face-to-face with my personal history and my family's reality as I read the horrific accounts of slaughter and saw the graphic images of suffering and death.

I was born in a refugee camp in the Gaza Strip to parents forced from their home and land in Asdod by the Israelis during the 1948 *Nakba*. That grim January in 2009, dispassionate news feeds gave us statistics but my telephone brought me news of the reality on the ground. My brothers and sisters still live in Gaza and, whenever they were able to get through, told us of Israeli bulldozers demolishing pitiful Gazan shacks at the coldest time of year; of power and water supplies being cut off; of gunfire and bombardment; of small children having mental breakdowns due to the inhuman levels of anxiety they were forced to endure.

One thousand four hundred Palestinians died in what the media insisted on calling a 'war', most of them women and children. Thirteen Israelis, ten of them soldiers, lost their lives in this latest episode of what must rank as one of the most unequal conflicts in human history.

I have lived in the UK for thirty-one years but my heart is still, and will always be, Palestinian. I respect and enjoy my adopted culture but I continue to speak English with an Arabic accent, stubbornly sticking to the same mistakes I have been making since my UNWRA teacher beat me with a stick for them back in the 1950s.

My journey from Gaza to London was a difficult one, undertaken alone, which took more than ten years and a lot of determination. At seventeen I was a refuse worker in Amman and afterwards laboured in the sweltering heat of a tomato-canning factory until I had enough money to fulfil my dream of studying at Cairo University, subsidised generously by my elder brother. When I said farewell to my fellow students, having graduated at the end of three years, I was the only student who could not exchange a forwarding address for I had no idea which country would next accept this Palestinian refugee.

Ironically, despite the great distance I have put between myself and my homeland, I find I am still unable to escape Israeli oppression. I have had death threats and a hate campaign launched against me by the Zionist lobby, which succeeded in making me *persona non grata* at the BBC for a couple of years. Lies about me litter the Internet thanks to the energetic efforts of the Hasbara (propaganda) department, and well-drilled Israeli students frequently disrupt my lectures at academic institutions.

Even when Gaza is not in the news, I have a black-and-white photograph of Deir al Balah refugee camp, where I was born, on my office wall, hidden behind a pillar where I can see it from my desk. Just a glance at the tents and tumbledown houses that passed for homes and the white waves pounding the beach beside them, takes me back and reminds me of my origins. Memories of the little mud house I was brought up in along with my eight siblings, the hardships we endured and the health problems caused by malnutrition prevent any possibility of arrogance or boastfulness on my part, no matter what I may have achieved.

That black-and-white photo brings back happy memories too: my beloved mother telling us stories in the winter dark; the fire crackling in the centre of the one room our house contained; the ceiling made of sticks and home to rats and fascinating insects; trips out to sea with the Gazan fishermen who used dynamite rather than nets to disable their prey before diving deep into the clear blue seas to scoop them up; stealing dates from the top of tall palm trees I would scale barefoot while a lazy guard slept beneath.

My three children speak more English than Arabic and are more at home on the streets of London than I will ever be. I took them to Gaza three times while my mother was still alive and she told me off for their Western ways but loved them deeply nonetheless. They will never forget what it is to be Palestinian, nor do they want to, because we often speak of the land and the pretty little house in Asdod that my distraught parents were forced to leave in 1948.

I will continue to insist on my right to return to that house, to that land, as long as there is breath in my body, and when my time comes I want to be buried there, finally back home.

The life and times of Ibrahim, father of the Editor. Ibrahim in military-style uniform before being conscripted to the Ottoman Army, Jerusalem, Palestine, c. 1911.

Ibrahim as a budding businessman, Tiberias, Palestine, 1921.

Ibrahim with his wife Aziza, a Damascene woman of Kurdish origin, on their wedding day in Tiberias, Palestine, 1923. Aziza's family had fled to Tiberias from Damascus after their only son was killed by a Senegalese soldier during the period of the French occupation of Syria.

'All these years we were there in a drawer, or perhaps on display, with Sido, in the heart of Ramallah.' Samer Abdelnour (left) with his brother Nader in a photograph he found in his late grandfather's apartment in Ramallah in Spring 2014.

Before the 'whirlwind' of the *Nakba*. Salman Abu Sitta (second from right) with his brothers in the orchard of their home in Al Ma'in, Beer Sheba District, 1944. It is the only photograph Salman owns from before the *Nakba* in 1948.

From *Mapping My Return: A Palestinian Memoir* by Salman Abu Sitta (AUC Press, 2015), courtesy of Salman Abu Sitta

Playing for Palestine. Lila Abu-Lughod's daughter, JJ (Yasmine) Mitchell, at training in Al-Ram Stadium for the Palestinian National Women's Football Team in January 2011.

'People keep on asking me where Palestine is on the map, so I have created it in the shape of my grandmother's words and face.' 'Map of Herstoric Palestine', a painting by Ibtisam Barakat, 2012.

On the brink of change. Ibtisam
Barakat aged three with her
brothers, Basel and Muhammad,
and parents Suleiman and
Mirriam at their home in
Ramallah, West Bank, 1967,
shortly before the Six-Day War.

Where it all starts. Ibtisam Barakat (left) teaching *dabke* to Arab-American children at
Al-Bustan Arab Culture Summer Camp in Philadelphia, USA in summer 2009.

Ida Audeh

Ida Audeh is an editor who grew up in the West Bank and now lives in Colorado. Her articles and interviews have been published by various electronic media, including Electronic Intifada *and* Countercurrents. *She is also the Editor of* Birzeit University: The Story of a National Institution, *published by Birzeit University in 2010.*

Ties that Bind, Ties that Sustain

The awareness of my identities as an Arab and a Palestinian was shaped in the United States, in the years following my arrival in 1980 as a twenty-two-year-old graduate student. My main concern when I decided to move was to avoid what I thought of as the predictable and conventional course my life would take if I were to return to my conservative hometown in the West Bank after graduating from the American University of Beirut. To escape that, I enrolled in a graduate programme at a university in Washington, DC; education being the only reason my parents might accept their unmarried daughter living in a foreign country.

It didn't take long for me to realise that the political and popular cultures of the country I was so eager to move to were profoundly hostile to Arabs, Palestinians and Muslims. Every news item that concerned Palestinians or Arabs generally was framed through an Israeli lens. I felt very strongly that I was part of a group that was considered suspect to a large extent because our existence thwarted Israel's grand plans.

Alienated, I turned to other Palestinians and Arabs for a sense of belonging. I participated in Arab community activities and joined a group whose mission was to educate the American public about Israel's illegal use of the massive US aid it receives annually, courtesy of the generous (and generally clueless) American taxpayer. This was when my education about the struggles I thought I had left behind actually began.

More than thirty years have gone by. Although I have spent almost my entire adult life in this country, I cannot see it as my own, and I do not want to grow old here. But the decision is no longer completely mine: having lost the 'correct' residency papers that might have allowed me to live in the West Bank, albeit under Israeli occupation, my US passport means that I can only return as a tourist, but (thanks to my ethnicity) my entry into the country is by no means assured. I am at the mercy of the Israeli who guards the point of entry – most likely an immigrant (or son or daughter of an immigrant) from the US, or Europe, or Australia – deciding who to admit and who to deny entry. The irony of my situation is not lost on me: when I could live there, I wanted out, but now that my entry is no longer assured, I am desperate to get the 'right' papers so I can return at will and stay as long as I please. But if I do, most of historic Palestine will be off limits to me (as it is now to West Bankers); I will be restricted to Bantustans defined by checkpoints, settlements, closures and the Apartheid Wall.

I go home as a tourist now and I pump my mother for stories of relatives and townspeople long dead. I want to hear about a time when people were living their lives in ways that made sense to them, doing the best with the circumstances they had, before anyone had ever heard of Zionism or the cataclysm it would cause. Simple, stubborn people, they travelled to North and South America to earn a little something to enable them to marry and set up a household, maybe buy a plot of land. Unlike other immigrants, these old-timers never intended to make a permanent home in foreign lands. I try to imagine the courage it must have taken for untravelled farmers to venture so far from home, relying only on their willingness to work and the few kinsmen who had preceded them. They left home knowing only that it would be a long time before they would find their way back.

It took my uncle twenty years to return home, but his was an involuntary exile. Arrested by the Israeli authorities for his activism as a labour union leader and a communist, he was one of many Palestinian leaders deported from the West Bank in the early 1970s. He returned after the Oslo capitulation (cynically described as the beginning of a 'peace process'); by then only one of his siblings was alive to welcome him home. The public mood was hopeful at the time, not because there were valid reasons to believe that the agreement would end Israel's domination, but because people were exhausted and needed to believe that the sacrifices made during the First Intifada were not in vain.

The need to believe that the seemingly impossible is within reach is not as delusional as it might seem. On 15 May 2011, Palestinians in Syria and

Lebanon marched towards the border with Occupied Palestine and, when it came into view, they ran across a field they were warned had been mined. I watched the video clips, dumbfounded. Who in their right mind would take such a risk? Fourteen were shot dead trying to return. But one of them, Syrian resident Hassan Hijazi, made it all the way to Jaffa. When questioned, he said simply: 'My dream is to reach Jaffa, the city where I am from. I don't want to go back to Syria, I want to stay here in my village, where my father and grandfather were born.'

To be Palestinian in these times is to live with contradictions. We are besieged, caged and increasingly impoverished, 'led' by spent old men who speak in a dead idiom and who are incapable of serving the Palestinian national interest. Never has Israel controlled Palestinian lives more maniacally, never has US government support for it been more absolute. We Palestinians have been pummelled by Israel and the US acting in concert, we have been betrayed, but the fact remains that we as a people have not surrendered.

When I get together with friends, the conversation inevitably touches on changes we have noticed in the coverage of Palestinian politics over the years. And it is certainly possible to find evidence that the conversation has been opened up to an extent. Thoughtful letters and op-eds are published in major newspapers by people who have done solidarity work in the occupied Palestinian territories or are otherwise sceptical of the US and Israeli official versions of events. In every major US demonstration for peace and social justice, Palestinian flags and demands have a prominent place: our cause has come out from the shadows and sits front and centre, impossible to ignore, related to other struggles.

Yet paradoxically, what makes me feel slightly less of an outsider in this country are not the signs of positive change toward Palestinians but rather signs of dissent on issues unrelated to the question of Palestine. Americans are undergoing a kind of Palestinian experience of their own. From the vociferous assaults on political expression and the criminalisation of dissent, to the protests launched by broken veterans who have returned from Iraq or Afghanistan appalled by the role they played in US empire-building, to the predatory economic policies that have made families destitute, Americans are learning what it feels like to be at the mercy of a powerful system that sees them as dispensable. Across the country, people are starting to fight back. I can stand in solidarity with that.

Omar Aysha

Omar Aysha is a computer science graduate from the American University in Cairo. He was a video game developer turned business IT consultant running a small UK consultancy. Near-death brought about a further career change and now he works on media projects and as a start-up writer/producer, and will soon be launching his own start-up.

Pal.I.Am

The painful truth is that I don't know what it's like to be *Filisteeni*, Palestinian. I've never been to Palestine. Cairo-born, I speak Egyptian Arabic, and I spent my formative years between Egypt, Kuwait and the UK. I visited my Palestinian family in Lebanon often, but the odd week or two here and there doesn't mean you share a culture. No, culturally speaking I'm Egyptian and English. I've always been a little ashamed of my lack of knowledge of Palestinian culture, of being Palestinian, being a 'proper' Palestinian, but most Palestinians born and raised in the diaspora have multiple cultural identities and have probably struggled at some points, like I have, to juggle these identities. It's natural; after all, you can't be from or understand a community or place unless you've lived in it as a native. And, by definition, we haven't lived in Palestine. Palestine's been denied us since birth, since before birth for most of us.

I've always felt Palestinian though. When I was a child in the 1970s I couldn't forget even if I'd wanted to: I had a Palestinian Refugee Travel Document, standard Lebanese issue. Going through Arab airports I got told by passport control to take a seat while my name was checked against 'The Black List'. Back in those days, with few computers and typical Arab inefficiency, this normally took hours. My younger brother, England-born and with a UK passport, went straight through. I was too young to understand why I got treated differently to him, we were brothers! Now I understand but don't accept it. Back then it made me frustrated, angry, sad and resigned;

it also made me think that being Palestinian was a mark of shame. It was something that had to be hidden; being Palestinian only caused you problems. Ironically, passport control at Heathrow Airport was painless and I was treated with respect. Britain, the country that denied me my birthright and made us refugees by instigating the creation of Israel through the Balfour Declaration of November 1917, was the first country that showed me what it is like to be respected as a human, even though its people also showed me some racism.

I loved and hated Britain; although the people were friendly, back then the news only showed Palestinians as the baddies. I loved the Arab countries and hated them too. I felt kinship and brotherhood there, but the authorities made life hard for me – they didn't want us. Childhood was confusing, filled with wildly conflicting emotions, but most of all I felt unwanted. Don't get me wrong, my family loved me and made me feel loved, but outside I felt I belonged nowhere. Being Palestinian was like being a leper, except even lepers have their own colony.

Growing up with my background it was impossible not to become politically aware, but I was too scared to be politically active. Even if no one said anything directly, it was clear that I was only allowed to be in any country at its government's pleasure, I had no right to be there. I feared that if I made a wrong move I'd be kicked out, 'bye-bye'. It felt like an axe hung over my head. Stay quiet, blend in and survive. It was hard to be proud of being Palestinian so I usually kept the fact hidden. On occasions I would tell Arabs I was Palestinian if I felt low and wanted easy sympathy, but no one in an official capacity if I could help it. Telling a Briton I was Palestinian was too much hassle and I was often met with a blank stare. Much easier to tell them I was Egyptian, at least they'd heard of Egypt – no tedious explaining to do.

Looking back now I realise what a privileged, comfortable life I had. Compared to what Palestinians go through daily under occupation I led a charmed life. But when I was a child my horizons were limited, and existential insecurity was ever-present in the background. My fears were real to me.

Then, in my mid-twenties, I became a British citizen. I had an officially recognised nationality, I officially belonged for the first time. I remember the day I got the paperwork and I wondered if people who were born with a nationality ever felt that joy, or knew how lucky they were. I felt safe, unbound. I went freelance and took contracts in Europe. Airports weren't scary anymore, I just showed my British passport and they waved me through. I didn't even have to get a visa, let alone apply months in advance; freedom of movement is amazing. Then I noticed that I began doing something wonderful. When I met someone new and they asked me where I was from, I'd say I was Palestinian! I wasn't scared to say it anymore, it was as if, as we say in Arabic, I'd 'got a back to lean on'. Getting a UK passport allowed me to express my Palestinian-ness.

My mixed heritage and frequent relocation as a child made it easy for me to mix with most people. When I started working freelance I was living or working in a new city biannually and because I liked to go out and party, like most Brits, I met lots and lots of new people. I was the first Palestinian many of these people had met and I found myself explaining and discussing the Palestinian issue over and over, but now it wasn't a hassle, I was accepted, I enjoyed it, I was doing good PR for Palestine; I'd become politically active by accident. My British identity meant I connected easily with Europeans because we shared a culture. I understood why Europeans felt a kinship with Ashkenazi Jews; they shared a culture and heritage. I also understood that it's much easier to be loud and proud and confident about your identity if you feel comfortable, because you feel fundamentally safe.

Just as I've become open and confident about being Palestinian, I've encountered many diaspora-born Palestinians who think the same. We are humans and we have rights. No one will give us our birthright so we must claim Palestine back. We now feel safe and confident enough to do just that. My father's generation had to focus on survival, so they instilled a bit too much fear in us, but my children and their generation will get to choose whether they stay in the diaspora or not. Being Palestinian now brings me hope.

Ibtisam Azem

Ibtisam Azem is a writer and journalist based in New York. She was born and raised in Taybat al-Muthallath and left from there to study at the Hebrew University of Jerusalem and then to Germany where she graduated with an MA in Islamic Studies and German and English Literature from the University of Freiburg. She is co-editor of Jadaliyya *e-zine. She has published two novels,* Sariq al-Nawm *(The Sleep Thief) in 2011 and* Sifr al-Ikhtifaa *(The Book of Disappearance) in 2014, both from Beirut.*

Things We Carry With Us

'Where are you from?' I hate this simple question that has haunted me in all the cities I have inhabited since I left Palestine fifteen years ago and went to Switzerland and then Germany. It still haunts me today in New York. My confusion as I attempt to answer it does not indicate any confusion in the identities I carry, it rather means that many of those I encounter see official maps as identical to reality. It also means that I have to explain and elaborate on what it means to be a Palestinian carrying an Israeli passport, and to do so without negating the 'Other' who denies my very existence. 'It is difficult to be a Palestinian', as the late Mahmoud Darwish said.

I do not wish to begin my conversation with anyone with a lecture on alternative history. My answer gets longer or shorter according to my mood, but it is always lacking. I might say 'from Palestine' without adding anything else, but I know the person will often think I am from the other occupied territories of 1967. I will add that I am from a city near Jaffa and my grandmother is from Jaffa, but she was displaced inside Palestine. She woke up one morning, she and an entire people, to find themselves refugees, or carrying passports that had nothing to do with who they were. The name of their country changed, as did the street names, the faces of people they used to know, the music, language; everything around now used to have a different name. Some of the new names were from the men who denied their existence and denied the *Nakba*, some who had committed massacres. And one still has to justify being Palestinian.

I realise this is not a good beginning when meeting someone for the first time, nor for small talk. After trying out a variety of answers, I have decided there is no need for explanation. I have started to say, 'From Taybat al-Muthallath, north of Jaffa, in Palestine.' If they want to know more they can ask, and they usually do!

The announcer on the radio speaks about building new 'housing units' in 'illegal' settlements.

'Is there such a thing as legal settlements?' I bark at the radio. 'The entire country is a giant settlement!' And I proceed to give the announcer a history lesson, but no one listens to me. His voice reaches hundreds of thousands of New York homes. The news brief becomes their news (the Americans) and I become an 'Other'. I scrutinise every word he utters not only about Palestine, but all the wretched and the marginalised. Those who are reduced to numbers and whose stories never make it to the news. Native Americans, African Americans, women, the Iraqis who have died and are dying, the Afghans. The list is long.

I leave my apartment and walk to my favourite spot in Washington Square Park. There is a man who plays the piano every afternoon in the summer. I sit on one of the benches, listening to him, and bathe in the sun's warmth and drink its light. The voice of an old woman wakes me up. We chat about New York, the weather and how talented the pianist is. She does not ask me where I'm from. Despite the accent, I am, as far as she is concerned, a New Yorker. She bids me farewell and leaves citing the unbearable heat. I watch the piano player and return to Palestine. In exile I always return to Palestine. And I wonder: when will the day come when we stop returning to Palestine in everything we see? The day when Palestine is like any other place. A place with which we feel bored. A place we hate, love, curse, or do whatever we please to. A place we call 'home', because home means feeling safe. I inherited feeling unsafe. No matter my status outside of Palestine, or how successful I am, or which passport I carry.

My grandmother's stories about Jaffa haunt me. The Jaffa where she was raised and from which she and her family were uprooted and scattered. The stories of bombs exploding, the bullets, the corpses and the cedars scattered on the streets. I carried these stories while in Palestine and I carried them here too, where I chose to live. I carry the stories of those who came to Palestine on ships from Europe's shores too. Our guests who became our masters. I never felt safe in Palestine. Do we inherit fear?

Fear follows me like a rabid dog. I feel it right behind me whenever I begin to feel safe here. There are days when I do not think of Palestine or Palestinians. I live these days like any other New Yorker. But I know that I am one of 'the people of tents'.[1] The *Nakba*'s memory haunts me even as I strike my roots in New York. Nothing liberates this memory from its burden unless its present is liberated. Unless we burn the tents. This is what I say to myself when I am tired of my fear. Away from Palestine I am comforted because I do not own things and thus they do not own me. I love streets and trees with an impartiality that increases or decreases according to my morning mood. I am happy or pained as much as anyone else. But my memory always returns to the first pain when that man yelled at me on the bus from Jerusalem to Tel Aviv. 'I hate Arabs,' he said when he saw me reading a book in Arabic. No one stood up or said anything to stop him. I, too, was silent. I shrunk in my seat like a lost ant. I was not even eighteen. We were all riding the same bus, but we went our separate ways. Twenty years later I am still haunted by that moment whenever I read a book in Arabic on the subway in New York. There is no safety, I say to myself. But then I remind myself that this is New York! This is New York! But in vain; the fear barks even louder inside me.

People of every colour and language surround the piano player in Washington Square Park. Elegant buildings are watching from above. Tourists are taking photographs of the famous arch. This spot is a perfect painting. But I search for the shadows in the painting I am in. The Washington Square Park painting. I search for its original name and for the first strokes, when it was still just a sketch. I remove the colours carefully to find the strokes on the canvas. I hear the screams of Native Americans and African slaves.

In my self-imposed and cherished exile I learnt to love the warm weather I did not like when I was in Palestine. I remembered that I love jasmines and bougainvillea. I planted them on my balcony and global warming helped the bougainvillea prosper. I love them because they remind me of the roads I took when I was young and I would smell the jasmine. When I kept saying that I wanted to leave that country. On lonely nights in New York, alienation lies waiting for me like a skeleton that can jump at any moment. I realise then that in exile there is even more exile.

The TV set shows images of Syrian refugees leaving their homes to flee the fangs of a ferocious war. Among them are Palestinians no one wants to receive. Their homeland's borders are shut before them. The announcer has nothing to say about that. I feel like a traitor when I return to visit my family in Palestine once a year. I feel like a traitor towards the refugees who cannot return. It was only a coincidence that my ancestors were able to stay. I also feel like a traitor because three years ago I found a city I call home. In this home I do feel safe . . . until further notice.

Note

1. Mamoud Darwish, 'Think of Others'.

Fuad Bahou

Fuad Bahou is a retired artist/poet/teacher. Born in Ramallah in 1935, he studied architecture, art and art history in Los Angeles, CA, and received his MFA from the University of California, Los Angeles (UCLA). He received grants from the National Endowment for the Arts in 1966, and the National Endowment for the Humanities in 1971. He has held teaching positions at UCLA, Santa Monica; Knoxville College and the University of Tennessee, Knoxville. He currently resides in Knoxville, TN.

The Sadness Continues

Palestine . . .
Palestine was always about simplicity
About fertility and dreaming
Always about the perfect hour, every hour
  The farmers
  The roaming sheep
Stone houses and windows old as looking
Stones everywhere, every size, every shape
Stones strewn across the landscape like pilgrims
It is in those stones I first realised
How large Palestine, how small the World
Now I realise the exact reverse.

I was born a stone's throw from Jerusalem, the heart and conscience of
 the world . . .
It was my destiny to have been born there
Now nearly seventy-five years later, it is my fate to sorrow for it
  Like a ribbon of shame tightened about my throat
  A bitter taste upon my lips
  Traces of cowardice in my heart
Now my mind is dizzy with the imagined pleasure of vengeance,

I am tangled with utter emotional fatigue
> My seeing severed from my hearing
> My memory severed from my flesh
> My speaking strained by my flawed silence.

I've become cynical and generic
My thoughts but molecules of inconsequence
My feelings as shapeless as migrant clouds
I am empty and contracted within
Palestine has become a distant lamp that shines with hesitation and
 difficulty.

> Once upon a childhood-time,
Palestine was my spring and my autumn
> My summer and my winter
> My very pigment, my light
> My territory, my geography, my psyche, my olive grove
Now – not even a part of my perception
Nor is it my breaking dawn
Now seemingly defeated
Grieving over the artificial and inevitable, I wait forlornly
I surrender all my cognitive faculties, consciously ignore all my
 anxieties
Diminish to a stifling halt all my memories
And with little to reminisce about
Remain neutral to all things and forces that embalm my mind
> with the thick of hollow hopes and dreams . . .

My Journey

I was thirteen when I first experienced the sound a bullet makes as it punctures the air with malice; the sound of tanks corrugating the asphalt of our roads. The concept of fear entered my mind, and my body succumbed to a sensation of oblivion and sweat, of skin turning blue. We were taken by surprise as the Israeli army conquered a good portion of our country, and before we woke from our sleep we had become refugees in our own land. My house, my father's shop, our fruit trees, all left behind, but for whom and why? I couldn't understand. I saw the winding mountain roads full of people leaving with a few belongings on their backs, heading south and east towards another town or refugee camp or whatever came first; multitudes of faces white as fear, now in flight towards a vague unknown. I was not prepared to become a refugee in my own country, my own mind.

From a distance like a beggar all I see is fog smearing the face of my memory and all I hear is garbled speech, the constant whining tongues of the oppressors. This garbled speech by now turns into craft, into a weapon of procrastination and vulgar delays. Time is lost now, innocence is obliterated, and the infrastructure of language, memory and yearning forever forsaken for the benefit of greed, making history a shambles and psychiatry an art form, fact and philosophy but a skeleton denuded of truth, an extravagance only the mentally deficient can claim to comprehend.

War is not about language nor even imagination, it's about bloodshed, about interruption and destruction, denigration, misguided passions and about feeling alien to, or elated by, someone else's misery and misfortune.

No one can understand what a strange and emasculating sensation this is until one is shamed, or made bitter and terrified by it personally. That is my dilemma right now. Events have a life of their own: alien walls erected, settlements built overnight on confiscated land . . . and the building continues. Millions of strangers populate the once-tranquil hills of Palestine, claiming their rights while trampling on the rights of others. Billions of dollars are spent universally on brainwashing and propaganda, all in defence of absurdity, a religious reconfiguration of a promise, a hollow purpose, a manufactured sentiment designed to torment and liquidate an ancient people of the Holy Land. The sadness continues, liberty and justice be damned.

Palestine: Memory / Hurt

> The heart yearns
> The mind desolate
> All matter in life subservient to human greed
>
> Justice goes by the wayside weeping day and night
> > Then comes the hurtful ache
> > The thwarted language
> > The hesitant eyes, lying lips

The pliable, condensed and caged memory
All in a matter of alien minutes

Now for sixty years I have witnessed the hawks rip my land apart
And with heavy hands reshape the content of our soul and the
  landscape of our heritage
Extracting venom from earth
Sage and pomegranates from the Dead Sea
Telling fables from naked desert stones
This is their time of anger, limp and raw:
Nearby a thousand olive trees mowed down
With cut throats they bleed and moan
It's not a comforting sight
It's uneasy and sad – it's heartless with indifferent shame.

Does the world really care?

And with acidic mirror eyes beneath a flock of silver clouds
        there the soldiers gather,
To swear and spit, shit and sleep
And with tongues dry they sing a song made of liquid foam
A fabrication, a vaporous fog laden with ill-omened shalom
Betrayal its middle name
A weaving of deception, threads thrown about in disarray
A glossy picture to blind the eyes of those who know
A broken vessel made of clay, irreparable
It will not hold water nor oxygen anymore
A whim much darker than a dream
A dream more violent than a nightmare
A hell of a dream . . . shame enmeshed with grief
God's gift in phantom, audacious garb
Unique to Man and his terrible ignoble brain!!

Aida Bamia

Aida A. Bamia, PhD University of London (School of Oriental and African Studies – SOAS), is Professor Emerita of Arabic Language and Literature. She taught in Algerian universities before joining the University of Florida in 1985. She publishes in Arabic literature and received the AUC Press Middle East Studies Award for her book, The Graying of the Raven *(2001). She is active in translation and contributes the essay on Arabic Literature to the* Year Book of the Encyclopaedia Britannica.

Childhood Curtailed

My victimisation as a Palestinian has instilled in me an acute sense of justice and fairness, the necessity to be inclusive rather than exclusive and to embrace others as my fellow compatriots. But my nightmare, like that of many Palestinians, has long been border crossings and the fear that I will be detained or turned back.

My life as a refugee began with a border crossing when I was nine years old. Our trip in the family car was to take us to Cairo for a few months of peace as we waited for the fighting in Palestine to subside. Crossing the Suez Canal was an exciting though scary experience – being unaware of the existence of ferries used on waterways! – but my elation after the safe crossing did not last long; we were suddenly in a different country with a different dialect. That night we stayed in a nondescript hotel room in Ismailia, which was not my idea of a pleasure trip. Once in Cairo my sense of estrangement deepened despite the help of friends, the attractions of the capital, the *feluka* rides over the Nile and the longer than expected summer vacation – we had left Jerusalem in April and the school year did not begin until September!

Everything changed in my life: social interactions, the power of the family name, its importance. No one knew who we were! Our Palestinian dialect amused merchants and our family name was a subject of jokes, while we stood helpless.[1] We had landed in a country with a great sense of humour, but being the victim of its jokes was not my idea of brotherly love!

Gradually, this simulacrum of a vacation turned into a nightmare, with worries about family members left behind, financial difficulties and no prospect of an immediate solution to our status as refugees. Despite my young age I could feel my parents' sense of loss, their mental *Shatat* as they faced the responsibility of caring for a family and dealing with the news of damage caused to my father's business in Jerusalem. I thought of ways to provide them with some joy; what better than to get good grades at school? Didn't my father always drill into our heads the importance of education, continuously repeating to my three siblings and I, 'Education is your fortune. No one can take it away from you'?

While waiting for a solution from the United Nations Security Council, we continued our education. But school was not neutral ground and geography lessons were particularly painful. I would search for my country's name on maps, only to discover its absence. My anger at the world's injustice led to heated debates in Europe where I pursued my higher education. The discussions often revealed people's ignorance of the historical and political facts surrounding the problem, especially in the sixties when Palestinian refugees were referred to as Jordanians. A Frenchwoman who learnt that I was from Jerusalem exclaimed, 'You are Jewish then.' When I said I was not, my interlocutor declared, sure of herself, 'So you are a convert from Judaism!'

In this frenzy my father tried to guarantee us the best education; spending money on anything else seemed to him pure madness! Following the 1956 aggression against Egypt and the rush of the Egyptian Jews to leave the country, there was an abundance of furniture for sale. In my usual impulsive manner I rushed home to announce the good news to my father: 'There is a piano for sale for only thirty pounds!' In his affectionate and diplomatic way, my father put an end to what would have been a great deal and a dream come true, saying, 'What would we do with a piano when we return to Palestine?' I was crushed, and to this day I still dream of owning a piano.

Travelling as a refugee is trying, and my academic work and research activities have suffered significantly over the years from my inability to enter certain countries, even Arab countries! When I finally obtained a tenure track position in the US, my department chair could not understand how I had failed to do research in Morocco while working next door in Algeria.

My dreams of settling down were continually crushed, increasing my sense of exile in exile as I travelled from Algeria, where I taught, to Egypt to spend my summer vacations with my family. During those trips the pleasure of seeing my family was marred, most of the time, by the passport authorities at the airport, especially if my visit coincided with a commando raid or a suicide bombing in Israel. There would be questioning, delays and endless waiting in the airport lounge.

However, when I did finally settle down in the US I discovered that a house, a car and the freedom to travel wherever I wanted did not fill the void within. It hurt to hear Israeli colleagues declare at the end of the academic year, 'I am going home', while I could not go to my home, or visit the tombs of deceased family members, or relive the memories of my happy childhood in Jerusalem and Kalandia, where I had enjoyed great freedom at my family's ranch, singing from the tops of trees, riding donkeys, and joining the caretaker on his night trips to burn wasp nests.

Armed with the optimism and the resilience that have helped Palestinians succeed and even thrive in countries where their rights have been limited, their movements restricted and their presence hardly tolerated, I still have some hope of returning to a Palestine I can call home, not a land under occupation which my American citizenship allows me to visit as a tourist. There is a glimmer of hope for me, but it is too late for my mother, whose deathbed wish could not be satisfied. She often wondered whether she would be able to see Jerusalem again before she died as she fondly remembered her own childhood, her school years and classmates, many of whom were Jewish.

My wish is to cross the Suez Canal in the opposite direction, with my young nephew, teasing him about driving on water to visit Palestine.

Note

1. *Bamia* means 'okra'. Egyptians enjoyed teasing us by asking how we liked to eat the *bamia*, because of the different ways to prepare it.

Ibtisam Barakat

Ibtisam Barakat is a bilingual author, poet, artist and the only Arab to win the International Reading Association's Best Book Award since the beginning of the prize in 1975, for her memoir Tasting the Sky, A Palestinian Childhood. *Her book* Al-Ta' Al-Marbouta Tateer *(Arabic) won the 'Read Everywhere' award. She has two new books forthcoming.*

Photo: Matt Peyton

Forty Days of Mourning

On 3 February at 10.35 pm Palestine time, my father died. When the phone rang with this message I was stunned. How could he not be alive? In the United States, where I lived, it was only 2.30 pm. So if he died at 10.35 pm, was he still alive in America? I bargained with God for eight more hours of his life, then set my alarm clock and waited.

One by one the hours escaped like moths fluttering towards the light and, as they did, I saw the face of my father. A quiet man, he was tall and strong – but afraid of the darkness, afraid of graveyards and their lonely silence. Living on the West Bank in harsh conditions following the 1967 Six-Day War and the occupation of Palestinian cities that followed, he was also afraid that he could neither protect nor provide for us.

My father was the one with the least schooling in our family, having finished only the first grade and half of the second. So as a teenager in the late 1970s, at the end of every week I sat with him, added up his work hours and helped him figure out his pay.

As I did this I was aware of his hands resting on the table near me. Weathered and wounded, they revealed the harsh reality of his life. When the work hours did not add up to what my father hoped, those hands clenched into fists. Snatching the pencil from me, he would demand a recalculation, then cried when my total remained the same. This meant that family purchases like meat or olive oil would need to be postponed.

What was never postponed throughout the years of my childhood and adolescence, however, were the little treats my father brought home with him at the end of each day. Sesame, popcorn, candy, salted seeds, nuts. They cost money, but he bought them anyway.

'The children need clothes more than they need these treats,' Mother would tell him.

'But these treats put happiness on their faces, even if just for a moment or two,' he insisted.

Now the clock announced 10.35 pm. My father was dead in both Ramallah time and America time. I felt a glimmer of desire to die too.

'Dad, do you want me to go with you?' I asked what I imagined was my father's soul venturing into the darkness alone.

I remembered that the one thing my father was never sure about was whether anyone would think about him after his death. The last time I saw him he gave me his *hatta* scarf and prayer rug and, tilting his head, said, '*It-thakkareeni*'. Remember me.

Now I wanted to give my father exactly what he would have asked for. I wanted to think of him, and to think of him in a way that honoured the traditions he believed in.

My father would not expect me to follow these traditions. In fact, he would be shocked! He knew me to be his free-spirited daughter who at the age of twenty-two, in spite of his protestations, had left for the West, an ocean away from home.

Perhaps I broke my father's heart a thousand times by challenging his traditional ways. But today I respect these traditions.

I decided to mourn for forty days, the traditional mourning period for Arabs. So I cancelled all of my appointments, set aside my work, put on dark clothes and recorded an outgoing voicemail message telling anyone who called me that I was in a period of mourning.

For the next forty days I did only basic shopping, I had no sugary foods for comfort, I didn't read books or watch movies or television to distract myself. Thinking about my dad would get my full attention.

I made a play dough sculpture of my father and began a forty-day conversation with him. I covered my walls with paper in order to draw large family scenes from my memory and to write giant letters on the wall.

A stack of Kleenex boxes that I bought for the strong rush of tears stood near the forty tall candles I would light – one for every day. I hoped they would conquer the dark and light up the road to the other world for my dad.

I put an extra set of plates on my table and as I served the food, I hummed *'ya dhalama al-layle khayyim'*, the only song I knew my dad loved. It said, 'Night, cover up the world like a tent; I am not afraid of your darkness. For after the darkness will always come a morning of love that rises and rises.'

As I progressed deeper and deeper into the days of mourning, I found myself going on a journey into the past. No amount of grief could stop me. Suddenly I was willing to feel again the events of my life, which had often seemed unbearable. Now, to remember was to think of my dad. To remember was to keep him alive in my life.

On day forty I wrote a farewell letter to my father, thanking him for his life, and forgiving him for having let me down sometimes. And I asked for forgiveness for having let him down at times too.

I drove to a creek at the edge of land owned by a friend because my father loved running water. My friend had left a shovel by the creek. 'Feel free to play the piano in my house afterwards', the yellow sticky note on the shovel read.

I dug the earth. In it I put the hardened play dough sculpture of my father, the farewell letter and the scarf that he had given me. I cut the prayer rug into two halves. Keeping the half where his feet used to stand five times a day, I buried the other half where he had put his forehead down in prayer.

I wanted to honour the fact that my father and I came from the same foot place, the same roots, but our minds had diverged into different worlds.

I faced the creek and once again sang his favourite song: 'Night, cover up the world like a tent; I am not afraid of your darkness.' I sang it over and over until there was only silence in me. Then I closed the earth as if it were an envelope, patted it affectionately, kissed it and went inside my friend's house.

I sat down at the piano and played with abandon. I did not feel even a whisper of unfinished sadness. I had cried all of my tears, felt all of my feelings, said all of my words. I played and played, swaying back and forth, the sunlight streaming on my fingers.

As I drove home I felt closer to my dad than I had ever felt during his life. I also became aware of a new place he had opened up in me, allowing new depths of my past to become accessible.

The next day, when the forty days of mourning were over, a stunning birth occurred. I began to write the book I had always wanted to write but had not been able to. It was about my childhood and war.

This story, beginning with the first night of the Six-Day War which took place between Israelis and Arabs in June 1967 when I was three and a half years old and had been accidentally separated from my father and my mother, had been hidden in a tent of darkness.

I had not been able to find these memories, no matter how hard I tried. Now I began to write. I wrote a chapter every two days, continuing until I finished two months later, writing as though I had entered a morning that never ended. And my father's song was with me.

'Night, cover up the world like a tent; I am not afraid of your darkness. For after the darkness will always come a morning of love that rises and rises.'

Ramzy Baroud

Ramzy Baroud is an internationally syndicated columnist, a media consultant and the Editor of PalestineChronicle.com. *He is the author of* Searching Jenin *and* The Second Palestinian Intifada: A Chronicle of a People's Struggle. *His latest book is* My Father Was a Freedom Fighter: Gaza's Untold Story. *He has a PhD in Palestine Studies from the University of Exeter.*

Seeking 'Home'

Just an hour earlier the scene outside the house had been a war zone, a one-sided war. Beseeching screams in Arabic, and commanding orders in Hebrew. We didn't have to see to understand what transpired that Friday afternoon.

'They must've killed him,' my father said sombrely in what seemed like a foretold prophecy. They must have indeed, for the moment the bullet was fired the voice of the young refugee pleading for his life was silenced.

I cannot recall the name of that particular victim, lauded as a martyr by the grieving refugees. I cannot even remember what led to the clashes between stone-throwing kids in my Gaza refugee camp and the Israeli army, all those years ago during the first uprising in 1987. But it has been a recurring scene since, manifesting itself in numerous ways, as it had for decades before. As a matter of fact, it defines the conflict between the Israeli occupation and the Palestinians, who live in a constant state of revolt.

I don't remember most of the details, but I vividly recall the sentiment: the heavy feeling of quietness that followed the violent scene after Israeli tanks moved on to another neighbourhood; my mother murmuring verses from the Quran to ward the evil deed away from her children; my father's stillness interrupted only by expressive puffs on his cheap cigarettes, one after the other. Although a child of twelve or so, the heaviness, deep sadness and permeating anger of that moment will never escape my memory.

That moment, alongside many such encounters, has continued to define me long after I left my refugee camp in Gaza for the United States. In a sense, everything I have said and written about Palestine – in fact, human suffering anywhere – has been, to some degree, connected to that very moment: the shrieks of the young man as he was brutally beaten before being shot to death, for no particular crime aside from being Palestinian.

I have lived in Seattle for many of the last twenty years, and in other parts of the world, but rarely have I not been aware of my identity as a Palestinian. I get reminded of my identity often: every time I cross a border, express an opinion, apply for a job or even have a random chat with a stranger in a coffee shop. Being Palestinian is like a perpetual political argument, and a heated one at that, and I learnt very early on that I needed to explain and at times defend myself for being Palestinian. Identity is not always a matter of course, it can be a constant struggle.

Yet I have never sought to sideline my identity as a Palestinian. Being Palestinian allows me to become immediately sensitive to and empathise – effortlessly so – with victims of human rights abuses and injustice, regardless of their identity, or that of the victimiser. On that terrible Friday in Gaza, many years ago, I hadn't caught a glimpse of the dying young man, nor did I see the faces of those who took his life, but it didn't matter. His face was masked by the thick air of unmitigated fear and his voice was muffled by the screams of the soldiers, but his suffering was real and, as with suffering anywhere, even when it isn't seen, pain is felt.

Similarly, I have never been to the village my family was expelled from in 1948. It was called Beit Daras and it was a peaceful village of mud houses, a mosque and a small elementary school. I was born twenty-four years after the village was erased from the face of the map, along with over five hundred others. Yet my rapport with Beit Daras has grown stronger with time. The stories passed down from my grandparents and the elders of my family made Beit Daras a place of bliss, a heaven, with a splendour that can only be understood when juxtaposed to the hell of the refugee camp.

Yet in that reality, between a peaceful village and a harrowing life in the camp, where I lived for most of my youth, my world continues to vacillate. In Seattle, Beit Daras remains my home. In London, the refugee camp occupies my thoughts.

On one occasion after I had travelled to the Middle East for work and excitedly returned home to the US to see my children, an officer at Seattle Airport inquired about the 'purpose and duration of my visit'.

'I am American,' I replied. 'I live in Seattle. I own a house there. My children are waiting for me across the hall.' I protested as to why I would be asked about the reason I was returning home?

'Sir, please answer the question,' he barked impatiently. He had discovered my Gaza connection and that was enough for him to overlook the colour of my American passport. For him, being Palestinian was loaded with all sorts of meanings and layers of suspicions. For me, it was a reminder that 'home' is somewhere else, a place that may no longer exist in the form of mud houses and an ailing mosque, but remains real in its significance and everlasting meaning.

Life is a succession of significant moments that, moulded together, define us, our values, our sense of direction, relationships and awareness of ourselves and our surroundings. For me, two decades of being Palestinian and living in the West has created a unique mould born out of many contradictions, longing, escape, hope, despair, struggle and pain – of one's self and others – but also an intense desire to one day find 'home' and never leave again.

Sahera Bleibleh

Sahera Bleibleh was a visiting scholar at the University of Washington, Seattle, where she received her PhD in Urban Design and Planning in 2012. Her research focuses on informal urbanism, everyday life and environment-behaviour studies, with particular focus on the spatial and behavioural consequences of political and military conflicts on communities and urban environments. She is currently an assistant professor at the Architectural Engineering Department of the United Arab Emirates University (UAEU) in the UAE.

Voices from Within

Listening to many voices from within, my sense of being Palestinian was shaped, but distorted, by growing up in occupied Palestine, creating a unique understanding of space and time that the world is not aware of because Palestine is *silenced* or not heard. I experience and hear this unique distortion in most aspects of everyday life, both inside and outside Palestine. It is a feeling that makes one search everywhere for what has been lost, even if the original site of loss is far away. This thought suddenly jumped to my mind while thousands of miles away from *home* in Global Village Dubai, when I found myself looking for where and how Palestine was represented in the mix of other places. When I made the connection to this long-embodied feeling, it reminded me that I am looking for Palestine outside as much as I am looking for it inside, and inside myself. Seeing Palestine in a piece of embroidery is as important for Palestinian identity as explaining how Palestine has been, and still is, fragmented by the occupation, and sadly by Palestinians too. Similarly, my conception of being Palestinian is deepened by my research on the ongoing trauma to our sense of space, examining Palestine's representation outside Palestine, talking with people about Palestine, and sharing what Palestine is and could be.

I thought identity distortion only happens while away, but during the Second Intifada I moved from Nablus to Ramallah due to the extraordinary difficulties in commuting with the endless number of Israeli checkpoints and barriers. It was one of the most difficult decisions I ever made. I tried to convince myself that it was only temporary and soon I would be back in Nablus. I rented a furnished studio to emphasise the temporariness of space and time, and to avoid the burden of resettling as soon as it became possible. This lasted for seven years, and God knows how many more if I hadn't left for graduate study in the USA. Reflecting back on that time, I better understand how tough it is to leave, especially when it's not optional. That experience not only undermined my sense of autonomy and ability to control my own destiny, but also the different ways in which I subconsciously resisted being internally displaced. Even though, once again, I was forced to accommodate the perceptions of what others thought of Palestinians, I believe there is an embodied power that emerges despite the fragility.

When registering to submit my dissertation at the University of Washington, Seattle, I was confronted by a denial of space and decided to speak up for a change. Filling out the list of requirements, I was unable to create an account because of an incomplete list. One of the requirements was 'nationality'. Well, Palestine, as usual, was not listed. After several trials to manipulate the registration, I failed. I decided to write to the website support, and I did. I wrote, 'Hello, Not sure if it's the right address to contact? I am trying to create an account to submit my dissertation . . . One of the requirements is country of citizenship. Palestine is not listed among the list of countries. Please advise. Thank you.' Surprisingly, I received an answer the second day: 'Thank you for contacting ETD Support. Indeed it is not. I will follow up with you when our developers add it to the list. Sorry for the inconvenience.' I wrote back to thank whoever answered my message, though I didn't expect much.

I had extreme thoughts then, including refusing to submit my dissertation via that system if my request was not processed. It was the least I could do to raise my voice about such 'invisibility'. Anxiously waiting, my little victory smoothly concluded with the nicest message I ever received: 'Dear Sahera, I am following up on your inquiry. Good news. Palestine has been added to the country of citizenship list. Regards.' I was wondering how other Palestinian students had managed to submit their works earlier! Not until I later shared this exciting experience with some friends, I learnt that other Palestinian colleagues had been trying to do this for many years. Acknowledging my sense of homeland, I was happy with my little victory.

But what do we carry with us when we leave 'home'?

I lived in a quiet residential neighbourhood close to the University of

Washington campus in Seattle, with Lake Washington nearby. It was a place where I often went for walks. But every time I walked I felt a need to carry my Palestinian ID. In my mind I needed proof of who I was in case any 'authority' stopped me. After several months I realised that it is only in Palestine, among the many places I have been to, that I needed to carry proof of self! Among the several built-in memories I carried was the implication of the helicopter sound. The flashbacks caused by this sound made me anticipate death. Each time I heard a helicopter I would say to myself '*Allah yustor*' (May God protect!). Later I figured out that it was because every time I heard this sound in Palestine someone was assassinated, or some sort of tragedy happened. In spite of the distance, I couldn't get this thought out of my head. I doubt that there would be any comparable misplaced correlations if I had lived all my life in diaspora.

For me, this demonstrates how experiencing place and time nurtures the ways in which we become sensitive to our surroundings. Luckily, I can have my therapy walks in the Old Town of Nablus, where I embrace my sense of place physically and spiritually. It is a place of many small details that reminds me of having a home that will one day gather us all. In the meantime, I will hold on to the beauty and peacefulness that resides in the Palestinians and their homeland.

Reja-e Busailah

Reja-e Busailah was born in Jerusalem, Palestine, before he was driven out by the Israelis in 1948. He studied at the University of Cairo, Egypt, and at New York University, where he obtained a PhD in English. He is now professor emeritus at Indiana University. He is a published poet and his memoir, In the Land of My Birth: Glimpses of a Palestinian Boyhood, *has recently been accepted for publication.*

The Tree

'Where were you born?' asks the officer.
      'Jerusalem, Palestine.'
'You mean Israel.'
'No, Palestine.'
'There is no Palestine.'
'There is, as there was when I was born.' The officer goes somewhere, comes back in a few minutes, and puts down Palestine . . .

Like the tongue wrenched out of your mouth, the tree was wrenched out of its native soil with all its roots exposed, dazed, writhing. And the roots were scattered and so were fragments of the trunk, and so were the branches and the leaves. They were scattered everywhere, each limb or member reaching out for the rest, for the whole; and when it failed in its reachings, it huddled to itself in order to keep what it could keep, a flavour, a memory, a dream.

But on the day his naturalisation was to be completed, the judge told him to preserve his 'heritage', for that would enrich the culture of his 'new country'. It did not exactly. Often it is hard for him and his new people to meet face-to-face and bosom-to-bosom; and so they end up meeting kind of sideways, and sometimes even back-to-back. Of his old tongue they know nothing. 'Doesn't he have his new tongue, funny as it may be?' they ask. He has mingled flesh and blood with them, has taught them Whitman and argued over Lincoln. But he won't eat their barbecues. He still can't stand the taste of sweetened meat. The fruit of the endeavour was much shell and little kernel.

He loves children, all children. Children are closer than adults to the air, the water, the plants, to beast and bird. Children know little of the law, and obey less of it. He goes with them in his new country. He moves along with them from the bough to the branch and down the trunk all the way to the ground. And there they part company. His roots are missing. Their roots are not his. It dawns upon him that they are by far more attracted to his guide dog than to him. When they hear him speak, they are uneasy, they shy away. Why? Doesn't he speak their tongue, he thinks to himself. Wasn't he given a tongue transplant? Doesn't he speak their tongue in his new tongue? Doesn't he teach them their own tongue? Why, he sings in their tongue, argues in their tongue, flirts and woos in their tongue. And yet both child and adult are still uneasy. 'Where do you come from?' The question continues to explode in his ears after more than fifty years. 'Are you British? Are you German? Are you Italian? Are you Greek? You sound French', with his answer always in the affirmative, 'Yes . . . uh-huh . . . yeah . . . you guessed it', and even 'yep' depending. So what! Most are still uneasy. He doesn't look right. He doesn't speak right. He is different. His accent is that of a foreigner, they are certain. He looks 'Middle Eastern', they are sure.

In his new country he hears the cardinal calling, and he likes him. But deeper he hears the *sinounou*[1] sweeping eastward from the Mediterranean, as he announces in a voice sharper than any cardinal's the coming of spring to where the tree was standing big and tall. And he hears the mourning doves in his new place, sad and monotonous. They are doves that do not know how to sing *'ya joukhti'*. Nor do they know how to remind the people to remember their God: *'coo-cu-coo, coo-cu-coo – uthkurou – rabbakun'* (Do remember your God).

When he was still green, and the tree stood high, he babbled songs under it in that tongue, songs he learnt, and songs he made. He wanted to sing of the tree, from its deep-reaching roots to its aspiring boughs. But the surgery pre-vented all that. He sings in his new tongue of the felling of the tree and the dispersion of its limbs. It is quite awkward. Isn't he like the Jew who came to Jerusalem from Europe, he asks himself, who composed Arabic music for the Arabs, with so much brain and so little heart? The woman who was driven out of Ethiopia into Jerusalem had a sad voice but a cute accent in which she promoted her roasted peanuts, *'fustu' ala kaifak'* (peanuts to your delight). His new tongue betrays him best or worst when temperatures rise, as tem-peratures have to rise sometimes. Then the tongue gets twisted, grows thick, and all is garbled. Then he cannot curse or swear with satisfaction, unless he resorts to the stubbles of the old tongue, his Arabic tongue.

He loves Buxtehude, Beethoven and Stravinsky as much as he does Paul Robeson, Harry Belafonte, the Weavers and Pete Seeger. He hums so much of them when the climate is cooperative, and yet they think he is odd because he sometimes misses *ataba* and *rababa* and the *oud* and the *nai* and the *shub-baba*,[2] all in the shade of the olive or oak tree and in the shade of the vine. He then withdraws as if ashamed to listen alone unheard. They think he is backward because he cannot tell Madonna from Dolly Parton, the Yankees from the Dodgers, or an inning from a home-run. They think he is weird when he starts at the thought of having smelled the fragrance of thyme or coffee with cardamom, or having tasted some lentil soup homemade on a faraway winter evening, or some hummus fetched from Mustafa's across the street.

But if he dares mention the story of the tree, then the exclamations: 'Huh . . . what . . . here we go again!' Something big breaks loose: something foggy, some pernicious veil arises between them and him, veil of woman locked up somewhere, calls of *Allahu Akber*, sinister Arabs and always Muslim terror lurking in the bush. Sometimes he recoils embarrassed or afraid. Sometimes he is enraged; but in vain. He is a liar about the tree, they persist, until he wonders to himself if he is not a liar after all! Maybe he was not there when it all happened: the grand theft in broad daylight, the wrenching, the uprooting, the saw and the shovel, the scattering and the surgery. Maybe he is not who he was. The commentator speaks of the 'so-called Islamic civilisation' of the 'so-called Arabian Knights', and the scholar declares that Arabic is a 'controversial language'. 'Am I controversial?' he wonders. Now he gets it: naïveté and knavery in his new tongue! Those who will never understand and those who will never be honest. That is it and nothing in-between.

At the defeat of Abd al-Nasir in 1967, he is stunned, dazed at the euphoria, at the orgy which possessed everyone around him, and which possessed the whole of his adopted country, a madness whose roots seem to strike deeper than any plant can – all because the man wanted to collect the fragments and knit them into a whole, a tree, a flourishing Arab tree to which he may belong again. The fragments again. And the limbs deformed and mutilated and dispersed again. In his dazed helplessness, he and his spouse want to 'adopt' a child – a virtue he has acquired in his adopted country. But he is told by the adoption agency, 'Because of your political views, you are not fit to be parents!' And the final stab in the back when the Reverend Martin Luther

King, looking at the napalmed children writhing, declares that the Israelis have the right to defend themselves. If only he could find a place in which to hide, to hide himself, his defeat, his shame!

But he is 'human', he stresses to himself, and wants to feel so, to prove it to himself. He grieves with the widow, the orphan, the bereaved father or mother. No! He is not fit to sympathise. You see, my friend, they can kill us seventy times over, yet woe to us if we dare say ouch! He is not wanted, unless he acquires a new identity, an identity authorised only by them, an identity which rejects, forgets or ignores his old one, his heritage. It troubles him to the core. It frightens him, so that like a child he now hugs his Quran, hugs it tight to his chest, his Quran which he used to take for granted before the uproot-ing; and he who used to pooh-pooh conversion now rejoices whenever he hears of a new conversion to his faith. 'One day . . . one day . . . ,' he whispers deep within himself, 'one day', yet deeper than any roots! As for now, if only he could be buried where the tree stood, or not far from where it stood . . .

Notes

1. A small bird with a blithe, piercing call. It comes from the west only in springtime. It is said he never lands because of his weak legs, and once on the ground he cannot take off again.
2. *Ataba* is the name for a type of folk song (with variations) common in Greater Syria. *Rababa* is a one-stringed instrument, common in Greater Syria and the surrounding desert. *Oud* is a musical instrument similar to the lute. *Nai* is a musical wind instrument, similar to the flute, made of reed. It has seven holes in Palestine and is used mostly by shepherds. *Shubbaba* is like the *nai* and the flute except it is made of metal.

Selma Dabbagh

Selma Dabbagh BA (Durham) LLM (University of London, School of Oriental and African Studies – SOAS) is a British Palestinian lawyer and fiction writer. She has lived in England, Saudi Arabia, Kuwait, France, the West Bank, Egypt and Bahrain. Her short stories have been published by International PEN and Granta. Her first novel, Out of It *(2011), is set between Gaza, London and the Gulf. She also wrote a radio play for BBC Radio 4,* The Brick. *She lives in London.*

Photo: Rowan Griffiths

A Road Taken

I once met a young lawyer who, like me, had an English mother and a Palestinian father. She had grown up in Surrey with no connection at all to her Palestinian side. 'I never knew where my father was from,' she confided, embarrassed. 'I just assumed that the foreign men who came to our house were Pakistanis.'

I remember a cousin of my mother's running down our driveway in High Wycombe exclaiming, 'Taysir! My favourite Arab!' and wondering why she was calling my father such a thing. I must have been five. I knew my father was from a place (I probably knew the word 'Palestine') where everything had been fine and the family was said to be a 'good' one. I knew that they had been attacked and expelled, an unjust war had ensued, that they had lost their country and were never able to return. This naturally led me to tell everyone at school that if it was not for the war I would have been a princess.

From as early as I can remember, my father told us stories about Palestine. When he was ten in Jaffa he had been hit by a grenade thrown by a member of a militant Jewish group. As children, we would ask to see his wounds – small, shiny patches of skin with jagged stitched edges, like suns drawn by nursery children – and he would feel for the place in his head where a speck of shrapnel is still lodged. This was all very exciting. Other stories of Palestine were about the sea, his dog and getting into trouble at school.

We moved to Kuwait from High Wycombe when I was eight (before that we had lived in Dundee, Reading and Jeddah), my older sister, Dina, was ten and Nadia, the youngest, was four. I cannot say that Palestinian culture, when we were introduced to it, was particularly attractive to us. Apart from receiving money at Eid, there was too much sitting around for our liking and our relatives often seemed to be depressed, particularly in connection to events in the news. The news was – and still is – omnipresent.

Most of the children at the English school we went to in Kuwait were Palestinian, but although I was in the top class they seemed far more studious than me and were not allowed to go out as much. My Arabic was nonexistent and efforts to learn were impaired by the lousy books prescribed by the Ministry of Education, the demotivated teachers and disinterested students. As an adult I have spent years studying Arabic, but it is still frustratingly broken.

My aunt, who was active in a branch of the women's PLO in Kuwait, once organised a fundraising event and I remember feeling surprised at how alien I felt being there, despite identifying strongly with the Palestinian cause. The *keffiyehs*, the 'I love Palestine' T-shirts and the paintings of bucolic lands meant little to me and, in truth, seemed a bit *naff*.

I still frequently feel like an outsider in Palestinian settings. I hate the '*beit meen?*' ('from which family?') middle-class conversations that are supposed to rank you, and I find the social and religious conservatism hard to deal with. I can also be irritated by the chauvinistic 'hierarchy of suffering' found in the more activist circles.

I believe that my English mother's politics formed a path to being Palestinian as much as my father's did: empathy with the underdog, intolerance of injustice and rejection of inequality informed everything both she and my father taught us. Without her outlook I am not sure I would have engaged with being Palestinian in the ways that I have.

In 1990 my father was trapped when Kuwait was invaded. We were in England for the summer holidays when we woke up one morning to find that he had been sucked down a political black hole. All forms of communication were cut. On the night of the invasion a badger came into our back garden and as the news was broadcast – jingoistic, misinformed and imageless – we kept referring back to the badger because we couldn't bring ourselves to talk about our dad.

It took him three weeks to get out, through Iraq and into Jordan on a fifteen-year-old expired Jordanian passport. Almost every member of my father's family, together with 300,000 or more Palestinians, were expelled from Kuwait over the following months. This is an expulsion that is rarely mentioned.

I was back at Durham for my second year at university, but nothing was the same. I wasn't the same. The news was unreliable and duplicitous and no one around me seemed to recognise it. I dropped a law course to take one on the politics of the Middle East. I became renowned for getting over-emotional at dinner parties.

From Durham I wrote to several non-governmental human rights organisations in the West Bank expressing my interest in working for them, to which they replied that they had absolutely no interest in me – I had no Arabic for a start and I had never lived there. I graduated and left the next day for Cairo to take a course on teaching English so that I could at least work in the West Bank while I learnt Arabic. In Cairo I wrote to an organisation in Jerusalem telling them I was coming to visit, to which they replied that they 'may have an opening'. I packed my bags and went.

And what did I find in the West Bank? Quotidian nobility. And who can dislodge the power of that?

Almost ten years later at a United Nations conference on Palestinian refugees I sat next to a man who had been with me at the human rights organisation I ended up working for in Jerusalem. We hadn't recognised each other at all and then got over-excited when we did. 'I remember you arriving,' he said. 'You were so young.'

'I was twenty-two,' I said. 'I wasn't that young!'

'Well, your face was really babyish and we all said, "That poor girl, now she has come here she's going to be stuck with Palestine for the rest of her life."'

I often think he was right.

Taysir Dabbagh

Taysir Dabbagh is a chartered civil engineer and a fellow of the Association for Consultancy and Engineering. He has worked as a consulting engineer in the UK and as an adviser for water-related economic development projects in many countries. Seventeen years ago he established a consulting engineering office in the UK and later in Tunisia.

Living in a World of Double Standards

The memory of our departure from Palestine will never fade from my mind. It anchors my Palestinian personality in a sense of humiliation and injustice, even though I have been a resident of the United Kingdom since 1959, I have an English wife and I am now the grandfather of eight delightful grandchildren.

It is now more than sixty-five years since I left Palestine. We were living in turmoil, faced by a well-organised and brutal enemy carrying out a vicious terrorist campaign. The horrors of the Deir Yassin massacre on 9 April 1948 had an immediate impact on Palestinian morale. Rumours that a similar massacre was imminent spread like wildfire without, sometimes, a single shot being fired. The prospect of being killed in cold blood or raped appalled the deeply traditional Arab society.

My father, fearing the worst, was in an agonising dilemma. Involuntarily, I perhaps provided him with a compelling reason for the departure of our family and our relations. The latter had been staying with us in Ajami neighbourhood in Jaffa, seeking relative security away from the clashes near Tel Aviv and other areas. As I was only ten and school was closed, I was busy entertaining myself with my dog and playing occasionally with our neighbours' children. During one such encounter on 27 April 1948, an invisible intruder hurled a grenade at us from the top of a hill adjacent to the alley where our houses stood.

Susan and I were wounded, but Coco (Nicholas) and Rajab (the nickname of Susan's sister for reasons I no longer recall) escaped unscathed. Feeling the hot blood trickling down the right side of my face, I realised what the grown-ups talked about anxiously had been translated into reality in a much more dramatic way than I could ever have anticipated.

In the lorry rushing me to the hospital it dawned on me that I might be dying and that I had better recite my final prayers. That night the Stern Gang, I learnt later, intensified their attack on Jaffa with a heavy bombardment that shook the glass of the doors and windows, and terrified the members of my family who came to see me in the hospital.

The next day I had to leave the hospital, which had become overcrowded, and go back to our house. Two days later I left Jaffa with my family and relatives. Our departure, on a lorry and at short notice, was humiliating, dangerous and terrifying. Snipers from the Jewish militia had been shooting at vehicles on the route out of Jaffa. As we left our house my abandoned dog chased the lorry, but lying on a stretcher and suffering from my wounds, I was unable to respond to his crying and whimpering. The older people calmed themselves by whispering verses of the Quran.

Embarrassed by the role of Britain in the creation of Israel, some of my English friends have tried to console me by saying warmly, 'You are English now Taysir!' I find it agonisingly difficult to agree, yet embarrassing and awkward to reject the compliment. This country has been very generous to me. People have gone out of their way to help me at every stage of my life in this 'green and pleasant land'. Indeed, the support I have received has been remarkable, whether moral support, financial help for my postgraduate studies, encouragement as a fresher student or in helping me to become a civil engineer.

When abroad on business assignments I long to return to England. I miss the smell of the fresh air and the walks in the countryside, the sense of humour, the small talk, the politeness, the BBC gardening programmes and even the weather!

Nevertheless, British foreign policy, towards Palestine in particular, and the Arab world in general, has remained perplexing. The double standards are blatantly obvious, and the pompousness and hypocrisy in overlooking injustice are sad and painful. British foreign policy has inhibited my love affair with this country and imposed itself on what I consider to be the logic of my anglicised mentality! 'How,' I keep asking my English friends, 'could people so congenial, modest, transparent and tolerant in their own country be so devious, aggressive and belligerent in the Middle East?'

This is why my Palestinian-ness is wedged in my inner soul. It is the agony I have to endure as a price for the good life I have in a country that continues to be oblivious to the immoral practices of the Israelis. Land-grabbing, home demolitions and settlement-building continue unabated, in the name of God and supported by military might and a powerful, biased media. This leaves me with little to be proud of. The majestic flight of the Concorde or winning a world-class football match may give me pleasure, but I don't feel fully entitled to it.

I never let the existence of Palestine become ancient history. Very emphatically I emphasise my origins to someone who might have misheard me: 'No! Not Pakistan . . . Palestine', I correct my questioner, however light-hearted their question may be. I also elaborate, 'I am a Palestinian Arab.' The bond between my Palestinian-ness and my Arab heritage provides me with a comforting face-saver. Being an Arab from an uprooted and exiled people, but belonging to a proud civilisation with its rich ancient culture and ethics, is an essential component of my identity.

Yet when I was asked, 'What would you do if you had your life to live all over again?', the question bewildered me and I had to think hard before I replied, 'I would live it all over again.' England has given me wide-ranging opportunities and sharpened my sense of freedom and objectivity. Being Palestinian has become synonymous with being stubborn and hard-working. I am content to be Palestinian, belonging to a determined and aspiring people who will never stop fighting against injustice. My children contribute effectively to the same sentiment and my grandchildren will most probably do the same until justice is accomplished.

Souad Dajani

Souad Dajani, PhD, is an American of Palestinian descent. Her works include Eyes without Country: Searching for a Palestinian Strategy of Liberation *(1994) and* Ruling Palestine: A History of the Legally Sanctioned Jewish-Israeli Seizure of Land and Housing in Palestine *(2005). She resides in Massachusetts.*

Walking in Her Years

The visa stamped in her passport, her *Palestinian* passport, is dated 26 April 1948. A sojourn with relatives in Tripoli, Lebanon until things quieted down. A week or two at most for Jaffa to be safe again, they thought, and then they'd return. My mother was twenty-one years old.

My grandfather reclines in an armchair in the middle of the room. His youngest son – a strikingly blond lad – sits on his lap. To his left sits one of his daughters; her hallmark sense of style evident in the bobbed hairdo she seemed to favour. A brother sits beside her. He never married and was to pass away in Lebanon. Seated to my grandfather's right is another daughter, with an impish smile darting across her face. Seated beside her is the eldest daughter, a gentle and nurturing soul and a pivotal figure in my mother's upbringing. Behind my grandfather stand his two eldest sons. One was to pass away a few years later. The other – he looks like a dashing movie star in photos of the time – was to become a renowned physician and college professor in Lebanon. Intricately woven tapestry hangs on the wall and thick curtains drape the windows behind them. Exquisite Ajami carpets line the floors. Seated on the carpet is an African youth who ran errands for the family; he later accompanied the family into exile. The photo was taken shortly before my mother was born, and a snapshot of a bygone era before Zionist forces seized Palestine and forced out most of its indigenous Arab inhabitants (see page 155).

My mother never knew her father. He passed away three days before she was born. He had been a distinguished and well-respected judge in Jaffa who, along with his brothers, had owned orange orchards – whence came the famed 'Jaffa oranges'. My mother grew up basking in his legacy. It seemed inconceivable that within two short decades the familiar routine of daily life in their ancestral home would be shattered.

Once Zionist forces encroached on Jaffa my grandmother gathered up her youngest children and fled to Lebanon. From there, my mother married and left Lebanon to accompany her husband to the USA. I was born a year later in 1953 as the first of five children. I vividly remember when my mother received the tragic news that her mother had passed away. I was four years old and too young to comprehend this terrible loss: how she must have relived the moment she had last laid eyes on her mother, not knowing then if she'd ever see that beloved face again. The *Nakba* ruptured this close-knit family and dispersed its members far and wide, taking my mother continents away from the family that anchored her. Now her mother, the most essential link to her past and her roots, was gone.

My mother was thirty-three when we made the return trip across the ocean to Beirut.

We were steeped in stories of their lives before the *Nakba*, the same reminiscences repeated over and over. I couldn't picture my parents as kids in Jaffa, let alone understand why they kept reliving these memories. But later I did. By recalling their past, my parents, aunts and uncles were struggling to ground themselves in the face of utter bewilderment and disbelief. Otherwise the enormity of what had befallen them, their permanent dispossession and exile from their homeland and the unrelenting denial and erasure of their lived history, was simply inconceivable.

Growing up in Beirut, I had still – somewhat defiantly – internalised Western values of individualism and (selective) historical amnesia. After finishing my master's degree, I made my way to Canada, escaping the civil war and leaving the Arab world behind. I was twenty-four years old and clueless.

1982 found me back in Lebanon. Israel's devastating invasion that summer had seared my Palestinian identity; this was my *Nakba*, my awakening. At twenty-nine, I finally grasped that to be Palestinian was to be vulnerable and demonised. It meant enduring the constant trumpeting of a most bizarre notion: that Jewish Zionist usurpers had a superior and more exclusive right to my mother's homeland than she did; that their claim to this land superseded and nullified her own.

My mother was fifty-six in 1983 when she, my father and youngest brother left Beirut to emigrate to Canada. My father passed away in 2004. A few years later we moved my mother to live with us in the US. We hoped she would live out her remaining years in comfort, free of any cares and worries. But we couldn't spare her from fresh misfortunes befalling the family. Several of her siblings had passed away years earlier, but the deaths of her two remaining sisters, within a couple of years of each other and in their different places of exile, seemed to do her in. Once again my mother relived memories of their last goodbyes, years or decades earlier. Their deaths seemed to seal the permanent severance of her last remaining ties to her roots and her past. She was old now and her family was gone for good, as was Palestine.

Then the unfathomable: my mother passed away. She had just turned eighty-six.

I wrestle with a profound sense of loss and grief. For too many years I had looked upon her simply as the mother figure, whose presence I had taken too much for granted. I try to remember what she was like at sixty, fifty-six, thirty-three . . . How did she experience herself then? Was it the same as I saw myself at those ages? My mother had always borne the burden of being wrenched from family and homeland with a quiet dignity so common to that generation of Palestinians. Unfailingly gracious and stoic, she held her decades of impenetrable loss and grief closely to herself. I find myself trying on the years that made up the stuff of her life.

I try to walk in her years and I am humbled.

Susan Muaddi Darraj

Susan Muaddi Darraj is a Palestinian American writer. She is the author of The Inheritance of Exile *(2007), a finalist in the AWP Book Awards. She co-founded* The Culture Collective, *a project dedicated to promoting ethnic awareness in modern fiction. She is also an editor at* Barrelhouse Magazine, *a literary journal that examines the intersection of literature and pop culture.*

Claiming Citizenship

Being Palestinian means that your identity is as fragmented as the landscape of your homeland. Being born in America, to Palestinian immigrants, does not exempt you from this identity crisis.

I was raised in Philadelphia, in a neighbourhood of Italian Americans, among whom, in the 1980s, it was popular to wear the map of Italy on a chain around the neck, embroidered on the back of a jacket, even on a licence plate. I envied them because their national borders were distinct: they had that amazing, boot-shaped country whose perimeter was uncontested, and their culture was received well in the United States. Among Americans, there was a general, albeit incomplete, understanding of what it meant to be Italian: it meant big family dinners, the Catholic Church and Frank Sinatra. There were more negative connotations as well, but as a kid I longed for that clarity of identity that the Italians seemed to possess.

Unlike most of my Italian American friends, who were third and fourth generation, I had a very close understanding of Palestine. I knew every inch of my parents' village in the West Bank, though I've only been there a few times in my life. I knew where the Greek Orthodox Church was and where the olive groves were. I knew the site of Al-Khader, the Roman ruins, where people still go to pray and to give thanks. I knew where the *qahwah* was and the school.

My father's stories filled in the picture for me, granting me citizenship to a town where I should have been born and raised, but for politics and war. On a cold winter night, if you set a cup of peppermint tea and a bowl of oranges in front of him, my father would reach for his pocket knife and unravel the fruit. And then he'd begin one of his nostalgic tales in which a poverty-stricken, war-torn childhood shone like a magical era. Hunting for rabbits. Colouring eggs for Easter with onion skins. Breaking in a new horse. Marching in the Boy Scouts.

I constructed my homeland on these words, bolstered by a few visits. Palestine, whose borders were so unclear, was at least clear in my mind, even though I could never find it on a world map or globe, could never pick it out as easily as my friends could find Italy and say, 'Here! This is where my parents were born. This is my homeland.'

One evening my middle-school friend, Anne Marie, was on the other end of the phone. I was telling her about the First Intifada. The evening news had just shown footage of soldiers trying to deliberately break the arm of a young man who was down on his knees. Children of the stones.[1] The Palestinian community in Philadelphia was organising a rally downtown that weekend, and my brother and I were planning to make and carry our own signs. My mother kept signalling for me to end my call soon because she needed the telephone to help coordinate the effort.

'Because the real problem is the settlements,' I said. 'They're illegal and . . .'

Anne Marie sighed.

I heard it gushing through the phone cable. Sigh. *How does this political stuff relate to me?* she probably wondered. Because in eighth grade her only concerns were the basketball team, the Philadelphia Eagles, the upcoming school talent show and whether or not Angelo S. liked her. Stone-throwing children with brown skin and fuzzy hair – across the ocean, to boot – weren't anything about which she had an opinion.

I understood, in the space of that sigh, how endangered most of my friendships would become, like wild animals fighting extinction.

To me, the First Intifada was a life-changing point in time. I was never the same again after watching the footage, marching in the demonstrations, signing petitions and writing letters to Congress.

To my friends, it was the year I became too annoying, too bothersome, too political.

Years later, during an undergraduate class on Middle Eastern history, the professor stated outright to twenty-five college sophomores and juniors that

Palestinians didn't really have a legitimate claim on the West Bank: 'They're actually considered Jordanians,' he said.

I sat, stunned, until I saw my classmates writing this information down. These words were about to become facts to them, another golden nugget of information to be studied, spat back in an essay or exam, or selected on a multiple-choice test. Quickly I raised my hand and the professor coughed and shuffled his notes. Perhaps he'd always suspected I'd be a problem.

'I respectfully disagree. I'm Palestinian,' I interjected. 'I don't consider myself Jordanian.'

He was ready for me. 'Okay, but the rest of the international community does.'

'I don't think so. I've never heard that . . .'

'Well, maybe not now, but in 1967 they did.' And he moved on. The West Bank was part of Transjordan, and thus Palestinians were actually Jordanians. Now please shut up, his eyes said, as he quickly moved on to the rest of his lecture. But I noticed, at least, that not everyone had continued writing.

That was the moment when I understood how, in America, being Palestinian was not just about being misunderstood. Palestinians were not as easily identified as other cultures or ethnic groups – I'd accepted that long ago. However, I had not realised until that moment how some people would try to rewrite your identity, to sweep over you like a mighty river, and how you would have to cling to an overhanging branch or a rock and refuse to be drowned. You're shivering and wet while you watch your friends glide by you in safe and sturdy boats, drifting further and further away from you.

It is twenty years later, December 2013. During a single coffee session, my cousin, our friend and I decide to start our own Arabic and *dabke* school for our eleven children so that they will understand their heritage. Over the next month we design a curriculum, organise a schedule, research textbooks and make a calendar. 'Let's do this,' my cousin says, and we all commit ourselves to the project.

This is how you refuse to be drowned.

Note

1. 'Children of the stones' (*atfal al-hijara* in Arabic) refers to the children who took part in the First Intifada.

Izzat Darwazeh

Izzat Darwazeh was born in 1963 in Syria and lived there until his family moved to Jordan when he was thirteen. He studied electrical engineering at the University of Jordan in Amman and moved to the UK in 1984 to study for his MSc and PhD at the University of Manchester. He has since pursued an academic career in the UK and has become a British citizen. He is now the Chair and Professor of Communications Engineering at University College London. He is married and lives in London.

Breathing Politics

I was born in the Syrian town of Homs. My parents and their parents and grandparents were all born in Nablus where my mother still owns land and a house, which she has been unable to live in or even visit since 1967. She is absolutely determined that her property remains in Palestinian hands and never falls into the hands of the Israeli occupiers. My mother had refugee status and my parents spent most of their adult lives as exiles, mourning a country lost and the friends and family they were separated from.

When people ask me where I am from I say Nablus, as that is where I feel my roots are, even though I only saw Nablus for the first time in my mid-thirties, armed with a British passport and my parents' mental maps of places they lived. It was a moving experience being in what would have been the town of my birth, if my parents had not been exiled. It was both strange and familiar, so much had my parents talked about their lives there, but I also felt like a foreigner, a bit lost and uncertain of my bearings.

I grew up in an atmosphere where politics was the air we breathed. My father was imprisoned in Syria two months after I was born and my mother recalls taking me to visit him in prison after her long days working as a doctor in one of Syria's deprived neighbourhoods. Some of my happiest child-hood memories are of the time I spent in my grandfather's modest house in Damascus, listening to stories of his struggles and adventures, stories that captivated my imagination as a child and continue to be a great source of pride in my family. My paternal grandfather, Mohammed Izzat Darwazeh, was born to a poor family in Nablus in 1887 and became a notable Muslim scholar, historian and political analyst, as well as a prolific diarist. He was a lifelong fighter against the British, and later Zionist, occupations of Palestine and was one of the leaders of the 1936 Palestinian revolt against the British. He was imprisoned for many years in Palestine and by the French in Syria, and he, his brother and my father spent more than four years exiled in Turkey in the early 1940s.

One of my earliest memories is hiding under the kitchen table during Israeli air raids on Damascus during the Six-Day War in 1967. Then, with my sister Mona, we stayed at my grandfather's house while my heavily pregnant mother volunteered to serve in hospitals. I have vivid memories of my aunts listening to Nasser's speeches and, feeling euphoric, promising that soon we would go home to Palestine. Little did they know that Palestine had just become much farther away! Even so, my earliest memory of actually feeling Palestinian was at school in Syria when I was teased by the teachers and other children for having a lunch box of cucumbers stuffed with rice and minced lamb, a Nabulsi peculiarity. Growing up in another Arabic-speaking country, it took me a while to understand that I was different; an exile in a 'sister' yet foreign country.

As a teenager, by now living in Jordan, I became increasingly aware of how I was disadvantaged both in the Arab world and internationally. I began to identify strongly with the oppression and suffering of Palestinians living under Israeli occupation. Many of my relatives in Palestine and outside had been killed by the Israelis and many of my friends and immediate family were imprisoned for political activities. As a university student in the early 1980s I got involved in clandestine student political activities. I remember how nervous we were of being harassed or possibly arrested for attending a poetry evening or playing Palestinian revolutionary music! Still, my parents were fully supportive and would always cover for us when the authorities came looking (my mother even sewing forbidden papers inside the cushions in our living room). Those were exhilarating and optimistic times when the prospect of freedom for Palestine seemed just around the corner for us with our youthful energy and unquenchable appetite for adventure. My friends and I even attempted to volunteer as fighters with the PLO during the 1982 Israeli invasion of Lebanon, with my father's full support, but we failed to make it to Beirut.

If we'd joined I wouldn't be here now. As it was, I swapped the potential life of a resistance fighter for the relative comfort of postgraduate studies at a British university where I got involved with the Palestine Solidarity Campaign, becoming a founding member of the Manchester branch in 1986, and other Arab and Palestinian political organisations, as well as British and third world political campaigns. I realised that the Palestinian struggle was not an isolated one but part of an international struggle against colonialism and neo-colonialism. In Britain, I experienced the relative luxury of being able to hold meetings in public and organise demonstrations with less fear of being arrested, albeit, dare I say, with less excitement. I found the British left, while often supportive of our Palestinian struggle, argumentative and somewhat self-important, leaving me with the uncomfortable feeling that the real struggle was elsewhere, somewhere I wanted to be but was unable to get to.

In 1980s Britain a Palestinian in the popular imagination wore a *keffiyeh* and knew how to use a Kalashnikov (I did neither!). When introduced to my then future wife's family, the first thing they wanted to know was whether I was in the PLO, read: was I a potential hijacker of planes? As a student I used to feel flattered, and more often amused, by the number of invitations I received to address meetings and the extent to which my views on political matters were sought, far beyond my immediate experience. I came to understand these reactions as subtle forms of racism or ignorance. Sometimes I experienced more obvious racism, such as the time a few of my colleagues at work complained about how foreigners were taking their jobs, or the lack of public outrage about a headline in one of the tabloid newspapers referring to 'Arab pigs'. Several of my Palestinian and Arab friends were randomly arrested and detained during the first invasion of Iraq in 1991. I went into hiding for a short while until the furore was over.

For me, being Palestinian is also about music and poetry. My mother used to play an old mandolin that she brought with her from Nablus and sing us to sleep with Fairuz songs about returning to Jerusalem and Jaffa. My father used to recite poetry to us as children, and the sounds, rhythms and feelings that poets and writers such as Mahmoud Darwish and Ghassan Kanafani evoke will always be a part of who I am.

Living in the Palestinian *Shatat*, particularly in London, means that I am always meeting other Palestinians, either other *Shatat* Palestinians, or those passing through. Politics, return to Palestine, current news and the Palestinian problem (*al-qaddiyah*) are always core topics of any conversation, normally preceded by a barrage of questions: Where in Palestine are you from? Who is your family/father/mother? When did they/you leave the homeland ('*al-blaad*')? Do you know Ms X or Mr Y? Inevitably you will find a link, a relation, a connection.

There is a strong sense of belonging among Palestinians living in exile. It feels like a huge extended family spread across the continents, where everyone looks out for everyone else. To me, this is perhaps one of the warmest aspects of 'being Palestinian'.

Dawoud El-Alami

Dawoud El-Alami, Licence en Droit (Cairo); PhD (Glasgow). Originally a lawyer, Dawoud has worked in British universities for twenty-five years. He is currently a senior teaching fellow at the University of Aberdeen.

Motherland

I was born in the mountains of Lebanon in 1953 in April, or perhaps October. The only thing anyone is sure about is that there was snow. Despite the fact that I was not born in Palestine, and have never lived there, throughout my childhood growing up in Egypt I knew I was a Palestinian in exile from my homeland. My eight siblings were born in Palestine before 1948 and the older ones, who have memories of life before the *Nakba*, have their own Palestinian identity. I had no direct experience of Palestine so my entire sense of being Palestinian has been mediated through my family. Being Palestinian, for me, begins and ends with my mother.

My mother was born to a life of comfort on her father's estates ten years before the fall of the Ottoman Empire. She married in her teens in Mandate Palestine and lived the first years of her married life in that precarious decade before World War II, unaware that her whole world was about to be shattered. How could she have foreseen the journey on which life was to take her? How could she have ever known that she would end her days in her ninety-sixth year in a late-Victorian house in west Wales in the twenty-first century?

In the way of strange connections, in the last years of her life, the biblical names of her homeland were all around her in the names of Welsh villages: Bethlehem, Horeb, Nebo, Nasareth, Peniel, Salem. The names have a resonance that conjures images of other landscapes and the sounds of other voices. They form a link to a map held in the heart in the same manner as the ritual of naming names and identifying connections that is always rehearsed whenever Palestinians meet: What family? From where? The jigsaw of place and genealogy is pieced together again and again and thereby preserved, its interlinking sections connected and the gaps filled. The recitation of names makes them real. Palestinians may have lived all their lives in Britain, America or other parts of the Arab world but they still identify themselves by lineage and the towns and villages of their family origin. Places may have been physically erased from the geography of the land but they are preserved in common memory.

My mother's journey from Asqalan to Ceredigion was a long one with many different lives lived along the way, but she carried Palestine with her and spread it out around her like a carpet wherever she lived: in the minutiae of daily life, the greetings and expressions, the social customs, the rituals of coffee and, above all, the food. There is a canon of dishes that is the common language of all Palestinians. Cooked by our great-grandmothers from the fruit of the land and passed on from mother to daughter over generations, these dishes connect us to the Palestine of our memories and to each other.

My mother left her home in 1948 and could never go back, but she had the strength to adapt and survive, to preserve the family in dignity and to carry the pain of my father who never recovered from the *Nakba*. My father lived the next forty years waiting to return, never really acknowledging the reality of the situation. He would stand on the shore in Alexandria and tell us that Palestine was just beyond the horizon, that he could almost see his orchards in Asqalan and that one day we would return, but my mother was a realist and knew that life was to be lived in the present and could not be postponed. She had already experienced loss: her brother and both her parents had died young. There was no negotiation in her expectation of each of us to succeed and to make our way in the world. We had no place to return to, nothing to fall back on and no one to depend on but ourselves – and her. She was our homeland and wherever she was, was home. Now, in her absence, we are adrift forever.

Najat El-Taji El-Khairy

Najat El-Taji El-Khairy is a porcelain artist of Palestinian origin born in 1948. After attending French private schools in Cairo, she completed a BA in English Literature at King Saud University in Riyadh. In 1988 she moved with her family to Montreal, Canada, where she studied painting on porcelain. She frequently researches, lectures and advocates on Palestinian art heritage and in 2005 she created 'embroidery on porcelain', an innovative patented method documenting Palestinian cross-stitch embroidery by painting them on porcelain tiles – a non-perishable medium. Her artwork is displayed in various museums and galleries throughout North America and Europe.

Painting my Way Back Home One Stitch at a Time

Being Palestinian defines every fibre of my being. It weaves my daily life with all its complexities. Whether living in the homeland or in the diaspora like myself, belonging to a land unjustly occupied by someone else is a stab in every Palestinian's heart.

Although I have never lived in Palestine, Palestine lives in me. It nourishes my veins with its exquisite culture, rich heritage and breathtaking landscapes. It calls for me wherever I go. I connect to my homeland with the scent of orange groves and the sight of olive and lemon trees. As I walk with my grandson along the Rhine in Basel, Switzerland, there she is in a small rock in the river that happens to be shaped like historic Palestine. We point to it and call it Palestine Island and pray for her displaced people. Despite our physical distance, Palestine is always close to me.

I was born with a twin sister in Cairo in 1948. As young children, we were oblivious to our nation's *Nakba*. Growing up, we kept hearing 'those twins were born during the year of the *Nakba*'. We overheard the elders recount our people's story, and with time came to realise that in the year we were brought to life, Palestinians lost the meaning of theirs. I sadly came to understand the reality of what became of my parents' and grandparents' mansions (Abdel Rahman El-Taji El-Farouki and Shukri El-Taji El-Farouki) and how my people were ethnically cleansed, robbed of their homes, farms and lands, and forced to leave their precious livelihoods behind.

A nostalgic, bittersweet feeling encompasses my soul when I imagine the blissful life my elders enjoyed, surrounded by orchards in peaceful towns and villages. Once upon a time in Palestine, Muslims, Christians and Jews were neighbours living happily on the same land. My ancestors lived with their extended families in comfortable roomy homes. Three generations: grand-mothers, mothers and daughters gathered to chat, embroider together and prepare delicious dishes of stuffed vine leaves, and *makloubet beitenjan*, a famous eggplant dish. The whole family ate together, enjoying *siniyet knafeh Nabulsieh* for dessert while sipping hot Turkish coffee on their verandas. Their laughter would resonate among the tall cypress trees surrounding their gardens.

What could have remained a beautiful story ended abruptly when in 1947 a United Nations decision allowed the creation of the State of Israel on Palestinian land. Just the thought of my ancestors losing their stable life to the Zionist movement is enough to stir my pain and agony. Families, like ours, who were fortunate enough to rebuild their lives elsewhere, were scat-tered all over the world. Suddenly, oceans divided siblings in the diaspora, as they went their separate ways to lead more decent lives for their families. Life as they knew it would never be the same. In their new countries they still reminisce and dream of lively family gatherings reuniting them once again. Like thousands of Palestinians who were unjustly uprooted and violently displaced, both my grandfathers died heartbroken, carrying the unresolved pain of being forced away from their precious lands.

As a Palestinian living in Montreal, Canada, my inborn duty towards my homeland is to preserve and assert our proud Palestinian identity in the diaspora. I take it upon myself to act as an ambassador to our lost country with a mission to reverse people's often negative images, which have been tainted by one-sided media. As an avid admirer and collector of Palestinian embroidered artefacts for as long as I can remember, and determined to get my message across, I chose to bring attention to our cause through culture and art, a universal language which transcends boundaries and touches the soul. Such a precious method, displayed in conferences and exhibitions, helps engage dialogue while inviting people to view and appreciate our distinct cross-stitch patterns. Each of the symbols embellishing our village women's dresses tells a wonderful story of the truly unique identity of a proud people.

Being a Palestinian abroad taught me to converse through art. Feeling deprived of living in my beloved homeland and needing to connect with my people, I decided to document the Palestinian cross-stitch embroidery designs by painting them on porcelain tiles – hence securing them in a permanent way. Each cross-stitch I paint brings me closer to my people enduring unimaginable suffering under an inhumane occupation. Each stroke is to reassure them of my commitment to our just cause. Realising that not only our land is stolen, but also our culture is being pirated, for example, by claiming our Palestinian national embroidered dresses and *keffiyeh* as their own, and declaring our traditional cuisine, such as falafel and hummus, to be Israeli dishes, I felt the need to protect and reclaim our heritage.

The Tree of Life and the strong vibrant olive trees I paint are a way of expressing my people's never-fading strength and determination, confirming our deeply rooted connection to our forefathers' land. Like their owners, they shall resist being uprooted and withstand all hardship, continuing to provide fruits of peace for generations to come.

The ugly Apartheid Wall being built by Israel is another important issue I feel compelled to raise awareness of in diaspora. The wall aims to alienate, humiliate, oppress and separate people from their work, farmers from their lands, and families from one another. I decided to depict the Palestinian resistance by drawing beautiful floral cross-stitch patterns climbing the wall in defiance, asserting our Palestinian resilience and perseverance despite all the obstacles we face. My message is that this suffering will not go in vain.

Living in the diaspora, I feel a constant longing for the day my people will return to their homeland. The heartbreaking realisation of my ancestors' fate marked a deep wound inside me and shaped who I am today: a proud Palestinian with a peaceful mission and a strong sense of duty towards her beloved, aching country. I exist, I belong, and I shall continue to keep our beautiful heritage alive in order to pave the way back for our children to our land – the land to which my connection is eternal – the land of peace-loving olive trees.

Sharif Elmusa

Sharif S. Elmusa, scholar, poet and translator, is currently an associate professor of political science at the American University in Cairo. He holds a PhD from Massachusetts Institute of Technology. Apart from his academic and journalistic publications, Elmusa is author of Flawed Landscape: Poems 1987–2008 *and co-editor, with Gregory Orfalea, of* Grape Leaves: A Century of Arab-American Poetry.

A Demon of Hope

> I said: I learned so much from you. I learned
> how to coach myself to row in the white
> Mediterranean Sea, searching
> through the dual matter of road and home.
> He ignored my praise. He offered me coffee,
> and he said: your Odysseus will return, safe,
> he will.

The foregoing stanza (my translation) from Mahmoud Darwish's poem 'A Vague Happening' recalls a conversation he had with the Greek poet Yannis Ritsos (d. 1988). It introduces the trope of Odysseus that Darwish and other Palestinian writers and poets, including myself, have tended to employ, especially after Yasser Arafat and many other PLO affiliates trekked in Greek boats to Piraeus in metropolitan Athens – their first port of call after their eviction from Lebanon by Israeli forces in 1982.

The analogy of the Palestinian journey with the story of Odysseus is fraught. Homer's hero was a leading Achaean, a sacker, not among the sacked, of Troy. He was guided by a coterie of thoughtful deities; alas, our chiefs have not been shepherded by such patrons. Odysseus' home remained intact, whereas Palestine has been transformed. Nonetheless, the tale is useful as iteration for reading the mind of a Palestinian exile, like myself, through the core idea of 'returning', which has never ceased to pester me.

I grew up in al-Nuwayma, 'in a desert/without the sinuous sands/of the movies, in a camp/by the gateless Jericho'.[1] My parents hailed from the village of al-Abbasiyya, now Yehud (part of the present-day Ben Gurion International Airport is built on land belonging to the former village). They were farmers who became landless in the first years of their expulsion when most of Palestine was made into Israel in 1948. They were sustained, like everyone else in the camp, by the hope that the *mughtasaba*, 'usurped', Palestine would be restored. Without that thought the camp-dwellers would have experienced utter disorientation.

In the tenth grade I was editor of a 'wall newspaper', *al-Awda*, 'The Return', which teemed with enthusiasm for fighting to liberate Palestine, angst at the defeatism of parents and Arab regimes, and rejection of the humiliating existence in the camps. I must admit though that participating in military battles, even for Palestine, has always intimidated me.

> My father remembered
> his twelve olive trees
> every day for ten years . . .
> Then one day he let go. Let go.
> My father was no Ulysses.
> He found a new land
> and stayed away on the farm,
> eking out some rough happiness.

And my mother?

> Her past was insatiable:
> The new house they had just built,
> with windows on four sides,
> windows tall and arched
> to let in the ample light,
> to spread out the prayers . . .

The poem is ambivalent and reverses the roles of Odysseus and Penelope. In reality my father told me about his olive trees in 1997: fifty, not ten, years after 1948. What he probably meant by letting go was that by this time he sensed the prospect of reuniting with his olive trees had dimmed. The ambivalence is a grey region between Ritsos' reassurance to Darwish that the Palestinian Odysseus would return and the scepticism of his fellow Greek poet C. P. Cavafy (d. 1936) who admonished the protagonist of the often-cited poem, 'Ithaca', not to rush back home, the value of which inhered in giving him the journey. Whereas Ritsos went back to Greece after being exiled, Darwish's body was laid in 2008 in a tomb on a hill near Ramallah – which he said was not his 'personal home' – overlooking Jerusalem. The village of his birth, al-Birwa in the Western Galilee, had been razed by the Israeli military in 1948.

What does the exile find or imagine finding upon return? We know what awaited Odysseus on his arrival. 'The Dream' from the *One Thousand and One Nights* conveys a like ending. A bankrupt merchant from Baghdad dreamed of a treasure in another city. He 'obeyed' the dream, as people did in those days, and travelled to that city. There, he ran into a stranger who recounted a dream of his own about a buried treasure. As the stranger described the place where the treasure was buried, it dawned on the merchant that it was his own house in Baghdad. I did a variation on 'The Dream' in which the merchant repaired from 'Technoville' back to his city 'Thirdstan', 'Swift as a bullet—/no meandering, no nymphs, no sirens'. Unlike Shahrazad's merchant, he was informed that his house had been sold to a young couple who, while renovating the structure,

> . . . unearthed a fine copper chest
> from under the fountain.
> They went wild,
> stomping the chest with their feet,
> sure the thing buzzed with ancient gold.
> But all they found were empty compartments,
> like hollowed teeth,
> like a childless house,
> begging to be filled.

In another poem, 'Homeward Bound', my narrator is going back home late at night, tired after long hours of work, and misses his stop. He loiters at the wrong station, eavesdrops on a couple's conversation, and ponders the motivations of ants filing up and down a wall until:

The body pokes the meddling mind
to mind its own business. It pricks up
its ears to listen for the sweet rumble
of the train. It craves the wide bed,
and the absent woman
to crawl beside.

No overjoyed Penelope waits for him.

It took Odysseus twenty years to land in Ithaca, after an existentially and physically trying and transforming voyage. It now takes me ten to twelve hours by plane, discounting the aggravations and delays of Israeli security, to go to or come back from Palestine – too swift for the enormity of the change. Speed not only annihilates time and space, it appears to also flatten depth. Would Odysseus go and stay in Ithaca if he could get there on Olympic Air in half an hour from Ogygia, the goddess Calypso's island? Well-heeled contemporary exiles shuttle back and forth or make their fictional characters do the same, and bask in being at home 'everywhere' and dread being at home 'nowhere'.

Would I, if allowed to return, continue to make such round trips, as I have been doing? Would I 'resettle' in America? Or would I remain forever unsettled? Perhaps, in the end, the ambivalence is the state in which I am meant to live, between the illusion of a perfect home and self, and the anxiety of being in abeyance. No matter, the desire for home seems unquenchable, like love in the song of the exiled Iraqi singer Kazim al-Saher, 'it burns us and itself does not burn'. My past, like my mother's, remains insatiable:

What is left of my heart
wants to beat in Palestine –
short on water
flowing with corrupt chiefs,
tiny and beautiful and exposed,
like the poppies of the field,
the land wherein I would not be an odd stranger.
From her ribs a strong hand
uprooted my family tree.

My mother is Maryam
and sister Fatima

and brother Ibrahim
and brother Ahmad
and uncle Mousa
and uncle Issa,
and cousin Sarah
and friend Isaac.

My brain has become warring cantons.
But a demon of hope stirs –
there will be unexpected *manna*.
My tongue keeps lashing at the conscience
of the farthest angels,
the clock gazing,
and my living rooms moving.

Note

1. All poetry in the essay is mine unless stated differently.

Doaa Elnakhala

Doaa Elnakhala is a freelance researcher. She has a PhD and an MA in political science from the University of Texas at Austin, USA. She has another MA and a BA from Birzeit University, Palestine, in International Studies and in English Language and Literature. Her research explores barriers on borders.

Contradictory Worlds

I never wanted to leave Palestine. Yes, I wanted to visit many countries but not more than merely visiting. The day I left, I was not at all certain I would make it out of the country. I had tried to leave four times before, but each time returned to my parents' house after four or more hours at Erez Checkpoint. The day I left, I told my parents 'see you in the afternoon'. I still remember my father's face peaking from the balcony watching my taxi as it drove away. Before leaving, I spent forty days in Gaza trying to get out. I spent this time trying to contact all officials and non-officials I could think of to ask for help to leave Gaza, which was under tight closure after the kidnapping of the Israeli soldier Gilad Shalit in late June 2006. Though about eight years have passed since that day, with many agonies, fears and happy moments, two feelings remain: uncertainty and fear. Uncertainty about what will happen to me after finishing my PhD. Will I be forced to go back to Gaza? Will I ever be able to return to Ramallah? Will I ever see my parents again? And fear about returning to Gaza, even for a visit.

The minute I crossed the borders, I felt so loaded with sadness and stories of the horror created by the occupation that I did not want to talk much. In Austin, Texas many colleagues and even professors wanted to meet me. I was not only the sole Palestinian on the PhD program at the Government Department of the University of Texas at Austin, but the only Arab as well. They all asked me questions: 'How is it to live there?', 'Why do young men and women bomb themselves?', 'How is it possible to live under occupation?',

'Are you a Muslim?', 'Why aren't you wearing a headscarf?' I literally felt I was in a zoo where a rare animal is on display and everyone wants to see. I also felt I should respond to the many stereotypes about a Palestinian Muslim woman calmly and diplomatically. I tried to swallow my anger about what I still think were stupid questions and remind myself that at least they had an interest in knowing what it is like to be a Palestinian woman. I later encountered many undergraduate students in Texas who never cared to know anything about what is going on in the Middle East, let alone Palestine.

In the US, one of the most surprising experiences I have had is flying without a visa, using only my driver's licence. It was so easy I did not believe this is how it works, and it always made me recall the different degrees of bad identity cards we have in Palestine. The worst in the bad scale is a Gazan Palestinian, which I am, followed by a West Bank Palestinian, a Jerusalemite Palestinian and the best is an Israeli Palestinian. The consequence of this classification is freedom of movement and access to services, no matter their source. It also made me recall the many years and occasions I had to pass alone in the West Bank without being able to visit my parents in Gaza.

In Texas everything was much bigger than I ever imagined. In fact everything is 'BIG in Texas'. The first month was among the toughest. After living in Ramallah, where I knew every corner, I needed to learn and understand how things worked. Simple things that I had taken for granted became an issue, such as how to get to school to take my classes from my apartment in Austin.

Another challenge came to the surface in one of my political science classes. We were having a discussion about the war in Iraq. The American students in the class (the majority) started giving opinions and analyses. I could not say much because I was absent-mindedly thinking of something rather minor given the subject of discussion. The question that puzzled me was: 'Who is "we"?' 'Am I included?': clearly not. The students were discussing the war, repeatedly saying 'we' should have done this and 'we' shouldn't have done that. For the first time, I was not a member of the 'we'. I felt so estranged and could not figure out how I could contribute to such a debate. I never felt a belonging to my surroundings in the US so my sense of 'Palestinian-ness' became increasingly important over time.

One of the most difficult moments was in late 2008/early 2009 while the Israeli 'Operation Cast Lead' was going on in Gaza. I was so worried about my family that I was calling them hundreds of times a day. While most of the time I could not get through, I was able to get in touch at least once a day. At the time I was in Virginia, but I did not want to be anywhere outside of Palestine because it felt as though Americans were completely indifferent to what was going on in Gaza. I was shocked by the American media, which presented Gaza as if it was a new conflict simply between Israel and Hamas, as though Gaza was the equivalent of Hamas. In fact, like every man anywhere else, my dad, who is an average Gazan, wants only to live in peace and provide good living conditions for his family. The American indifference angered me so many times I wanted to stop my car in the middle of the highway and yell at everyone.

Being in the US has deepened my Palestinian identity. In Palestine I never got involved in activism or politics outside of my academic studies. But in the US I realised the importance of discussing politics to change people's perceptions of Palestinian women and the Palestinian question. As a result, on different occasions, I have found myself talking to random people on the metro, or in airports and on buses, making sure they know I am Palestinian. By doing so, I am unconsciously trying to bring my two worlds, America and Palestine, closer together.

Amal Eqeiq

Amal Eqeiq is a native Palestinian born in the city of Al-Taybeh. She is a writer, scholar, activist and an occasional poet. She holds a PhD in comparative literature from the University of Washington. Currently she is a visiting assistant professor of Arabic and comparative literature at Williams College, Massachusetts.

Bint Liblaad **on the Road**

When I was invited to write for *Being Palestinian*, I was surprised. Although I have been living outside Palestine since 2004, I don't qualify as part of the diaspora. First of all, leaving Palestine to pursue doctoral studies in the US was a choice *I* made. In fact, it was more of a realisation of an age-old dream to travel, to explore new horizons and to discover all the selves that I could possibly be. Second, and most importantly, I can *always* return. I can return if I don't wish to pursue an academic career in the US, or if I run out of poems inspired by spectacular North American landscapes: the eerie sunsets in the distant Pacific Northwest, the majestic summits of the Olympic Mountains, the Cascades and the Rockies, and the crystallising whiteness of death in the frozen lakes of New England. I can also return when I stop recognising familial features in the physiognomy of very exhausted poor people, mostly of colour, running around the map to chase 'America the Beautiful', as they saw it on TV. I can *always* return despite Ben Gurion (the vision) and through Ben Gurion (the airport). After all, I am from Palestine '48, *al-dakhel* ('the inside'), historic Palestine, the west side of the Apartheid Wall, inside the invisible Green Line. I am a Palestinian 'from' Israel. I hold an Israeli passport and, according to Ben Gurion's Declaration of Independence, I should be grateful for my great fortune to have been born in a Jewish democratic state! The first *exile*!

'So how is it to be a Palestinian with an Israeli passport?' is a question that I am often asked by people who are curious about anomalies. 'At Ben

Gurion I am treated like shit, but Uncle Sam welcomes me with a big smile,' I respond, and continue to describe the adventures of racial profiling at Ben Gurion. My blue passport, with a menorah engraved on its front page, does not protect me, as a Palestinian, from being strip-searched, getting tags in a *different* colour on my luggage and body, confiscation of *sumac* and other valuable national souvenirs, insidious interrogations about my personal life and, most importantly, the destruction of the harmony that my mother creates inside my suitcases with her neat, geometric organisation of my belongings. I look at her standing on the other side of the security line observing the special security team turning her labour of love into chaos. If only I could uproot that anguish from her eyes! I try to reassure her from my side of the security line. I send comforting smiles. I wave with random hand gestures like an amateur actress: 'I am fine. Nothing broke. I am not afraid of Ben Gurion's grandchildren.' I wave to my father, whose feet move restlessly behind the security dividing line. I signal to them (again): 'Proceed to the other side of the exit behind the special screening gate. Order coffee there and wait.' They know the routine!

August 2005, Mexico. I am sitting next to Graciela Lucero-Hammer, a professor of Spanish literature from Córdoba, Argentina. We are on an early bus ride from Querétaro to Guanajuato. 'This landscape reminds me of my country,' Graciela says, and points to the rusty green mountains of La Tierra Fria with affectionate eyes. These green mountains look oddly familiar to me too, and so are the brown bodies of Mexican *campesinos* bending hard to cultivate life around them. Between these rusty green mountains I imagine myself driving through Wadi 'Ara and going up the road north to the Galilee. I want to tell Graciela that I feel the same; that this landscape reminds me of my country too, but I cringe in my seat tongue-tied. I ask her if there is another way to say 'my country' in Spanish without using '*mi país*'. My tongue just won't utter 'my state'. Bewildered by my intense, sudden silence, she answers: '*Mi tierra*. Your land is your country too.'

'Yes, this sounds better.' I nod contentedly like a small child who has just learnt a new word. My forehead touches the bus window. I look outside more closely. When Graciela later reflects on what seemed to her as a lost in translation issue, I interject to assert: 'I belong to the land, but the state that exists on it is foreign to me. It also treats me as if I were a foreigner.'

I was born in 1976 at Golda Meir Hospital in Kfar-Saba, another Jewish town with a deformed Palestinian name. Portraits of the woman who declared to the world in 1969 that Palestinians 'did not exist' can be found all over the hospital walls. I often wonder how my mother and the rest of the women from my small town and the other neighbouring Palestinian villages felt giving birth there. Did Golda's ghost haunt them in the delivery room? Did they hear her screams from the picture: 'Do not listen to the doctors! You have nothing inside!' I never asked my mother these questions, but I know that she pushed really hard. When she left the hospital she carried me, her fourth child, together with a birth certificate printed with a Golda Meir Hospital letterhead. Several lines under Golda, my name appears in modern Hebrew script. The Jewish doctors told my mother I was a healthy child. They said nothing about raising healthy children with chronic alienation!

From 2000 to 2004 I commuted from my hometown Al-Taybeh to Tel Aviv University. The almost daily thirty-five-minute drive has left a critical mark on the formation of my exilic consciousness. For almost two years the transportation of heavy machines would create more traffic than usual, and the thirty-five minutes would become an hour. Radio Ajyal from Ramallah became my best friend. I would listen to it while I watched the trucks diverge left to the construction site of the Apartheid Wall near Qalqilia. While the people from Qaqilia and their farmlands slowly 'disappeared' in front of my eyes behind the rapidly rising militarised concrete, their voices and the voices of other Palestinians behind the Apartheid Wall rang out in the morning radio talk shows. Some called to complain about the misery of occupation and the corruption of the Palestinian Authority; some called to comment on social issues, or to ask the radio presenters to play their favourite song; some dubbed their voices for commercial advertisements. The voices sounded familiar, close and intimate. They became my faithful companions on the road, keeping me tuned to the life that still existed behind the wall. These voices would stay with me until I approached the first traffic light in north-eastern Tel Aviv, at the major intersection in Kfar Hayarouk (The Green Village). I don't know what used to be the Palestinian name of the area buried underneath this jammed intersection. But there, when the radio wave was lost, I realised I had just crossed an invisible border. For years to come, I would ponder why I didn't call the radio to greet the people of Qalqilia? I should have told them that I still see them, despite witnessing how the wall had sealed them off.

Randa Farah

Randa Farah is an associate professor at the University of Western Ontario who has written extensively and continues to write on Palestinian refugees, memory / identity, the United Nations Relief and Works Agency for Palestine Refugees in the Near East (UNRWA) and, to a lesser extent, on refugees of Western Sahara. She was an associate researcher at the Refugee Studies Centre (RSC) at the University of Oxford.

Darker Shades of Exile

It is bitter cold this morning. I wrap my Palestinian scarf tighter around my neck and look down to avoid the razor-sharp wind blowing my face. I notice the deep traces my boots imprint in the Canadian snow. It is early and the quiet of the vanishing night lingers except for the swooshing sound of my footsteps, exaggerating the dissonance I feel with the vast landscape. Beneath me are historical layers attesting to a colonial history that robbed indigenous peoples of their land, corralled them into reservations and snatched their children to 'civilise' them in 'residential schools'. How deep must be the sorrow etched in their/our soul, in memory and in Mother Earth?

A student once asked me if I consider myself part of the Palestinian diaspora. In response I reflected on Edward Said's deliberations on exile, for it resonates with my unsettled existence, unlike the term 'diaspora' which vitiates the struggle against the ongoing violent eviction of the Palestinians, invoking instead nostalgic longing for some ancient mythical homeland. I am neither the 'Wandering Jew', a phrase often used in diaspora studies, who is living by or awaiting biblical prophecies to be realised, nor am I a migrant who journeys north from a post-colonial world seeking a better life. Exile or refugee are more appropriate terms to describe the ruptures, temporariness, violence I and other Palestinians suffered, and to summon our right of return.

But my Palestinian being has been deeply moulded by my attachment to my homeland and my past, as much as by its public negation in Canada and in Western societies in general. In Canada, to explain who I am, I try to describe rather than define: I cannot take my son to Palestine to places where I and my family hail from, and if I can it is only by permission from the coloniser, in contrast to Canadian Jews who have a concocted 'birthright' to come and go as they please, only because they are Jews. But to ordinary Canadians, such descriptions are often alien and suspect – always needing ample proof, as if they signal danger. Sometimes I resort to material culture to assert an identity, but then walk by tables in university halls where *za'tar*, hummus or *tabbouleh* are presented as Israeli food. It is the end of the term and, as usual, there is a problem – someone has complained I was 'one-sided' in my lecture.

Thus, so much of my Palestinian identity remains memory-locked. Exile and Palestine have become almost inseparable partners. What am I doing here and where is 'there'? I search through labyrinths of memory to find an answer, but the metaphor illuminates alleyways in Palestinian refugee camps, where I spent years doing research and recording refugee life-histories. There, I had learnt from Imm Muhammad, who originates from Dayr Aban, a village in the district of Jerusalem that was depopulated and destroyed in 1948, and from many others, about other histories and anguished journeys of exile, and how they intersected or diverged from mine. The ethnic cleansing of Palestine shaded every story, dotted with many losses and dislocations. I often wonder: do birds have to fly across all the skies before they begin their journey back? How I miss Darwish.

Refugee life-histories interweave past recollections together with pressing matters about everyday life, forming a suspended tapestry wherein permanence and temporariness are engaged in an intense battle, much like mine. Yes, I am a Canadian citizen, but I can only be fully so when my Palestinian self is not excluded, and when my stories and my politics become recognisable and acknowledged.

But how do I represent the life-histories of refugees, or my own, in a Western society that celebrates Israel's 'miraculous birth' and excludes or problematises mine/ours? I think of my elderly parents in Toronto, both carrying stories almost a century old, some transmitted, others untold, with so many dreams of return unfulfilled. How ancient I feel with those memories. Indeed, exile has a long history in my family. My maternal grandmother, along with other Palestinian Christians, was exiled by the Ottomans to Urfa, also known as Edessa, in what is today Turkey. When they arrived they were given the option to live in the erstwhile houses of Armenians, the victims of the 1915 genocide, but they adamantly refused. I now often 'return' to my parents, and shudder to think of the inevitable: how will I connect with my personal past-present when my parents are gone? The burden of memory is getting heavier, like a growing chain concatenating one generation to the next, one exile to another.

I travel further in time to when I left footmarks on the sandy beaches of Haifa, and watched them disappear when a wave settled briefly on the seashore, only to be gulped back by the sea. There, my parents would tell us that the sea held centuries-old stories about civilisations, merchants and visitors arriving by ships to Haifa's harbour, lured to the city by its curvy coastal contours and by al-Karmel, the enchanting mountain watching over the city. Together with my sister and two brothers I would swim against waves, build castles and closely watch busy crabs hurrying sideways on the shore. That same harbour had carried expelled Palestinians in flimsy boats away from their beloved city; when will they sail back?

I feel a deepening *ghurba*, the Arabic word for exile, alienation and estrangement, and try to dispel the desolation with the words of an old song: 'our *ghurba* is one day longer, our return one day closer'! But am I closer to Haifa, the *belle* city where I lived as a third-class 'non-Jew'? That perhaps was the deepest of exiles, yet most tolerable since it was where I could locate, hang, see and live my memories: place and people are imbricated in shaping and reshaping our being. My childhood memories of the late 1950s and 1960s are of segregated schools for 'dirty Arabs' where it was forbidden to study our history, where our movement was restricted by law, where we were humiliated and excluded from Jewish-only spaces. I wonder how it would have felt had I lived in an independent Palestine, a thought that reminds me of Imm Yousef, a refugee living in Marka camp in Jordan, who told me: 'A dog in his Homeland is a Sultan.'

I remembered my school in Jerusalem before and after the Israeli occupation of 1967 when the bus my sister and I took was frequently stopped by European-looking soldiers who searched our school bags. I rush to 'find friends' on Facebook, seeking solace and continuity between the past and present, and between exile and a place of origin. The phone rings, a voice from the past! A childhood friend from Haifa in Canada at long last. The bridge I needed to begin composing a coherent self. I followed up with friends from Jerusalem, Ramallah, Beirut, Washington, DC, London and Amman and wondered if this is how I would eventually conquer exile, or at least begin stitching my scattered self together.

But for now I am tired of being a present absentee, constantly having to defend my right *to be*, to *have been* and *my future right to be* a Palestinian. Today, I am sliced in two: an internal world of memories and Palestinian ways of being, and an external life which I mechanically navigate, often unsuccessfully, in a Western society. It is still bitter cold and I walk faster, I am eager to reach my house so I can listen to the news, and live virtually in the Arab world. Who knows? I might be a day closer to return.

'A snapshot of a bygone era'. Souad Dajani's maternal grandfather sits in the centre surrounded by his children and an African youth who ran errands for the family, at their home in Jaffa, Palestine, in the 1920s.

Demonstrating in the diaspora. Izzat Darwazeh on a demonstration during the First
Palestinian Intifada in Manchester in late 1987 carrying the banner of the Manchester
Palestine Solidarity Campaign, a group he co-founded in 1986 which continues to this day.

'Being a Palestinian abroad taught me to converse through art.' Najat El-Taji El-Khairy's cross-stitch embroidery designs painted on porcelain tiles. 'Three Generation Picnic Scene': 'grandmother to mother to daughter relaying traditions, culture and heritage'.

© www.najat.ca

'Rebelled Spirits': 'Spirits rebelling, determined to keep olive tree strongly rooted in beloved Palestine'.

'The images I make as a visual artist are simultaneously beautiful and tragic.' 'Hamed Moussa, 1910(?) – 2013' from John Halaka's multi-disciplinary project, 'Portraits of Denial & Desire'.

Khaled Hroub in front of the Church of the Nativity in Bethlehem, Palestine on Christmas Day, 2014.

Fady Joudah's father, Ahmad Joudah, behind his derelict grammar school in Isdud/Ashdod. When Ahmad was a child, trees from an orange orchard ran along the back wall of the school.

Rawan Hadid

Rawan Hadid is the Editor of [wherever]: *an out of place journal. She is an ardent advocate for the necessity and durability of the printed word. Her life has dictated that she travel a lot, and she has translated that necessity into her work. She lives in New York, sort of.*

Present in Absence

The diversity of the modern Palestinian experience astounds me. Refugees, privileged global citizens, now Jordanians, now Puerto Ricans and citizens of Israel. The assumption is that many of them must share a kinship: one of shared sadness. Loss, anger, frustration, to varying degrees and to variable levels of intensity, are what unite us.

The majority of people associate being Palestinian with an intractable, existential and political sense of being. I am approaching thirty and for the majority of these years this has not been the case. I have been privileged enough to have remained for the most part sheltered from the harsh reality of Palestinian politics. That, however, has not protected me from a nascent, and growing, existential crisis. One that is admittedly as much a product of the times we live in, as it is a product of the rootlessness of my family.

Despite the time I have spent pondering and assessing what being Palestinian means to me, this short essay remains excruciatingly difficult to write. How to make public the most personal of identity . . . predicaments? Do I discuss my childhood? How has the trauma of my grandfather, the last man to leave Safad, who left his key under the front door mat, manifested in my life? It must be related to why I perpetually over-pack, despite being a seasoned traveller who really should know better.

I discovered Palestine, in a civic sense, with a general political awakening that many people experience at university. I wrote for the student paper, joined student associations and discovered that injustice and censorship were far more common than my liberal upbringing would have had me believe. Prior to university, Palestine was the funny names of my grandmothers and their friends, my mother's cooking, stubborn stereotypes and an otherwise mystical place my grandparents all came from but about which they seemed to have very little to say. I now recognise that this was a result of the shock and suffering from the ordeal – their loss is one I am sure I will never comprehend and one that they never came to terms with. So, like a hysterical relative or a dead sibling, Palestine was rarely discussed but always omnipresent.

I began my undergraduate studies in business school, but within a year it became clear that my interests lay elsewhere. I enrolled in only one degree course each semester and chose four electives. I explored the history of my region, which I did not yet know very much about, dabbled in political theory and philosophy, and generally tried to make sense of the world around me, and my place in it. Eventually I transferred to a communication studies programme, designed to provide me with the tools to tell stories. I graduated feeling dissatisfied and proceeded to the academic home of the late Edward Said in the hope of finding answers, and stories to tell. Naturally, more dissatisfaction ensued, for academia cannot resolve inquiries of the heart. Today I write and edit the stories of others, tracing their travails and travels as they wander the world. My work has become, in part, an effort to create a printed reflection of people who are moving around, taking the time to embark on some self-exploration and feeling restless or confused about their place in the world. There are so many stories.

My parents, both born after 1948, could offer little insight into what Palestine feels like. Ultimately, I have no idea how Palestine smells or what it feels like to be there – I can only imagine. My maternal grandmother still refers to Stanton Street in Haifa. My great-grandparents, alive and healthy until a few years ago, lived in Southern Lebanon, a short drive from their homes in Haifa. They grew new fields and groves and I heard that they kept a box full of legal deeds authenticating all the property they left behind. It is from their stories that I have come to know the land, and while I only came to understand why my belonging to Palestine matters and how it shapes me later in life – and separately from them – my sense of belonging remains rooted in theirs: a family home on a narrow street; my grandfather feeding the chickens before leaving, confident that they would remain his; my great-grandmother's box of tattered legal documents; and her daughter, my grandmother, painting a picture of the steps to her house in the Hadar neighbourhood of Haifa from childhood memories.

Fortunately, or unfortunately, my sense of being Palestinian is intrinsically linked to these people, my family, my relationship with them and their disjunctured relationship with Palestine.

And so, being Palestinian, Palestine is in the details. Palestine sets the scene for the venue where I met my Palestinian husband in New York City. Our recent wedding in Andalusia was full of Palestine, in the particulars that were present and in all that was absent as well. We cannot return to her, but she stays with us everywhere.

John Halaka

John Halaka is a visual artist, documentary filmmaker and Professor of Visual Arts at the University of San Diego, California, where he has taught since 1991. His artwork has been exhibited and his films screened both nationally and internationally.[1]

Photo: Raeda Taha

Inside as an Outsider

I am not sure how my childhood idea of Palestine developed. Maybe it was the winds of Arab nationalism blowing over my subconscious, or an accumulation of things I overheard as a child, when my father would visit with my uncles. But as I think back about it now, my childhood visions of Palestine appear as a brooding and turbulent storm that loomed on the horizon of my consciousness and shaped my fertile imagination. In the solitude of my youthful reverie, Palestine was an imminent tempest that would send floods of biblical proportions, spark lightning that would scorch the earth and unleash winds that would devastate cities. Yet this turbulent land of my imaginary Armageddon also held a sweet and magical mystery that would appear briefly, like a rainbow emerging from gloomy squalls.

Without fully understanding it at the time, the Palestine of my childhood imagination was a land where good and evil were battling for dominance. More than fifty years later, I view Palestine as a stage where an ensemble of colonial actors are repeating timeless tragedies of forced hegemony and racial supremacy.

I was born in El Mansoura, Egypt, in 1957, to a Palestinian father and a Lebanese mother. My paternal grandfather was born and raised in Ramle, Palestine, and my grandmother was born and raised in Jaffa. They moved to Egypt a few decades before the *Nakba* under circumstances that are unknown to me and others in my family. I heard stories of war, famine and epidemics that drove them out of Palestine, but the details were buried with my grandfather when he died in 1934.

My father was not politically engaged and rarely spoke to me of Palestine, as he seemed too busy (or too nervous) trying to shape a basic middle-class existence in Gamal Abdel Nasser's Egypt. My mother worked as a seamstress and my father worked in a bank. Even though neither of them went to university, they greatly valued education and lovingly scraped together enough money to send my two siblings and me to private schools. In the French Jesuit school I attended in Egypt, I was subjected to what I would later understand to be the Western colonial tradition of education. In my first seven grades at school in Cairo, I learnt Arabic as a foreign language and knew a lot more about French history than Arab history. Suffice to say that when my family emigrated to the US in 1970 I was rather confused about who I had been, who I was and who I was becoming.

My personal metamorphosis as an immigrant to America was accompanied by a temporary amnesia of most things Arab. One's identity is created by remembering as well as forgetting, and by concealing as well as revealing.

This cultural amnesia began to lift at university as I gradually became aware of the active struggles for civil rights, indigenous rights and human rights in the Americas. It was the survivance[2] of the oppressed and the marginalised of the Western world that re-introduced me to the existential fight of the Palestinians. Survivance is the desire and will of a people that reject being swept away by ongoing ethnic cleansing, and is an active indigenous presence against political, physical and psychological absence, whether that absence is from their homeland, or an absence in the international discourse on human rights, or an internal absence caused by the acceptance of defeat. Survivance highlights the process of active survival that is shaped by creative and moral resistance to oppression, resistance to institutional manipulation, to neglect and to dehumanisation. Survivance underlines the will of the individual and underscores the power of the collective.

The apocalyptic storms that once filled my youthful imagination were being increasingly illuminated as the anti-colonial struggle of the indigenous Palestinians who, like other subjects of colonialism, have been and continue to be treated as a disposable people.

My identity as a Palestinian was being shaped and reshaped by a growing understanding of my identity as an outsider. I was born an outsider to my homeland, Palestine, and I felt like an outsider in my birth-land, Egypt, and I was being treated as an outsider in my host-land, America. But I very gradually began to feel on the 'inside' as an outsider, as Palestine is the quintessential non-nation of outsiders, enduring a global diaspora of nearly ten million refugees. It wasn't until a number of years later that I realised my critical advantage as an observer from the margins, operating in the gap between inside and outside. I began to understand that being Palestinian is an identity developed by occupying undefined liminal spaces, and worlds not desired. It is a way of living as a serial refugee, an outsider to pockets of tranquillity and an insider to seas of flux. My identity as a Palestinian, as an artist and as a citizen, is defined by my relationship to the seemingly oppositional forces of feeling continually restless and at rest with my restlessness.

I am not a refugee or the son of a refugee, yet my worldview as a Palestinian in America has been in large part shaped by the experiences of Palestinian displacement, resilience and resistance. For a little over three decades, my work as a visual artist has explored the aesthetics of instability. I have attempted to bring into visual expression the feelings of being pulled and pushed off balance, our struggle to reclaim an internal balance and our resistance to forces that undermine our stability. These recurring motifs in my paintings and drawings have also informed my recent projects in documentary film and photography. The sources of instability that I address in my artwork are political, sociological and psychological. The experiences of Palestinian refugees and the political history of Palestinian displacement have been at the core of my reflections on exile, resistance and survival.

The images I make as a visual artist are simultaneously beautiful and tragic. It is in the gap between these seemingly opposing experiences that I feel most comfortable as an artist and as a Palestinian. The tension between beauty and tragedy, between desire and denial, between decay and the possibilities of rebirth, is my way of reflecting, through a range of visual media, on a few of the experiences of being Palestinian. The pressure between the horrific and the seductive, as represented in my work, is a meditation on humanity's potential for greatness, our proclivity for self-destruction and our impulse for the repression of others. Being Palestinian is simply being human, with its countless virtues and endless vices.

Notes

1. Selections of John Halaka's artwork can be viewed on his art website: www.johnhalaka.com. His documentary projects can be viewed on his film website: www.sittingcrowproductions.com.
2. The term 'survivance' was coined by the Native American scholar Gerald Vizenor to describe the creative resilience of the indigenous people of the Americas against cultural and physical genocide. The word is a combination of survival and resistance and applies fully to the struggle of the Palestinians. Survivance is a concept that creatively employs memories, personal and communal stories, as well as tales of ancient customs and evolving traditions, to convey a living culture that refuses to die and disappear.

Anwar Hamed

*Anwar Hamed, a Palestinian novelist, poet, literary critic and BBC
journalist, was born in the West Bank in 1957. He holds an MA
degree in literary theory from the University of Budapest. He has
published five novels in Arabic and Hungarian, a multilingual poem
collection in Arabic, English and Hungarian, a book on literary
theory and dozens of articles. His novel,* Jaffa Prepares Morning
Coffee, *was long-listed for the International Prize for Arabic Fiction
in 2013. He is a member of 'Bush Writers', a society of writers
whose members have worked for the BBC since it was launched.*

Caught Between the Taste of Sunshine and Chopin Nocturnes

Each time I try to approach the Palestinian narrative in a way that could
make sense to non-Palestinians, a certain scene jumps to the surface of
my memory.

I was nineteen, a first-year student at Middle East Technical University
in Ankara, Turkey. My brother, Omar, had just graduated from Aleppo
University as a civil engineer and was working in Latakia, a coastal Syrian
city, not far from the Turkish border. I hadn't seen him since he left the West
Bank to pursue his university studies in 1966. The 1967 war broke out while
he was abroad, so, according to the laws of the Israeli occupiers of the West
Bank, he had no right to visit his family there. The only chance for me to see
him was by visiting him in Syria, which only became possible when I moved
to study in Turkey, eleven years after we had said goodbye to each other in
the West Bank.

When I arrived in Latakia, not knowing his home address, I headed
directly for his workplace. One of his Syrian colleagues offered to give me
a lift to his place. When we got there the colleague pointed to a young man
opening the door of a SUV vehicle. 'There's your brother, Omar,' he said. I
looked at him and I could just about recognise his face. When I had last seen
him he was twenty; eleven years later his face had not changed much. I got
out of the car and approached him, smiling. He looked back at me and didn't

seem to recognise me. My smile froze on my face. His Syrian colleague who witnessed that strange scene volunteered to resolve the tension.

'Here is your brother, Anwar.'

He, the stranger, introduced us to each other.

We did not waste much time lamenting the absurdity of the moment. Omar gave me a warm hug and we spent the next two weeks putting together the missing chapters of our lives.

With my other brother, Osama, the missing life chapters were even more. Sixteen years had passed since I had said goodbye to him at Amman International Airport, from where he flew to California to do his postgraduate studies, until we met again in Budapest where I had settled down and had a family. We had been missing each other on our irregular visits to the West Bank until then.

This is how our coerced lifestyle turns family members into strangers, and this is why I decided to make the whole world my home.

I spent four years in Turkey before I moved to Hungary where I received an MA degree in literary theory. I fell in love with a Hungarian girl, whom I later married and with whom I had two children. It was in Hungary that I wrote and published my first novel. Needless to say, Palestine was at the heart of it. The novel was an illustration of my complex identity: a Palestinian who looks at the scene in his country from a distance, trying to view it from different angles. I was in a lucky position as a Palestinian who had become acquainted with other cultures, met people from all over the world and had hot political and cultural debates with them. These experiences set me on a journey of self-discovery, in which the basis of my political and cultural awareness was shaken by my encounter with new, unfamiliar questions. My writing career has been an attempt to find answers to these questions.

There I was, stuck between two completely different cultures, Palestinian and Hungarian, two sets of moral codes and value systems, facing the task of raising two children in a way that would help them to find a healthy balance between the two. What was the right path to follow? To allow them to find their own way or to interfere? We decided to expose them to the two cultures, and allow them to develop their personalities freely.

Now they are both over twenty, they both speak several languages and have friends from diverse cultural backgrounds. They relate to all kinds of religion, including their mother's and their father's, in a healthy, tolerant way.

Ten years ago we decided to move to London, the city of my dreams.

Living in Budapest – where people were used to one variety of things: one language (Hungarian), one skin colour (white), one religion (Christianity) – I always longed for diversity.

London is the place where I am defined in professional and human terms, rather than narrow national terms, as was the case in Budapest. Here I can answer the phone on a bus in Arabic, Hungarian or French without anybody finding that extraordinary. I can have a French meal in a restaurant whose owner is Columbian and whose chef is Indian, without this affecting the taste of the dish in any way. In London I rediscovered my cultural roots, and I am back to writing and publishing in my native language, besides Hungarian and English.

Now, after thirty-eight years of living abroad, crossing all kinds of national and cultural borders, with two European passports in my possession, how far (or close) have I got to my Palestine? Where do I feel at home? In Anabta (my Palestinian hometown)? In Budapest (where I spent twenty-five years of my life)? Or in London, whose cosmopolitan streets make me feel like a 'world citizen'?

The answer is not easy, but what I can say is the following: I relate to the music of the Hungarian Franz Liszt (Liszt Ferenc), I read the plays of Harold Pinter and I dance *dabke*, all with the same ease.

Yet, in those rare moments when I manage to dive deep into my inner self, I hear a voice calling me from a distance to family reunions on summer roof-tops, the echoes of a lonely shepherd's '*dal'ona*' songs[1] coming from a neighbouring hill, and sleepy whispers at dawn of vague figures of men, women and children heading to the neighbouring field to harvest dewy olives.

Note

1. A traditional Palestinian song which accompanies the popular dance, *dabke*.

Sousan Hammad

Sousan Hammad has lived in Paris, New York, Houston and Haifa. She is a contributing writer for Al Jazeera America, and has had short fiction and essays appear in Guernica, *the* Boston Review Blog *and* [wherever] *magazine. As a translator, she has worked on a selection of Najwan Darwish's poems on Haifa. She is presently working on her first novel.*

I see Palestine in my Rear-View Mirror

I plucked a flower for you today. Funny how the one tree you can't seem to grow properly in Houston is the same one I find in my Haifa garden. I don't mean to say that it's *funny*, but this got me thinking about all the other plants you so persistently tended. They were the same plants I found myself picking from when I first moved here. I suppose I did it without much thought, like the way you carried on with your gardening in a *joie mystique* that never required words. But if you must know why I am writing to you, Mom, it's because I'm having difficulties understanding the map you drew for me.

Last week I drove to Jerusalem to look for clues you might have left out of your last letter, like why the American playground is such a focal point in your map when it shut down years before you were born. The good news is that your house still stands, so says a shopkeeper who remembers Sitti. I suppose it's more her house since you only lived there for seven years, but still, the playground, people are saying, shut down decades ago. I don't know whether this is important, but I think it's here that we can find a clue to the plumeria. You say that the aromas of this flower had a way of floating in the Old City air, migrating from the playground and sometimes drifting through your window, and that the perfumes even followed you to Amman, when you and Sitti and everyone else walked all the way across a forgotten landscape, in the wrong direction.

Somewhere between spring and autumn, I looked in Jerusalem for this beloved flower that you've planted in your childhood memory, but it wasn't there, not even in the cemetery. The caretaker at Mamilla told me that he knows all about *fitna,* how some people believe these short-lived flowers provide shelter to djinns and how it's a flower often associated with death. But the only plumeria trees I found were in Haifa in the final days of autumn, summering by the sea, some with petals scattered in the shadows of a blossoming tree. Could it be that you mistook the smell of jasmine for plumeria? Both flowers are white, and most fragrant at night. They say, anyway, that memory is never constant, or you remember what you want to forget and forget what you want to remember. The truth (if we can call it truth) is that the flower doesn't exist in Jerusalem, and that it wasn't brought to Haifa until after you left. Mom, I don't know what it means that the one plant you keep trying to cultivate, only to see it grow but never bloom, is the one species that isn't native to Palestine. The friend who I rented my apartment from told me the tree was brought to the Levant – to everywhere but your childhood city – by Europeans, along with many other plants foreign to the place you call home.

I suppose I could call it the same – home – but Palestine for you is grief. For me it's an injustice. Maybe that's why I don't exactly embrace this idea that I'm the daughter of *dépaysement,* whether living in France, America or Palestine. Lately, when I drive, I find myself captivated by the rear-view mirror that shapes my surroundings, like the glare on your face when you gardened on those hot Texas days. Funny (and again I don't exactly mean *funny*) how landscapes are so much more beautiful in a frame.

That's why everything you planted in the backyard of our Texas home took me to the places of your past: the thyme, rosemary, sage and lavender – all of those plants are like framed moments from your lost chapters in Palestine, reincarnated as witnesses to our everyday realities in Texas. I never knew, until now, what those gardens meant to you, even though I went along with you in your adventures shopping for species, wandering up and down the aisles of nearly every garden store in north Houston because you didn't know the names of plants in English and were too shy to ask. In the end you managed just fine and recreated a forest of your native home.

It's true that it would have made *my* search easier if I had a picture of your Jerusalem home, so that I could become a witness and trace your first memories in the winding alleyways of the Old City. In a way it almost seems deliberate that you left behind all your pictures from Palestine when you went to America. But maybe the imagined forms I know, thanks to you, are more liberating than we think?

This is why it doesn't matter if you invented the plumeria story, because they do exist, somewhere, between the spaces of familiar things we share, like the smells that soap our mourned cities. If there's one thing I learnt growing up in a household of only women, it's to appreciate that it's the city – which is always feminine in Arabic – that opens the possibility to share experiences with the people or places we love. For me it is Haifa. I made a choice to live here, and Haifa, to me, smells like sweetened humidity on the day of liberation. For Dad, it was always Gaza. I'll never know why he left us when I was only nine, but Gaza, I do know, is the smell of his corpse. And you, Mom, you have Jerusalem, you'll always have Jerusalem and the smell of your home that still stands, whether we get it back or not, because sometimes the objects that seem so distant are actually closer than they appear.

Laila Hamzi

Laila Hamzi, LLB, BSc (University of Melbourne), GDLP, is a Palestinian, Lebanese, Australian lawyer now studying a Master of Laws at the London School of Economics. She has worked as a corporate lawyer in Australia and has also spent time interning with a defence team at the International Criminal Tribunal for the Former Yugoslavia. She also managed a non-profit organisation in Australia with alumni from the University of Melbourne and worked with the advocacy group Australians for Palestine. She continues to be involved in Palestinian advocacy work in London.

I Am, and I Am Always Becoming

It is quite an unusual task to have to reflect on what it means to simultaneously be something you are and something you are fighting to be. I do not mean fighting to belong, but rather something distinct from the otherwise assumed or comfortable constituents of identity that we will never be challenged on. To me, for better or for worse, being Palestinian involves both of these types of identity. On the one hand, I just *am* Palestinian, in the same way I am human: I am a product of my conditions and whether or not I indulge the idiosyncrasies of my culture and heritage, or resist and challenge them, I am born of a context which, consciously or subconsciously, shapes me. On the other hand, this never seems enough and it's not the end of my story. There is a part which is more complicated and bestows on me a duty I cannot ignore. To this extent I never just *am* Palestinian, but I am shaped and defined by the need to *be* Palestinian, a free Palestinian.

I grew up in Australia in quite a typical Palestinian Lebanese home where my parents pushed me to excel in school, took me to Arabic school and where we went on an annual pilgrimage back to the ever-longed-for homeland. I was lucky enough that my father never let us speak English at home and that I always spent my summers in the Middle East with my cousins, rather than on the beaches of Australia. I was also lucky that my parents raised my brother and I with such a strong sense of identity and knowledge of who we are, that

I never struggled to reconcile my 'Levantine-ness' with my 'Australian-ness' – the partnership came naturally and I just was who I was. As a result, my culture has always been an integral and unconscious part of my development and I have remained incredibly attached to the land I was born in. Perhaps unsurprisingly, the overt manifestations of being Palestinian are all there: I love eating hummus, falafel and *knafeh*, and reading Edward Said. I love listening to Mohammed Assaf just because he has a great voice, and I think Palestine is magnificent. I cherish the importance of family, and I love that there are times when English simply won't do and I have to revert to Arabic. When I get married I want a traditional Palestinian *zaffeh*, and my mother will certainly be wearing a *thob*, and I know that I can rely on my aunts to take the dancing seriously.

These are conventional indicators of what it means to belong to a people. They are uniting traditions, rituals and artefacts that transcend territory and follow us into the diaspora. In many cases I suspect they describe very well what it means to be part of a nation, yet I feel like they barely scratch the surface. It is the more personal and silent elements that embed themselves, that transform and define. These are truly constitutional, rarely identified and much less discussed. Looking back now, I think my parents had a hidden agenda that was not so clear to me growing up. Imbued in all of the speeches about our history, our people and empire, lying in the interstices of everyday life was the slow cultivation of a cause, and this cause is one of the constitutional elements of my identity. It does not deny other aspects of being Palestinian, or how these have shaped my mind and personality but, on the contrary, it is a powerful stand-alone pillar that informs my sense of being Palestinian.

From a very young age I recognised the power of identity and belonging. However, for me this never involved slotting into an involuntary diaspora community, or silently accepting my place in a story of dispossession while embracing the fruits of exile. It meant, and still means, having the freedom to define the terms of my identity and choosing how my belonging relates to my past, present and future, and that of other Palestinians.

I have never been comfortable with labels or categories that define what identity should or shouldn't be, or that make choices for me. As a Palestinian woman who has grown up in Australia and now lives in London, my identity is certainly fluid but it is, at the very least, what I say it is. For now, I can say with resounding confidence that an interconnectedness with my fellow pre-colonised, pre-occupied Palestinians defines my identity in untold ways, regardless of where I am. It is this unity, a cord of resilience linking us to one another, which pushes me forward and is what it means, for me, to be Palestinian. This is a force that may begin in diaspora, but it certainly does not end there.

Nathalie Handal

Nathalie Handal is from Bethlehem, and has lived in Europe, Latin America, the US and the Arab world. Described as 'one of the most important voices of her generation', her most recent books include the acclaimed Poet in Andalucía; Love and Strange Horses, *winner of the Gold Medal Independent Publisher Book Award; and the landmark anthology* Language for a New Century: Contemporary Poetry from the Middle East, Asia & Beyond.

Guide to Being Palestinian

If you are darker than most,
have a beard or wear a hijab,
it's wise not to speak too loud
when you reach an airport
or any exit.

If your father begged for his house,
was dragged away,
and returned the next day
without his eyes or his honour,
don't judge him.

If your mother told you to watch
his humiliation,
it wasn't to hurt you
but to help you
understand where you are from.

If you are exiled
don't expect an open field,
a smile, a new home –
most likely you will always be a stranger.
Stand close enough to see their eyes,
far enough to protect your heart.

If you think you can write
about all the days you are missing
in your town or city,
think again –
it's another's myth now,
and if you are afraid of forgetfulness,
apathy is even more dangerous.

If you take your longing
everywhere you go,
keep the keys to your old house
even if it's inhabited by others –
it's a clue you should also keep everything else:
the photos, the art, the folklore and even the stones.

If you laugh and feel guilty,
love and feel like you shouldn't,
remember all aching begins with desire.

If your ancestors gave you a map of your country
but didn't give you one for dispossession,
weave the distances with your history.

If our father calls you father – *baba* –
when you are his son or daughter,
asks you, *you know the name of your birthplace?*
answer in Arabic
even if you are told to speak it
only at home – for your safety.

And if the day comes
while far away
you are asked,
who gave you that name?
remember what matters
is that the land knows
your face, your voice,
the origin of your silence –
and that, what's holy is alive
in who you are,
not in who you are told
you should be.

Jean Hanna

Jean Hanna was born in Amman, Jordan to Palestinian parents. She emigrated to the US with her family in 1956 and settled in St Paul, Minnesota. She has a BA degree in Arabic and Middle Eastern Studies from the University of Minnesota. She is an active board member in various local and national organisations, including the Arab American University Graduates and the Arab American Anti-Discrimination Committee, and she continues to represent the Near Eastern Collection of Archival Materials to the Immigration History Research Center Archives, University of Minnesota.

Memories that Live

I was only four years old when my Palestinian parents emigrated to the United States of America. My only fond recollections of this momentous occasion were the playful days my brother and I had on the deck of the ship during the fifteen-day trip, and the smell of the vast ocean air. It was not until my early twenties that I encountered that wonderful smell again when I was visiting a close friend in North Carolina and we spent several days on the Outer Banks, along the Atlantic Ocean. A sense overcame me that reminded me of the trip we made when I was a young child.

When my family and I arrived in New York, we went by train to live in St Paul, Minnesota, where we were to start life anew – in the middle of the USA and far away from oceans. Not having relatives around us was sad for me as I did not grow up knowing my cousins. My father worked hard to help us assimilate into our new country and the culture around us. Although my father knew English, the rest of us had to learn it quickly. However, we still spoke Arabic at home so we would not forget our culture and traditions. My father brought slides and pictures of his beloved Palestine to show to us. It was through this medium that he would explain our story. He wanted to make sure that we would never forget our ancestral homeland, Palestine.

Upon becoming naturalised citizens of the US, my father decided to change our native names so as to ease our assimilation into American culture.

He worried that American people had a difficult time pronouncing and spelling our names so he chose easy and common Western-sounding names for all of us: my eldest brother Najib became James, my sister Wardeh changed to Rose, Nabil to Bill, Nadim to Ned, and I went from Najwa to Jean. My youngest brother was born in the USA so he was given the name of George. My mother was not pleased; she loved our cultural names and she would still call us by those names at home.

After living in the USA for only six years my father was diagnosed with acute leukaemia and passed away. My mother was left with the responsibility of raising four children, who ranged in age from three to thirteen, on her own. The main focus for my mother now was to keep our family together and to ensure her children received a proper education. A friend of my mother's had a catering business and she asked her to come and work with her since my mother loved to cook. This gave my mother a lot of exposure in the community. She slowly added Middle Eastern foods to her selection of catering options – which were well received. She went on to do Middle Eastern cooking classes through the Community Adult Education programme sponsored by the St Paul Public Schools system.

Since my mother had a heavy accent, we would often be asked where we came from, and of course my mother would gladly reply 'Palestine, in the Middle East', and then set out to explain our immigration story. At first this was easy to take, but as I grew older it seemed such a burden to always have to encounter this type of discussion with new people. I often wished, in secret, that we had been born in Sweden or Norway so we did not have to stand out and be so different from our friends around us who were of Scandinavian background. When I was younger, I suppose I did not appreciate spending so much time explaining myself to others; I just wanted to blend in with everyone else.

However, as I grew older I began to appreciate my ethnic and cultural background and I wanted to learn more about our culture and history. When I graduated from high school I chose to attend the University of Minnesota where I studied the written Arabic language and the history of the region, from the ancient Near East to the contemporary Middle East.

While studying, I became acquainted with students from the Middle East who came to study in the US. This was the first time I met others who were like me and it gave me a chance to learn about their desires and aspirations. They came to study engineering, medicine or business, so as to return and help develop their countries of origin and people. I finally felt a connection to my roots. There was an Arab-American Club at the university where we would share our cultural backgrounds. This club provided social events to create and enhance a better understanding of music, foods and ways of living in our respective countries. What I found most memorable was listening to musical instruments from the Middle East and dancing *dabke*.

A difference between my mother and me was that I grew up living in a city, far away from the country life she knew. However, my mother did have a garden in our backyard. She would grow vegetables that were native to our culture. This included light-green zucchini, not the dark-green zucchini which was more common, and *mulukhiyya*, a green leafy vegetable which we called 'Arabic spinach'. She even had her own grape leaf vine for making fresh stuffed grape leaves. I was proud of my mother's knowledge and experience of country life, but I was a city dweller at heart. Then one weekend I went camping with my college friends at a rustic campground in Minnesota. Unbeknown to me, they brought a real live sheep with them which was to be our meat for the long three-day weekend. At first I was shocked and amazed, but then I thought: well, in the Middle East they would slaughter a lamb, and cook and serve the meat fresh to guests for certain special occasions. It truly was the best barbecued lamb I have ever tasted.

Living as a Palestinian in the diaspora keeps me focused on who I am, as a Palestinian with a rich legacy of culture and traditions. This is something that cannot ever be taken away from me.

Marwan Hassan

Marwan Hassan was born in Nazareth and earned his PhD in hydrology from the Hebrew University of Jerusalem. He is currently a professor in the Department of Geography at the University of British Columbia. He lives in Vancouver, Canada with his family.

A Boy from Mash-had

To the memory of my mother who left this world too soon!
To my kids who have yet to learn their history!

August is the hottest month of the year in the village of Mash-had, near Nazareth. Even though he has just awakened, the boy can already feel the heat of the day. He is standing outside his family's house on the hill where his village is built. He is looking east, across the valley towards the Sea of Galilee. Tall yellow grasses cover the surrounding hills, dotted with large white rocks and small trees and shrubs. He wonders about a story told to him a few days before by his mother, about Saladin, the general of the armies that battled the Crusaders. Later, the boy will learn in school that Saladin was a Muslim leader, a general, who fought against the Third Crusade led by Richard the Lionheart (1187–92).

Suddenly, in front of his eyes, the plains erupt in a mixture of colours that interrupt the quiet harmony of the landscape. He sees men on horses and men running all over the plains. He smells the smoke from the burning grass and the dust from the horses and hears the noise of fighting, the clash of battle. Bodies litter the ground in front of him, covering the grass. He sees the sultan, Saladin, sitting in his tent, gazing at the Crusaders' leaders who have been captured in battle. He is victorious, smiling, savouring the moment. Then the sultan offers his enemies water from his own gilded drinking bowl. This place holds the burden of history and the boy feels the weight of it. His family would have witnessed this battle as they have lived on this hill for centuries, well before the time of the Crusades.

That afternoon the boy finds himself walking with his friends, picking grapes and figs from the trees and the fields surrounding the destroyed houses of a nearby Palestinian village. The boy is struck by the calm and quietness of the place. He hears the buzzing of insects and sees grasshoppers jumping through brown grasses and butterflies moving lightly through the air. He hikes up to the remains of the Crusader castle and sees the entire landscape surrounding him, the trees and orchards. He can barely see the ruins of houses in the destroyed village. It is as though the village has become part of the landscape, part of the land. The houses follow the landscape's rise and fall, the same height as the trees, in a way that is hidden, protected by them.

In the distance he sees a few new buildings, all of them with red roofs, like mushrooms. They are above the landscape, the colours are clashing, they do not match the hills, or the grass, or the trees. They feel alien. The boy wonders about this contrast between the destroyed village and the new buildings nearby; it puzzles and confuses him. He doesn't know how to think or how to feel about this change. The new settlement is off limits. He cannot go there. The boy remembers his mother's story of the time the soldiers from the new settlement came to the house and searched. One of the soldiers saw a photograph of the Egyptian leader Nasser on the wall and demanded that it be destroyed. His mother grabbed a broom and said: 'Don't touch it or I will break your hands with this broom.' They stared at her, then left. The boy imagines the Crusaders roaming this area much as these soldiers do.

The scattered, destroyed houses around the castle are organised in terraces, stacked nearly on top of each other and hidden by the neglected fruit trees. His parents told him that this village had been one of the largest and the wealthiest in the region. The village resisted Israeli advances for a long time. When it was finally captured, its citizens were ordered out and forbidden to return. Some became refugees in Nazareth, others were pushed to refugee camps in Lebanon. The boy wanders into a half-demolished house. He can imagine the family sitting on the sun deck during the summer evenings, discussing daily affairs, while the kids, running, screaming, laughing, refuse to come into the house and play with their friends in the dusty streets. The boy notices the small kitchen and the place where the family once stored olive oil and wheat. He wonders if the family had time to take their oil and wheat with them when they fled, or if someone else scavenged the remains. He still smells the aromas of freshly cooked food, pita bread in the wooden oven with olive oil and *za'tar*. In the living room he smells the roasted coffee beans, strong and fresh, like the smells in his house every morning. He hears the father calling one of his kids to come and carry coffee to the guests. In the kitchen, the kids are grabbing the pita and *za'tar*, their mother asking them to sit and eat slowly.

The boy gazes at the settlement in the distance and at the destroyed houses, and realises that he has a lot of work to do. He needs to clean the house and guard the land and the trees until the family returns. He is sure that they will come in the summer. He looks around and tells himself that they can sleep under the grapevine and the fig tree until the house is fixed. The boy will be there with them when they come back, he is sure about that.

Ghazi Hassoun

Ghazi Q. Hassoun was born on 21 June 1935 in Haifa, while Palestine was under the British Mandate, and became a refugee in Lebanon in 1948. He received a BS in Physics in 1956 from the American University of Beirut and his PhD in theoretical physics in 1963 from the University of Minnesota. He is currently professor emeritus at North Dakota State University. In 2013, he published his memoir, Walking Out into the Sunshine.

Reconciling Araby and America

Ever since my eyes saw the light of day in Haifa, my identity as a Palestinian was a self-evident given. My parents and ancestors of untold generations were native Palestinians of a strong Islamic/Arab character. I was weaned on Quranic recitals, old and modern Arabic literature and native Palestinian folklore, attire, food, music, dancing, styles of celebrations/festivities, and the like.

The 1948 *Nakba*, which led to my prospering family becoming refugees in Tyre, Lebanon, has been central to my life. Loss of home, community and country had a profound, shattering impact. It transformed me from a simple medieval boy, leading a carefree and playful life, into a dispossessed and charity-dependent refugee boy. At age thirteen, I, with two older friends, decided to post homemade leaflets to a free food ration distribution centre for refugees. The posters demanded 'NO to hand-outs' and 'RETURN to our homes in Palestine'. Weeks later, I saw some schoolboys going back to their homes in the afternoon and a question flashed in my head: 'How come I am not going to school?' In the evening I asked my mother if I could go. It had been over fifteen months since my schooling had been interrupted by the collapse of law and order in Haifa, accompanied by an upsurge of communal armed clashes. Mother lovingly said, 'Tomorrow morning I'll take you to the school and find out what it will take to enrol you.' It was a private school that had, a few months earlier, started a small section of a Palestinian-based educational programme made up of two grades, with a handful of students attending. Tyre and its surroundings had by then thousands of Palestinian school-age children unprovided for. I was very fortunate to have been enrolled and placed in one of the grades that same day!

With the *Nakba*, Palestinian identity, a sub-identity of the larger Arab identity, developed a sharper and narrower *Palestinian* focus. It was accentuated by the inhospitable and demeaning treatment of the neighbouring official Arab host countries, affording the Palestinians little status and few rights. This tended to set the Palestinians apart. The *Nakba* awakened in me a passion for education at all levels, feeling it was the way to close the gap with the West and redress the wrong. I began to dream of going to America: for education, for economic opportunities and a dignified life. At the American University of Beirut, I majored in physics because it is a basic science and a leading tool for modernisation, or so I thought. Within a year of my graduation I departed for the US. Saying farewell to family, friends and the land of 'Araby' at large was one of the most painful things I had done up to that point.

In the US, I experienced culture shock and insecurity for the first few months. To bring about a semblance of security and emotional stability, I sought a mate, a partner, to share my hopes and struggles with. I was blessed by meeting early on a high-minded college co-ed of a beautiful spirit. We were wed by the end of my first year.

With my graduate studies completed in the summer of 1963, I eagerly returned to visit my family in several Arab countries. To my dismay, I found out that my specialty, theoretical physics, was of no immediate use for the prevailing socio-political infrastructure, nor was it a medicine for what ailed it. I turned westward to make the best of the opportunity I had to pursue an academic career. It seemed logical and ostensibly straightforward, but the execution was another story.

My mind was crowded with questions. Was it right to commit my life to a career in physics and citizenship in America? It would entail setting aside much of my other human concerns, especially related to Palestine. Was I ready to detach myself from the past and the emotions, motivations and hopes that, at its very core, had propelled my pursuits heretofore? How was I to reconcile the Islamic/Palestinian/Arab precepts, values, aspirations and way of life, deeply ingrained in me at a tender age, with those of a country with a starkly different history, social fabric and worldview? What would all this do to my identity as a Palestinian?

I wrestled extensively with these issues for over two decades before I began to glimpse a pathway towards meaningful answers. It entailed a process of reinventing or 'reformatting' my psyche. The soul-searching transcended traditional views of nationalism, religion and identity. I saw these as time and place dependent, relative, culturally intertwined and evolving models for living. With the phenomenal explosion of knowledge and its dissemination in our technological age, I saw the trajectory of the evolution of these models to be momentous, accelerating towards larger and higher models, encompassing greater universal values and inclusive of all humanity. My love for wider horizons and greater knowledge and the satisfaction of sharing these with others became my guiding light. The higher my perspicacity, the freer I felt. The path became clear: be resilient, evolve, adjust, adapt and keep up. The affiliations and identity need not be given up, but they may take a different form and/or be exercised differently.

My connection to Palestine and its people continues to be an integral part of my life. Beyond the US, I have kept steady and close contact with family and friends spread all over Palestine/Israel and several Arab Middle Eastern countries through repeated visits, attending conferences and heart-to-heart exchanges. Forty years after I came to America, as I was nearing retirement, I found myself compulsively writing down recollections and reflections of my Palestinian experience which I published fifteen years later, in 2013, as my memoir: a living testimony and resource for future generations to study and learn from. My memoir is a manifest expression that my Palestinian identity is alive and well and I expect it will remain so to my last breath.

Johnny Hazboun

Johnny Hazboun, MPA 2014, Harvard Kennedy School, BS San Francisco State University, is co-founder of a software company in Boston and a technical consultant for election systems development in North Africa and the Middle East. He has served as a management consultant to the United Nations Development Programme (UNDP) and the EU Commission in Jerusalem, and directed various healthcare and IT sector economic development projects in Abu Dhabi, San Francisco and Ramallah. He is currently working on human capital development projects in the Middle East.

When Will it be Vacant?

One of Harvard Kennedy School's traditions is for new students to introduce themselves in a fifteen-second presentation to the entire school. The presentation has two rules: state your name, followed by which country you are from. The remaining time is for the student to say what he or she wishes. In my school records, the country of my origin is 'Palestinian Territories, Occupied'. So my fifteen seconds went like this: 'My name is Johnny Hazboun, I am from the Palestinian Territories, comma, Occupied. Occupied is the word I see on the water closet door of an aeroplane – and the first thought is always, when will it be "vacant"?'

I left my hometown, Bethlehem, for the US in 1989, two years into the First Intifada, in pursuit of higher education. Beginning my college life in the US, I remember one of my first encounters with an American student. He started the conversation by asking, 'Where are you from?', a question which is preceded only by the obligatory, 'What is your name?' I said, 'Palestine'.

He subconsciously corrected me: 'Ah, Israel, wow, cool, you guys have a powerful army.'

Having grown up in the 1970s and 1980s, my education until high school was based on a Jordanian curriculum, managed by the Israeli government. In practice, this meant the word Palestine, its flag and any related literature was prohibited. A conversation about Palestine in my community was accompanied with deep paranoia and fear of spies among us; being an informant for Israel would prove a ticket to a 'better' life for some, causing for others harsh retribution and prison terms.

The innocent American question sparked in me a million thoughts: overwhelming astonishment, anger and bewilderment. What stood out at that time was my inability to respond. I did not know where to begin, because I did not know enough. I lacked the necessary education. My school did not offer classes on the history of Palestine, the history of Israel, or the history of Israel's military occupation. Instead, the curriculum focused on Arab-Islamic history, World War II and the development of Western Europe. The best I could convey to my newfound American friend was my own experience – stripped of a framework, facts or references. Looking back, I think this encounter was the moment when the challenge of being Palestinian awoke in me. Subsequent encounters, in America and around the world, probing and questioning my homeland and upbringing, have offered a fertile environment for the germination of an articulated Palestinian character, perhaps residing in the seed of my DNA.

It was never a question of whether I was interested in learning about 'my' history. This was a seed that, once sprouted, demanded nourishment. Twenty years on, after countless inspiring and despairing conversations, and work on many concrete projects for the betterment of my community, I have concluded that being Palestinian is not a role to be negotiated, but an identity to be embraced, internalised and elucidated.

Hence my choice of 'Occupied Palestinian' as the title to my fifteen-second introduction to the group of three hundred Harvard students, faculty and the Dean, upon enrolment in the fall of 2013.

What will change more in the coming years: my narrative of being Palestinian or the context in which it is received? I don't know. But I stand prepared to work and adapt to the changes constructively where they will – and can – occur. That's why I chose to leave work and invest a year in Harvard, and maybe that's why the School made an investment in me.

Being Palestinian will remain a polarised, and perhaps intractable, domain of identity politics in my lifetime. My brief introduction before my class at Harvard will most likely have determined who will work with me, and who will not. What awaits is adaptive work.

What awaits future generations? The same, or something different?

The curiosity that sends us out to discover more about who we are, is also carried forward to, and by, our young. A sense of identity survives in spite of – or sometimes because of – repression and, in the Palestinian case, Israel's occupation of our land. Ignited perhaps in what my now eight-year-old daughter conceived when, two years younger, she had to cross three Israeli checkpoints to see her grandmother in our ancestral home between Ramallah and Bethlehem. Sparked again possibly when she noticed the bright lights of the well-to-do Israeli colonies surrounding Bethlehem. Observations of a not-so-fair state of affairs were further reinforced when we walked together by the thirty-foot concrete wall surrounding Bethlehem.

In this particular case, our daughter brought a lesson – in the form of a question – to her first-grade teacher at the International School of Boston, MA: 'Why is there no Palestinian flag flying with the [many dozen] others at our school gym?' The teacher brought the issue before the school council and, after a four-month debate, a new flag was raised. The fate and challenge of being Palestinian comes alive in a new way and in a new person.

Khaled Hroub

Khaled Hroub keeps wandering around cities, falling in love with them, puffing shishas in their cafés and exploring the limitlessness of being human and Palestinian. He is grateful to what makes that possible, including his specialty in political Islam and Arab media and culture, along with his academic life with Cambridge University, Birzeit University and Northwestern University in Qatar.

Living in Letters or the Arrogance of a Cityless Man

Lieber Thomas,
Berlin

You wouldn't believe it. I write to you from Wadi Foukeen, my village near Bethlehem. And guess what: my sister's house is now 'wired' and has got Internet access. Her kids can now say good morning to the outside world. My village lies by the so-called Green Line that divides the so-called Israel from the so-called West Bank. Half of my grandfather's land, as that of the rest of the old villagers here, was lost in the 1948 war and got included behind that Line. Since then it has become part of what would be called Israel. Because of that war and the one that followed in 1967, half of the inhabitants of my village left their homes, including my grandfather and his family.

Anyway my friend, we are now in the year 2005. And what I can see through the window of my sister's living room is the ugliest thing you could ever imagine: a huge concrete wall that encloses all the villages in the area. It only leaves a narrow passage for their people to reach Bethlehem and the surrounding areas. Everybody here hates this edifice of discrimination. Why do such walls elsewhere fall down but in Palestine a vile new one is put up? All wonders here!

I guess you ask how come I think of you here and now. OK, yesterday I visited the only school in the village, the elementary school where my sister

Najah teaches. Her colleagues wanted to meet her brother, me, who came all the way from London to visit. I was so joyful as everyone was very welcoming to me. On the wall of one of the classes, Thomas, I read these words: 'The Wall in Berlin was destroyed, and the Wall in Palestine will be destroyed too.' I was overwhelmed. For a moment, and I don't know why, I imagined you next to me, looking at and reading those words, as if you could read and understand Arabic.

Reading the name of your city, Berlin, in my remote and nearly unknown village surprised me. I bet you nobody in Berlin would know the name, or anything, about Wadi Foukeen, my village. And you know what, I just wonder too how many of all these little kids here know what and where Berlin is? But for me, as you know, I fell in love with your city from the first visit. And since that day when you showed me around I have kept warm memories. The thing that I loved most about the guided tour you gave me around Berlin was the idea of stepping on the traces of that gruesome wall that used to divide your city. I was happy but a bit saddened too: happy, of course, to see that the wall had gone. Listening to your comments about the places, streets, cafés and their histories was wonderful. Seeing life blossom anew above the no-man's-land of the wall was spiritual, no doubt.

But there was something else in the air. Your immersion in the small details of your city made me discover something missing in me. I realised that I was a man without a city. There was no city for me to take people around and show them. My early departure from Bethlehem had left my attachment to it more notional than real. When I left Bethlehem I was only four years old. I hardly remember anything, and I never thought that it was necessary anyway. To be honest with you, my feelings towards Bethlehem are mixed, and maybe I will explain that to you later.

Leaving Palestine, I moved and lived in many cities, and continents. I created a theory to console myself and justify living in the present, whatever present it was at the time: I'm a timeless and cityless man. I belong to nowhere and to everywhere. I move between cities. I love them and stay in them, or dislike them and leave them, just like an unfaithful lover. That tour of Berlin you took me on destroyed my theory and arrogance, Thomas. It left me as an orphan. A lonely man thrown in the middle of the wilderness, without a place, without a city. Since your tour I repented my faithlessness to Bethlehem and decided to go search for it!

Ciao Cecilia,
Pisa

You may have already forgotten about me. It has been almost ten years by now. But I didn't forget you, your family and your city. It is me, Khaled, the Jesus-look-alike guy from Bethlehem. I was amused by the wonderment in your eyes when you heard that I was from Bethlehem. A sweet feeling it was, uplifting and really satisfying. Funnily enough, at the dinner in your house, surrounded by you, your husband and your two little kids, I felt a little like Jesus. Those eyes around the table were exploring me. Your shy husband could not help but ask how it could be that I was a Muslim from Bethlehem. He also was curious about the interior of the Church of the Nativity. Suddenly, I felt ashamed inside. I had never visited 'my city' as an adult. I could not tell him a lot. I struggled hard to remember what I had read in some books. And yet, looking like Jesus, everything I said to him was received with such deep reverence and conviction.

When I spent a few nights in the nearby monastery, there was a portrait of Jesus in my room. I kept staring at his face. Definitely it is a beautiful face. Cecilia, I remember that you were slightly shocked that the real Jesus would look more like me than the Jesus in the portrait. It was a new fact for you that his hair should be dark, not blonde, and his eyes brown not blue. Alas, the most beautiful thing about him is his being from my city. He is my bridge to you and the world. I hid my doubts and qualms with all religions and gods when I spoke to you. All the time I had blamed God and questioned his wisdom in crowding Palestine with so many prophets. It is a very narrow strip of land to be crammed with so many prophets and sacred texts. Over centuries the followers of these prophets have fought each other for absurd reasons. I keep pondering whether we might have lived in more peace had the prophets been better distributed across the four corners of the world.

Sarah Ihmoud

Sarah E. Ihmoud is a doctoral candidate in social/activist anthropology at the University of Texas at Austin. Her research interests centre on race and racism, gender and sexuality, militarisation and settler colonial violence. She has conducted fieldwork in Guatemala and Palestine, and holds fellowships from the National Science Foundation, the Palestinian American Research Center and the Wenner-Gren Foundation.

Palestine in the *Nepantla*

Five years ago, I found myself wandering the cobblestone streets of Trinidad, a colonial city in the Sancti Spiritus province of central Cuba. Following the decline of the Ottoman Empire, like many men of his generation, my great-uncle Mahmoud had migrated to Latin America in 1918, at the age of twenty-four, to help support our family in Turmos 'Ayya, a small village between Nablus and Ramallah. It took him three months by freight ship to arrive in Havana. He went on to change his name to Jose Julián Aliz and to become, as family rumours would have it, one of the wealthiest men in Cuba, owning several farms, a cattle ranch and one of the biggest cigar factories on the island.

We would never see him again. Though he had always planned to return to Palestine, the political times in which he found himself embroiled thirty years later, between colonial contests over his homeland and the stirrings of revolution in his new country, foreclosed any such possibility. Our families lost touch sometime around the beginning of the Cuban Revolution. The last letter my grandfather, his brother, received from him was in 1954.

Here I was now, half a century later, in Trinidad de Cuba, with nothing but a name and this history, searching for strangers. As I walked the streets, speaking to elderly women and knocking on doors, I considered whether, if I did find them, they would embrace me as their kin. To what degree would they see themselves as Cuban? Would they still identify as Palestinian after nearly a century of separation from the homeland? Was the dream of return something that my great-uncle had passed on to his children?

I wondered then, as I still do today, how Palestinian identity is lived across different geographies. My longing for an imagined homeland of my own did not begin with my father's story of exile or dispossession. Though I would eventually seek out and attempt to assemble a collection of memories, images and histories of Palestinian culture and identity, including of my own family, those fragments were not unearthed until later.

My Palestinian revolution began in Latin America. I was nineteen years old. Sitting in a café in Managua one humid summer afternoon, a guitarist strumming *musica trova* in the corner, I listened intently to the story of a former fighter in the Sandinista uprising when he uttered the words 'Palestine Liberation Organisation'. Why had he mentioned Palestine in the context of his own country's rebellion? I insisted the *compañero* elaborate. The Sandinistas, he explained, had seen the liberation of the Palestinian people, an anti-colonial struggle, as bound up with their own struggle for national liberation. The PLO, he said, had been active in supporting not only the Sandinistas, but also other revolutionary movements in the region. These ties, I would later learn, were first forged in 1966, when Cuban leader Fidel Castro hosted an international conference to build solidarity between revolutionary movements worldwide. 'The road to Jerusalem leads through Managua', PLO Chairman Yasir Arafat once stated.

I was captivated by this encounter, not only because of the compelling history it revealed, but also because the coming together of these worlds seemed to be an expression of my own complex identity. My mother was Mexican, my father from Palestine. Growing up, I had always felt 'out of place', though I attributed this not to the condition of being Palestinian, but rather to the condition of being poor and brown in America.

The pieces of Palestine I gathered in Nicaragua were further developed in travels to El Salvador and Guatemala the following year. In El Salvador I discovered a thriving Palestinian community that was active across the political spectrum. In Guatemala I learnt that identifying with Palestine had a strong resonance with the indigenous communities among which I lived and worked. The country had recently ended a long civil war, in which state security forces were found guilty of committing genocide against the indigenous peoples. My friend Maria Tulia, who herself had joined the guerrilla after her father was 'disappeared' by the *ejercito* (army), explained to me that it was not just a struggle for land and resources that indigenous Guatemalans shared with the Palestinians, but that Israel had played its own hand in the dirty wars of Latin America during the Cold War era. When human rights abuses forced the Carter Administration to halt military aid to Guatemala, Israel became a surrogate for the United States, supplying not only weapons but also training to the military regime during the height of genocide of indigenous communities. Palestine and the Palestinian struggle had left its imprint on an unlikely region across the world.

This history of internationalist anti-colonial solidarity and resistance, recounted on the ground by the very people who had participated in revolutionary movements throughout the Americas, was my introduction to what it means to be Palestinian. My exposure to the Palestinian experience in Latin America drove me to uncover my own family's history in the region, and led me to Cuba where, finally, after nearly an hour of wandering in Trinidad, I was directed to a blue building. There, I was surprised to find a woman in her mid-thirties answer the door, a small child pulling at her skirt, both of whom looked remarkably Palestinian. It must have seemed a strange request when I asked her to recall whether her family had had another name – a name they had called themselves before 'Aliz'. She did not reply with words, but rather walked over to the bureau in the corner of the living room and opened a small drawer. She returned with a stack of letters in her hand, written in Arabic, and a map of Palestine with a circle drawn around our village. She reached out and pulled me towards her, and we stood there, embracing each other in silence for a long while.

My relatives in Cuba had identified with Palestine, but as part of their past, their origins – an identity of their forefathers. They had come of age immersed in Cuban culture and identity, and had no other place to call home. My relatives in the occupied West Bank, on the other hand, though having lived throughout South America and the United States for decades, identified strongly with Palestine as their home, the only place to which they would ever truly belong. My diasporic family's sense of identity, home and belonging, I found, were shaped by processes of forced or voluntary migration, colonisation and contestation, producing multiple and distinct experiences of being Palestinian.

What have I myself been searching for between these spaces – between my Mexican mother and Palestinian father, between the colonial debris of history and memory, between Latin America and Palestine? Perhaps I once believed that by traversing these distant lands, and physically reconnecting my family, I might somehow recover some lost or vacant part of myself, a part of my identity that had been stolen as a result of my father's exile. Yet in seeking out my diaspora, I myself became diasporic.

I have learnt that Palestine is not just a land or place, or even a collection of memories. To be Palestinian is not a unified identity, an essence, but rather an identity that is constantly being reshaped, and one that must be claimed by each new generation in the *Shatat*. Palestine lives wherever we, Palestinians, live. I have found Palestine not only among the hills of my father's village, Turmos 'Ayya, but also among the diasporic communities in Latin America, and in the embrace of my family in Cuba.

And for me, ultimately, being Palestinian is not a given, but a becoming. Being a *Shatat* Palestinian means living in and indeed embracing what Chicana feminist Gloria Anzaldúa calls the *Nepantla* – the liminal space between worlds, not as a source of tension or confusion, but of strength and possibility. It is a space rich with creative insights. One that we might cultivate and draw upon in further developing our identities, collectivities and cultural-political practices, devoted to expressing our full humanity, seeking justice and liberation.

Mohamad Issa

Mohamad Issa is a retired professor of physics. He has worked as a lecturer in institutions in several countries, including Jordan, Iraq, the UK and Qatar. After twenty-five years at Qatar University, he retired to Scotland. He is a committee member of the Dundee–Nablus Twinning Association.

Enduring Ties

My full name is Mohamad Ragheb Ahmad Hassan Mohamad Ibrahim Issa Mahmoud Wadi Al Ramahi, later changed to Mohamad Ragheb Issa for administrative ease. Despite having such a distinguished list of Palestinian forebears there is no record of my date or place of birth. You will just have to trust my account. I was born in 1948, the year of the *Nakba*, in Muzera'h, a small village razed to the ground, literally wiped from the map and swallowed by the State of Israel. During the 1967 War and Israel's occupation of the West Bank I was a freshman at Jordan University with dreams of returning to my homeland. These dreams were shattered within six short days. Having completed my studies, I should have graduated in 1970 but the ceremony was cancelled due to political tensions (better late than never, the graduation ceremony was held in 2007!). As my life appeared to be dictated by seemingly arbitrary decisions and events beyond my control, fuelled by profound feelings of injustice and dislocation, I decided to leave.

As I approach retirement age, after years in academia, memories have become more vivid and my need to reflect stronger. Although I have lived more than three-quarters of my life outside Palestine, one constant remains: my Palestinian identity. My early experiences shaped my character and life in exile forged my identity.

Too young to fully appreciate the full implications of the *Nakba*, my earliest memories centre on the villages of Beit Rema and Deir Ghassanah. Despite the hardships faced by my father and mother following their expulsion from

Muzera'h, life for a young boy was exciting, especially after the long harsh winter months when we emerged from our small one-room basement flat and headed for the orchards near the village. Sweet tea flavoured with *maramia* (sage) greeted us in the morning as we waited for my mother to return with hot bread from the communal stone ovens. After breakfast my brothers and sisters ran wild through the endless fields of red poppies, only returning to pick fresh fruit from fig and vine trees or gather eggs from the chickens. These carefree days were punctuated by large family weddings often accompanied by the rhythm of the *tablah*, the *dabke*, the high-pitched *zaghareed*, the chant of women recalling the family history of young couples. Too romantic? Perhaps. Yet despite the poverty, these halcyon days and the sense of freedom, innocence and belonging they engendered have remained with me.

Like many members of the diaspora, before I arrived in my new country I was given an extensive list of family and fellow Palestinians who had made the journey earlier. This shared identity and common history creates strong bonds borne of a desire to preserve our Palestinian nationality. Yet these ties are much more practical in nature. They offer security. Heated debates concerning Palestinian politics often take place behind closed doors because nothing should jeopardise economic and family security. In exile, the need to survive and support the wider extended family is of paramount importance. Work permits can be withdrawn at any time and the cost can be very high – especially for those whose travel documents are dependent on the arbitrary decisions of foreign governments.

I realise I was more fortunate than many Palestinians. In my mid-thirties I settled with my Scottish wife in Qatar. A relaxed and hospitable country, Qatar was an ideal place to raise a family. Life was easy but passing on my Palestinian heritage to my daughters less so. Despite having the benefits of a good education in private schools with a sound grounding in Arabic and Islamic studies, they displayed a frustrating lack of interest in their Palestinian identity. When asked where they were from, they would simply reply that their father was Palestinian and their mother Scottish. How could they be Palestinian when they had no knowledge of Palestine? The connection had been severed long before they had been born. Needless to say, I felt that I had failed my daughters.

My disappointment, however, was short-lived, for when my daughters left Qatar to study in Scotland, an amazing transformation occurred. They actively sought out other Palestinian and Arab students, students who understood the history and culture of the region. For the first time, phone calls home were in Palestinian dialect rather than English. As their social network of friends expanded, Palestinian recipes were exchanged and dinner dates arranged. After graduation, both married Palestinians and found their true identities. As for me, I learnt that cultural and political identity cannot be taught or extinguished. It is not merely an abstract concept, it is a reality that inhabits the soul.

Being Palestinian and Scottish offers a freedom of expression that had hitherto been suppressed. Since coming to Scotland I am constantly amazed by the young Palestinians I meet. Neither born nor brought up in Palestine, they are proud, educated and confident ambassadors. Perhaps I shouldn't be surprised. In my experience in Scotland, my adopted homeland, there appears to be an ability to empathise with those who suffer injustice and a desire to understand their plight. Many devote their time and energy to supporting causes that embody the notion of justice.

Having recently become a British citizen, my dream of visiting Palestine can now become a reality. Yet if truth be told, I fear that if I visit Palestine my childhood memories may be crushed under the harsh reality of life under military occupation. How can I possibly understand the life of my fellow Palestinians from the perspective of a comfortable retirement in Scotland? One of the challenges I faced when applying for my British passport was choosing the place of my birth. I was only given two computer-generated options. Should I choose Israel or the Palestinian Authority? The only answer was 'not applicable'! Yet administrative obstacles pale in significance when compared to endless checkpoints or arbitrary arrests endured by those who live under occupation. Would a short visit satisfy my desire to return? Perhaps it is better to demand my right to return to the land of my birth; only in this way can my belief in justice be kept alive.

Asma Jaber

Asma Jaber is a Palestinian-American graduate of Harvard University's Kennedy School of Government. She has worked on civil rights issues with the US Department of Justice, as well as on humanitarian affairs with the United Nations in Palestine. She is currently pursuing her own start-up, PIVOT, which will streamline digital cultural preservation, first within Palestine/Israel, and eventually throughout the world.

The Pain and Beauty of Dispossession

'The old will die, and the young will forget.' For the Palestinian people, the first part of this statement is true, as it is for anyone. But the second is wrong. It is wrong because my being Palestinian was based upon not forgetting.

I used the first pay cheque I received from my job out of college to take my father on a trip back to his homeland of Occupied Palestine. I chose to go to Palestine because *I* did not forget.

I did not forget the story after story about Palestine that my father told us, whether during a car ride, or over the breakfast table. Stories about Palestine's hills and fruits, the land he tilled and the kilos of grapes he picked. Stories of his day-long hikes as a boy scout in Jerusalem, exploring the alleys, smells and sights of the Old City.

And then there were the heart-wrenching stories of dispossession.

Stories of how his parents hastily packed up their belongings (and their child, my father) in Nazareth during the 1948 *Nakba* which led to the expulsion of approximately 750,000 Palestinians from their homes. They thought it was temporary; it has now been sixty-seven years.

One dispossession led to another: my father's exile at the Allenby Bridge, the now border crossing between Jordan and Occupied Palestine. After the 1967 War my father tried to travel back home (as he was living elsewhere at the time). He recalled how just days before my grandmother had been ecstatic that my father would see their remodelled apartment, a result of his hard-earned remittances. But he never saw it.

Instead, he saw his mother's face only a few metres away on the other side. She looked on as her son was denied entry into the only home he ever knew. They were later stripped of their residency, as were a quarter of a million Palestinians. My father's family gathered their belongings and left; once again they thought it would only be temporary. It has now been close to half a century.

The Allenby Bridge is the main entry point for Palestinians abroad seeking to enter the West Bank. It has kept generations away from their land and has torn loved ones apart. Mourid Barghouti writes that the bridge is 'no longer than a few metres of wood and thirty years of exile'. The bridge not only symbolises the humiliation inflicted upon Palestinian lives, but also the endurance that Palestinians must have when crossing it.

My father hated that bridge with a passion, and he could never fully recall the story because it was too painful to do so. I was constantly surrounded by such recollections as a child. As I grew older, I knew that his stories were my stories and our history. I had to save them for my children and their children. I had to save them to show that there is a Palestinian people with a right to self-determination, equality and freedom.

Being Palestinian meant feeling disconnected with my surroundings in South Carolina, the only place I ever physically knew as home. But, somehow, I also felt less 'Palestinian' than others, as if being born in the diaspora diluted my identity.

I longed to feel rooted, to at least know my family in Palestine and to explore our homeland myself. It is when I recently returned to live in Palestine that I felt a connectedness that I had never felt before. I felt that I had known my family there for decades, though it was my first time really getting to know them. As for the friends I made, I felt I was torn apart from them in child-hood, though it was the first time I had met them.

I felt a connection and love in Palestine. I felt pain and loss. Ironically, it was Palestine that made me feel alive again. I experienced grape season; I'd call and tell my dad. I went on the same hikes that he went on as a child; I'd call and tell him. I mapped checkpoints, roadblocks and interviewed child prisoners who were under house arrest and could no longer attend school; I'd call and tell my dad. And cry.

In what turned out to be one of my last conversations with my father, I recounted to him an incident that had occurred while I was working in Jerusalem. I waited to hail a cab when a young Jewish couple close by engaged me in small talk. When the couple realised that we were all Americans travelling to the Old City, they offered me a ride in their cab, should they find one first.

After discovering that I grew up in South Carolina, the husband remarked, 'I didn't realise there were many Jewish folks in South Carolina.'

'There aren't many,' I replied. 'And I'm actually not Jewish. I'm Palestinian.'

Suddenly, whatever we had in common no longer mattered. The man stopped, looked at his wife, and then motioned me to the left: '*Your* buses are over there.' The couple got into a cab, and I stood there trying to comprehend what had just happened. The humiliation and hurt coursed through me. Despite the heart-breaking story, my father was proud of my will – and that of so many Palestinians – to return and fight for equal rights, rather than endure the humiliation of being told to ride segregated buses.

I was counting down the days to go back to South Carolina and really debrief my dad about my work and to tell him about all the villages I now knew intimately; I even wanted to bring him and drive him to his village. But my life began to unravel in the next few hours as the news of my parents' car accident reached me. I was creating a digitised map for my father of his land in Palestine at the very moment I learnt he was not going to make it. I hastily packed my bags and made my way to Tel Aviv Airport, my eyes swollen from tears. I was taking the very same path he took in his youth to go spend his last moments with him.

Barely able to speak, I told the Israeli airport officials my situation, but I was still strip-searched en route to see my dad one last time by the same occupying power that displaced him – and me.

My dad passed away three hours after my hands interlocked with his. His mind, his memories and his extraordinary resilience, however, will never die because they live on in every Palestinian.

So what does being Palestinian mean to me?

It is incompleteness. It is a remodelled home for which you tirelessly worked, but that you never enjoyed.

Being Palestinian is eating grapes in South Carolina but missing the taste of your own.

While recently picking figs from the thirty-year-old fig tree my father planted in our backyard, it hit me: he had done everything in his power to reinvent Palestine in South Carolina – to plant the fig, olive and plum trees he knew from his childhood and to adorn our fence with grape vines – just to gain a semblance of home. But none of it tasted or felt the same, I'm now sure.

Being Palestinian is reclaiming a right and finding love.

It is recently meeting my fiancé (who was on his own path to explore his Palestinian roots) at the same bridge from which my father was exiled – at the cusp of the diaspora. Instead of seeing my grandmother's face of despair at that bridge, I saw my soon-to-be husband and the faces of a future Palestinian generation crossing that same bridge, this time going *back*.

Being Palestinian is going back, no matter how many articles of clothing are stripped off your body by the occupier.

It is purging your emails and browsing history so that the mere mention of the word 'Palestine' doesn't cause you to be deported from your own home.

Being Palestinian is going back, no matter how many walls are built on the beautiful land that our ancestors tilled.

It's growing into the shoes of your ancestors and somehow carrying a burden too heavy to ignore.

Being Palestinian is missing something you've never had, and it is loving it even more.

There is meaning to the fact that I began to know my homeland inside out at the same time my father was taking his last breaths. Being Palestinian is not forgetting, no matter who gets old and dies. My dad has died, but I have not forgotten. *We* have not forgotten.

Salma Khadra Jayyusi

Salma Khadra Jayyusi, poet, critic, literary historian and professor of Arabic literature, is founder and director of The Project of the Translation of Arabic (1980) and the East–West Nexus (1990) for studies on Arabic civilisation, which includes The Legacy of Muslim Spain. *She lives between Cambridge, MA and Jordan.*

The Durable Cords of Memory

When all was finally over and the whole of my extended family became refugees, I found myself in the grip of estrangement and I slowly developed a feeling of permanent loss. This feeling worked itself inside me as an independent entity, accompanying me wherever I went, even to Palestine itself. What can one do to endure this parting, this tearing away of a whole life, of a whole intimacy with place?

What could one do later to reach happiness? I was born with a sunny outlook on life, but I still could not be totally true to the short-lived élan that sometimes filled my soul. My confidence in a steady future seemed totally unreachable, even though I felt fulfilled in the work I chose to do. Throughout the years happiness was reached only in moments so transient that they merited mention in my poetry: 'We've always lived on moments', I reminisced in my poem 'Shudan'.

Memory became a constant reminder. Certain places kept appearing to me: the Safad stone alleys, slippery and polished to perfection by myriad feet throughout the centuries, and I, a child of four, carried on the shoulders of one of my cousins and taken, half asleep, to or away from some other cousin's wedding. Then there was 'Akka (Acre), city of my childhood and early adolescence and its western shore, al-Gharbi, with its jutting rocks and rough, brown-reddish sands (*zifzif*) where we often went to see the sun sink into the Mediterranean. On the horizon were the Haifa city lights looking like an open jewel chest, unbelievably beautiful. I see myself running wildly across the open 'Akka meadows, or climbing the Napoleon Hill east of the city with the old French guns perched on the top which we used to climb with immense joy, never aware of the evil they represented as an invader's tools. They were just rusting guns, huge toys for us children. 'You keep soiling your dresses on those guns, Salma!' Umm Muhammad, our house help, would say wearily.

But aside from the bouncing memory of play, I, as a child, also carried later into my diaspora the bitterness of that pre-1948 epoch of warped values and cruel intentions. I had seen, with unbelieving eyes, the victims of an erroneous world order, suffering, groaning, incarcerated, often falling into destitution, sometimes carried to their graves.

Images still haunt me, unabashed. I have no idea why I, a girl of ten, was standing near the door in that grieving woman's house, witnessing one of the saddest dramas of final farewells: 'I want my husband! Give my husband back to me!' repeated over and over again. He had been killed by a British soldier. She was heavily pregnant, maybe in her eighth month. I went home pale and trembling and was immediately put to bed, all shutters down.

Growing up in Palestine, I became ever more aware of the differences between city and village people. Spending a summer during my early puberty in the village of Farradyeh, near Safad, I became secretly infatuated with the handsome Atif, the Mukhtar's son. But I, proud city girl that I was, peered at him through the openings in the window shutters and never gave him a second look when I passed him by. As an adult, after our diaspora had begun, my greatest concern centred on our peasants, ousted from their homes and leading the sedentary life of a segment of society whose identity had been doubly snatched from them: as Palestinians, and as tillers, planters and harvesters of their own land. I could never forgive the world for having accepted their eradication from their ancestral homeland, from exercising their birthrights as peasants who had lived with dignity and pride on the land of their forefathers. I keep seeing our villagers in my mind exposing their chests to British guns in defence of their country, then to Zionist guns, then to a sudden, violent expulsion beyond imagination. This scenario was greatly enhanced when I heard Reem Kelani, the great Palestinian singer/musician and patriot, singing those peasants' heart-breaking songs, inherited from time immemorial, on the stages of Europe.

However, many Palestinians in the diaspora refuse to sink into the abyss.

Exile, with its aloneness and alienation, its helpless need for the other, continues to bring out their inner strength.

In a lecture on Palestinian identity I gave at Brown University in April,
1997, I said:

> When Palestinians think of themselves, they always think of 'us', the
> Palestinians, the afflicted, the impoverished, those robbed of home, iden-
> tity and possessions, those thrown into destitution, terrorised, tortured,
> abandoned by the world and buried alive; but they also think of themselves
> as dedicated, self-sacrificing, courageous, intelligent, successful, pioneering,
> enterprising and – despite their tragedies – robustly alive.

When Jinan Coulter brought me her documentary film *Searching for Saris*,
requesting help to translate the Arabic interviews into English for the selection of subtitles, I was surprised to discover, in these remarkable interviews,
the deep understanding of the Palestinian predicament by men and women
from Saris village. A young boxer from Saris says: 'Balfour did not own
Palestine nor did Britain own it, yet he gave it to the Jews who did not own
it either.' The validity of this simple equation has escaped world notice. The
failure to comprehend this reality is staggering.

Palestinians in the diaspora, I among them, carry their forced exile with
them everywhere, together with the courage to live, endure and, often,
to achieve. My own personal love of travel, of seeing the world and its
peoples, has never diminished my deep awareness of my exiled state.
Images of exile have shown up mainly in my poetry, where the inner perception is alert:

Khartoum 1

> *And I? a restless tent,*
> *I raised my house on the horizon*
> *I fixed my signpost in the wind!*

A Tale

> *And I?*
> *a wound in the traveling brow*
> *a seal on the wind,*
> *a marriage contract with exile*
> *my people dead and dying,*
> *my little ones are lamps*
> *in an ever moving chamber.*

And the diaspora continues.

Salwa Affara Jones

Salwa Affara Jones was born in December 1944 in Aden. At the age of ten and a half her family moved to Edinburgh where she completed her schooling. After obtaining a degree from the University of Edinburgh, she pursued a teaching career in both primary and secondary schools. For several years she also worked as an information and communication technology support officer with the City of Edinburgh Schools and Families Department. She has one daughter and one granddaughter.

Mujaddara – **Arabian Haggis!**

Looking back over my life I can see that my sense of identity has evolved over time and place. Now, when I am asked where I come from, I say Scotland. I feel Scottish because Scotland is my adopted country and its people are my people. Having spent fifty-eight of my sixty-nine years in Scotland, I no longer feel the need to explain that I'm an Arab with a Palestinian mother and a Yemeni father. Today I'm comfortable saying I come from Scotland. After all these years it would be almost disloyal to say otherwise! But in so doing I do not renounce my Palestinian and Yemeni identities, but embrace my adopted country as my own, recognising its immense contribution to me as an individual.

My previous need to explain my origins came from a deep-seated sense of loyalty to my Arab identity as a Palestinian and Yemeni. After all, I was brought up to be proud of both cultures. Perhaps this was a way of clinging to my Palestinian and Yemeni roots as my Scottish surroundings exerted a greater influence on my life. I was also fearful of finding myself with no identity at all: not Scottish, not Palestinian and not Yemeni.

I am not of the diaspora but was first exposed to it at the age of five. My mother and aunt had heard that a temporary camp of Yemeni Jews had been set up in the desert near Sheikh Othman, Aden. Hearing that these people were waiting to be airlifted to the infant State of Israel, they decided to visit and I was taken along. Years later I realised that this was the clandestine 'Operation Magic Carpet' (1949–50). Though very young at the time, I remember begging arms stretching through the boundary wires of the camp and my mother and aunt, the latter a newly dispossessed refugee from Ramle in Palestine, finding out that these ragged highland people had travelled from their homes in the Imam's Yemen to the British-administered Aden Protectorate. At the time I was told they were Jews, but they were so different from Miryom, Rosa and Hanno, Jewish friends from Aden who were frequent visitors to our family home. I sensed my mother and aunt were disturbed after the encounter. Even though I was still very young, I realised that something was amiss. It was then that I became aware of Palestine as my mother's homeland.

My arrival in Scotland at the age of ten was traumatic. I remember crying myself to sleep at night because I missed my friends and hometown, Sheikh Othman. To make matters worse, I suffered dreadfully from the bitter cold of the Scottish winter – there was no central heating in those days. Thankfully my school in Edinburgh was wonderfully supportive and our family was welcomed by the local community. Although we missed South Arabia, we embraced our new life with enthusiasm. However, I clung tenaciously to my mother tongue and all things Arab, both Palestinian and Yemeni, for fear of losing these precious links to my heritage. Arab students were regular visitors to our home, where we enjoyed preparing and eating traditional dishes such as *mujaddara, malfouf* and stuffed pastries while exchanging news, jokes and reminiscences in Arabic. I welcomed these opportunities as most Arabic speakers were eager to practise their English! To this day I love speaking in Arabic and it's a cause of great personal frustration that my language skills are deteriorating.

During my Scottish childhood my Palestinian identity was already fading to memories of family holidays to Ramallah where my grandparents and cousins lived, and a few visits from Palestinian friends and family to Edinburgh. Encouraged by my mother, we wore embroidered Palestinian dresses on special occasions and prepared traditional dishes on feast days. We loved listening to tales of her life as a child in Nazareth and later her work as a nurse and midwife in the Old City, Jerusalem. It was while working in a hospital in Hebron during a typhoid epidemic that she met my father, a Yemeni doctor. She was a great storyteller who laid the foundations of my Palestinian sense of self, although I still identified strongly with South Yemen, where I was born and had spent my early childhood.

While I grew to love my new country, I still couldn't call myself Scottish. In those days, had I said I was from Scotland I would have been asked to explain where I was *really* from. Brown faces were not as ubiquitous in Scotland back then as they are now.

It took the Suez Crisis of 1956 to awaken my Palestinian identity. In trying to understand the conflict that was dominating the news headlines in Scotland, I learnt about the troubled recent history of the Palestinians from both my parents. It was a seminal moment as my memories of 'Operation Magic Carpet' clicked into place. As I understood it, Britain, along with France, had joined forces with Israel to fight a war with Egypt. Israel was the country that was guilty of stealing a huge part of my mother's homeland and dispossessing thousands of people, including many relatives. It was no friend of the Palestinians.

The Arab–Israeli War of 1967 firmly established my Palestinian consciousness. It was an alienating time for Palestinians as few Scots knew the truth about how Israel, always perceived as the victim, was created. Anger, disappointment and sheer frustration at the injustice of what was happening only served to intensify my Palestinian identity. In the years since then, the ongoing conflict, the many atrocities committed against the Palestinian people, the publicising of our cause and the actions of an increasingly belligerent Israel have slowly shifted public opinion in Scotland towards a greater understanding of the historical and human rights issues at the centre of the conflict. It is as if my adopted family is finally starting to understand.

Even now I feel my identity is still evolving. The rise of instant communication and mass travel has broken down national boundaries, and change in many societies has gathered pace. New identities are constantly being formed while old ones are questioned and in some cases discarded. Global environmental and economic conditions are creating a new identity: the world citizen. I still identify with Palestine and Yemen, for my ties are strong and my loyalty to both countries is steadfast. Yet my daughter and granddaughter are Scottish and Scotland is where my home is. It is the country that nurtured me. These multiple identities are not a source of conflict for me as I slowly embrace another one: a citizen of a fragile Earth.

Fady Joudah

Fady Joudah is a poet, translator and physician (originally from Isdud/Ashdod). He is the author of three poetry collections, most recently Alight *and* Textu. *His first poetry collection was awarded the Yale Younger Poets prize in 2007. His translations of Palestinian poetry, especially that of Mahmoud Darwish and Ghassan Zaqtan, have earned him the Banipal prize (2008), the PEN USA award (2010) and the Griffin International Poetry prize (2013). He became a Guggenheim Fellow in poetry in 2014. He is a physician of internal medicine and lives in Houston, Texas.*

Still Life[1]

You write your name on unstained glass
So you're either broken or seen through

When it came time for the affidavit
The panel asked how much art
Over the blood of strangers the word

Mentioned the weather and the sleepers
Under the weather all this
Was preceded by tension enzymatic
To the hills behind us and the forests ahead

Where children don't sleep
In resting tremor and shelling
The earth is a pomegranate

A helmet ochre or copper sinks
In buoyant salt water
Divers seek its womb despite its
Dura mater

And it hangs on trees like pregnant mistletoes
I'll stand next to one
And have my German lover

Remember me on a Mediterranean island
Though she would eventually wed
An Israeli once she'd realised
What she wanted from life

A mother of two
On the nose of Mount Carmel
Where my wife's father was born driven out
But there lies the rub O Lord

My father's hands depearl
The fruit in a few minutes add a drop
Of rose water some shredded coconut
For us to gather around him

He will lead his grandchildren out transfer
Bundles of pine branches in the yard to where
His tomatoes and cucumbers grow in summer

Let them let them
Gather the dried pine needles forever he says
They will refuse to believe the fire dies

And they will listen to his first fire
On a cold night in a forest of eucalyptus trees
The British had planted as natural reserve
Outside Gaza

Note

1. Fady Joudah, 'Still Life' from *Alright*. © 2013 by Fady Joudah. Reprinted with the permission of The Permissions Company, Inc. on behalf of Copper Canyon Press, www.coppercanyonpress.org

Khalid Kamhawi

Khalid Kamhawi was born and raised in Jordan, where he became a founding member of the 24th March Coalition, a non-violent movement calling for democracy. He has lived in the USA and the UK, and holds a PhD in mathematics from Imperial College London. As of yet, he has never been to Palestine.

Subversive Abstraction

To me, being Palestinian is an unyielding moral assertion that demands political engagement with the world. It is a statement of both individual freedom and universal justice; resistance hand-in-hand with forgiveness; an act of liberation within the context of coexistence. It is a fearless humanism that cannot be overcome by grief or anger, and an endless determination to prevail without malice. Ultimately, it is a personal stand against defeatism and apathy.

Like the fading memory of a plethora of flowers, mine is a reality of Palestinian non-experience.

Palestine – its desert and seas, its ancient olive fields almost touching the horizon, the old neighbourhoods and streets, Jerusalem – is dislocated from my experience. The injustices that continue to befall its occupied and exiled people – my people – have turned our notion of home into a remembrance of an imagined past, illusory and perfect. Amid those remembrances are stories as sweet as honey, told over and over in reminiscence –some of which I choose to believe. One is about my grandfather spending his youth building a maternity hospital in Nablus, only to donate all of its beds and medical equipment a few years later to the Algerian revolution. Another is of how (if one listens intently) the hills around Hebron call out to the Gazan shore at sunset.

And with every sunset, time passes into permanence.

As it does, our lives are turned into their own stories. Yet, the history of my life cannot be reduced into a generic narrative of the *Shatat*. It is not a life lived simply from the outside. For although I can trace its trajectory so far, heartbeat following heartbeat, city to city, starting from Amman, where I first fell in love, to Pittsburgh, where I experienced the New World's portent, and then London, in which the moon seemed to be eternally suspended as I walked in its parks and cemeteries, back to Amman, and London once again . . . Palestine was always present as a moral compass, prohibiting me from internalising exile into an identity of alienation, constantly defying such capitulations. I have always refused the *Shatat* the chance to indulge in negative space.

There is a subversive abstraction in being Palestinian.

It manifests itself as a blustering ethical identity that entices one to fight for *all* who are wanting of a dignified life. From a very young age, I refused to see myself as an outsider. The implications would have been metaphysically severe: could I become a mere observer who, although able to reflect, has no choice but to accept the world as unchallengeable fact? No. Standing idle was always abhorrent to me, for it required that I embrace the occupation, the discrimination and the expulsion. To be an active member of the global body politic is the manner by which I uphold my identity. Only as a literal cosmopolitan, participating in the sharing of hopes and the building of aspirations, can I break through the *Shatat*'s enclosing walls. This universal belonging underlines my moral obligation to other causes for justice, the most recent of which are the current Arab revolutions.

I was in London when the Arab Spring swept across the streets of Tunisia and Egypt. The sun lit brighter, and there was no hesitation in my decision to return immediately to Jordan, where I grew up, to help support the establishment of a fair and equitable democracy. Not to act was not an option, to be intellectually involved from afar was a compromise. I knew I had to engage with the historical moment in both body and spirit. The choice to leave my prospects in the UK was not stipulated on any preferential demarcation of the *Shatat*. On the contrary, the landscape of exile is characterised by demands for liberty and prosperity, and yet it is my impetus to exercise Palestinian-hood as political action which determines where I stand in its sprawling desert.

I left the steady course of a quiet future behind me, and leapt towards the unknown.

Against the migrating birds, I went south in the spring. As soon as I arrived back in Amman, I reacquainted myself with its winding streets. Protesting was the creation of public space, extending the idea of parliament to neighbourhoods, breaking the barriers to free speech with silent marches. I became a founding member of the 24th March Coalition, an association of men and women hungering for liberty. We actively organise and participate in the stubborn non-violent movement that calls for an effective representative government in the country. That fight is no more or less important than striving for the liberation of Palestine, and reflects the underlying justifications for it. Once established, a democratic Jordan (valuable in and of itself) will be a stronger support to the Palestinian cause. *Ab uno disce omnesa*,[1] a freer world will surely be a fairer world, and with it the general apathy towards injustice will diminish.

Palestine has never felt closer.

The early Zionist programme perpetuated the false claim that Palestine was a land without a people. Rather than a people without a land, out of the historical injustices there has risen a nation with a moral covenant. Being Palestinian is much more than nostalgia and longing for a homeland – of course there is a constant yearning in our hearts, poetry, music and an unquenchable determination for liberation – but what I believe defines us is a proud kernel of moral dignity that is upheld, no matter where we are.

Note

1. Translation: 'From one, learn all.'

Ghada Kanafani

Ghada Kanafani was born in Beirut, Lebanon. She emigrated to the USA in 1985. A published writer, poet, speaker and trainer, some of her writings are taught in library schools and are included in anthologies. In 2005, she published A Life in Pencil, *a collection of her poetry. Her work and activism are highly recognised and have received numerous local community and national awards, including the Elise Boulding Peacemaker of the Year Award in 2009.*

Photo: Rolf Kjolseth

Where to Now?

Exile is the identity of a Palestinian. To be born Palestinian is to be born exiled, regardless of the place of residence. My identity exists without me. There are no defining lines between my people, me and our struggle for justice.

At an early age I questioned my humanity and, since then, I have realised that injustice is the norm. The United Nations Declaration of Human Rights only serves as an answer to an ongoing question: am I, are we, humans? It seems not. If we are, why does the world continue to stand idle to the fact that we are denied basic human rights? Why does the world turn away in oblivion when these continue to be taken away? We live in survival mode.

I am a stranger to myself. I am a revised version of me, a version that conforms to concepts that are not relevant to my true identity. I am sheltered in foreign lands, a lonely bird in a hostile sky. I find myself in others but I continue to be unrecognisable to them, even to the ones with the best of intentions. Most of the time I exist for their own benefit.

My name is غادة but I live exiled from my own name. My name lives in a past I don't want to remember, yet the voice carrying me home is the voice that says غادة. What of a name but the familiar, the voice of a lost beloved and of what a parent had in mind. My name is buried in a new place and is lost to a new people.

Outside forces and endless wars have torn off pieces, and sometimes bigger parts, of my being. The living part of me is displaced and my association with place is cut off. I go on living with unfulfilled emotional connections and experience rejection every step of the way.

As an exile, I live a great sense of grief and numbing despair, I live with anxieties and unbearable, sometimes self-inflicted, inner tortures simply because I survived. Sometimes I even reject my physical existence at the sight of my handwriting, when others are gone forever, simply because of their writing.

I live in loneliness and isolation and feel confined. I insist on withdrawal and retreat, yet I yearn for justice, freedom and a true refuge. I am frozen because any sign of warmth will not last. Angry but determined, my only choice is to survive.

In a last and desperate effort, I make sure that my personal memories are told to younger generations. I hope they will be able to make things right, or that I might protect them from the 'immediate' history readily available to them, written by the victor. I overlook the fact that my personal memories are scarring them, a contributor to our historical trauma.

I have a strong sense of belonging to the past. I long to come full circle: to restore a past I am not nostalgic for as a whole, just some fond memories I choose to hold on to, through which I am better able to see the future or at least anticipate it. I deny the present; I can hardly relate to any of its brutal components. I work tirelessly for a better and just future for all.

As an exile I have developed a tolerance for contradictions and ambiguities. I seem to have acquired a great enough momentum to strike down obstacles and to keep my focus on the goals I want to achieve, rather than my own person and well-being.

I live in-between two languages; I desperately hold on to the Arabic language that's left in me, it's my only refuge. I protect and defend her words from becoming mere unrecognisable sounds.

Art happens to exiles like me: poetry, music, painting, dance and food. I have to use all my senses, including the sixth that is known by the code name 'intuition'. As a Palestinian, it's in my genes. It has developed, been nurtured and later evolved into a life of its own for survival purposes.

My artistic expressions as well as my activism are full of the anxiety of banishment I carry in my soul, but visions of salvation keep me going. I know how hard and slow salvation is forthcoming, and that if it comes at all, it comes as an escape.

I carry my roots around; I gave up on trying to plant them in foreign earth.

I am the only person I know of who is unable to grow mint or *za'tar*. They refuse to grow even in the most fertile soil, for the same exact reason my elderly parents refused to emigrate: 'Do you want us to die in foreign lands?'

I realise that there's no more home for me. There was never a home in the first place, not even for my ashes.

The We and the I's eternal question continues to have no answer: 'Where to now?'

Ghada Karmi

Ghada Karmi is a physician, writer and academic at the University of Exeter's Institute of Arab and Islamic Studies. She fled from her birthplace, Jerusalem, in 1948 and settled in London, where she has lived ever since. This experience is described in her widely acclaimed memoir, In Search of Fatima, *reissued in 2009.*

Fitting Nowhere

For most of my life, being Palestinian has been interchangeable with being miserable. By this I do not mean being in a state of active unhappiness or weepy wretchedness, but rather a low-grade background gloom. This might seem odd, for unlike so many Palestinians forced from the homeland, my family had not ended up in a refugee camp, or living from hand to mouth in a country of exile. We were readily privileged, having found refuge in England where I grew up and was educated.

For much of the time, this gloomy feeling, compounded of insecurity and sadness, lurked just below the surface of consciousness, leaving me able to believe that my life was normal, not unlike many of those around me. I judged my achievements and failures by reference to those of people in my social and educational milieu, unaware of any fundamental difference between us. I had come as a child to England in 1949, and grew up much as a middle-class English child might have done, not because my family was remotely English or could be defined in English class terms, but because of the good education I received and the company I kept as a result of it. As I grew up, the memory of Palestine, where I was born, and the ties my family had fostered towards it and the rest of the Arab world, grew fainter and less relevant. How could the shadowy recollection of a sunlit house in Jerusalem that I had barely known before being uprooted from it compete with the living reality of my school in London, and then of university in Bristol?

Indeed it could not, until one day in 1960 when I was a young student, eagerly embracing my new university life with the others in my year. I had developed a troublesome bout of urinary infections, which led to my admission to hospital. I was given a bed in a small ward, whose other occupant was a young woman roughly my own age. She was fair-haired and pretty and we made friendly conversation. It turned out she was also at university, reading English, and had a similar complaint. Her background was clearly what one would have called at the time 'county': genteel and charmingly self-confident. When our medical investigations were completed and we had recovered on the ward, I prepared to dress and leave the hospital. I was alone. No one had brought me there and no one was taking me back. She, on the other hand, sat on the edge of her bed waiting to be collected. As I packed my tiny bag, her parents suddenly appeared. They were both exactly as one might predict, genteel and very English.

'Hello, darling,' said her father, taking her bag and helping her up. Her mother put her arm round her daughter protectively. 'The car's just outside and Aunt Mary's there. We're going to Uncle James for lunch.' They glanced at me and smiled. The girl and I shook hands. I think I murmured something about wishing her well, and she reciprocated. They left ahead of me and I never saw her again.

A small incident, but I remember how keenly in that instant I felt the difference between her and me. She, fitting naturally into her environment, secure, loved and knowing her place in the world, and I precisely the opposite. I would never be English in the way she was or in any way at all. I would never have a home and family that was so much a part of the country I now lived in. And I would never know her natural self-assurance and sheer sense of rightness in her own skin. I imagined her finishing her studies, marrying a man from her own class and background, and living a long and happy life.

By contrast, and like all displaced Palestinians, I fitted nowhere. There was no comparable feeling of belonging and no secure future. The fear that stalked me was that I might never know how it felt to live in my own land and take my rightful place in it, visiting the places of my childhood and those of my forebears as something natural, not as a tourist courtesy of the Israeli authorities. Ours had not been a story of immigration, and we had not planned to leave our country and settle in another. Nor was it a tragedy that had overtaken us long ago, whose memory would dim with time. It was ever-present, ongoing and relentless, and therefore impossible to forget. We were not normal people with normal lives and never would be. Saddest of all, if Palestine came back and we all returned, it would never be right, as it had been right for that girl in Bristol long ago. Something shattered for us when our country was taken away, and it will never be whole again.

'Ever since my father set foot in the British Isles he has become very fond of islands'. Victor Kattan, aged four (front right), with his father and sister, and the late Joe Hazboun (back left), and his son, on the South Pacific Island of Vanuatu.

Reem Kelani performing at World Music Shanghai in July 2011.
Photo courtesy of Nono Hu

From Jerusalem to Georgia: old friends meet in diaspora. Father George Makhlouf with His Eminence Archbishop Atallah Hanna of Sebastia at the Hall of St Elias Antiochian Orthodox Church in Atlanta, GA. Archbishop Atallah Hanna was invited to deliver the keynote speech for the commemoration of Land Day on 30 March 2014.

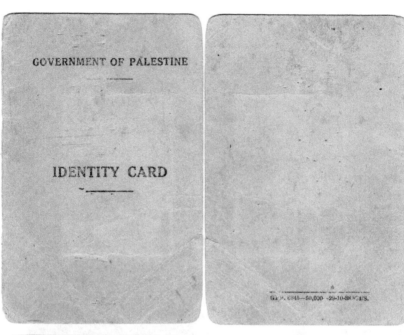

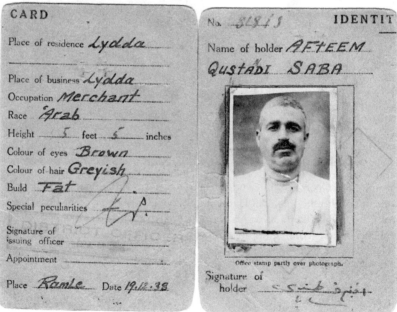

Documenting dislocation. **Above**: The Palestine Identity Card of Aftim Saba's grandfather, Afteem Qustandi Saba, a merchant in Lydda, Palestine, issued on 19 December 1938 by the British Mandate Authority. **Opposite**: The refugee identity card of Aftim's father, Amin Afteem Saba, aged twenty-seven. It was the forty-sixth identity card issued by the Gaza Egyptian administration in 1948 shortly after the *Nakba*.

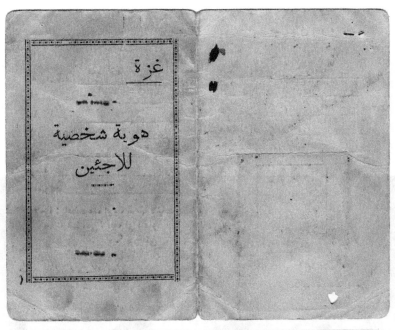

غزة

هوية شخصية
للاجئين
IDENTITY CARD

رقم الهوية ٥٠٠٠٤٦

اسم حامل الهوية حكيم اسميه انيس سابا

الجنسية عربى فلسطينى

محل الميلاد اللد

الجهة التى هاجر منها اللد

العمر ٤٧ سنة

محل الاقامة غزة سريون

المهنة السابقة موظف سكك حديد

المهنة الحالية

لون العيون بني

لون الشعر بني

البنية متوسط

الميزات

ملاحظة : أعطيت هذه الوثيقة لحاملها لأثبات
هويته فقط وهي لا تمنحه اى امتياز

التوقيع ٢٨ يوزباشى

المشرف على المهاجرين

Aftim Saba's niece Reem Jubran, (front left), performs *dabke* with the Bay Area *dabke* troupe, 'Aljuthoor [Roots] of the Arab Shatat' at Palestine Day in the Hall of Flowers Golden Gate Park, San Francisco in September 2013.

Photo courtesy of Ramsey El-Qare

'. . . the savouring of a sweet fig in the cool summer morning is a joy no matter where the picking is'. Figs grown in Aftim Saba's garden in Arizona, October 2014.

Victor Kattan

Victor Kattan is a senior research fellow at the Middle East Institute and an associate fellow at the Faculty of Law at the National University of Singapore (NUS). He was a legal adviser to the Palestinian Negotiations Support Project on secondment from the United Nations Development Programme from 2012 to 2013. He teaches a course on the use of force in international law at NUS and previously taught international law at the School of Oriental and African Studies (SOAS), University of London, where he obtained his doctorate. He is the author of From Coexistence to Conquest: International Law and the Origins of the Arab–Israeli Conflict 1891–1949 *(2009) and* The Palestine Question in International Law *(London: The British Institute of International and Comparative Law, 2008).*

Home is Where the Heart is. But Where is Home?

I am often asked where my surname comes from. Depending on who is asking the question, I usually say that my surname is 'Middle Eastern'. If they persist, I will say that it is 'Palestinian', and if they ask about my religion, I will point out that there are Christian, Jewish and Muslim 'Kattan's, which might be spelt in Latin as 'Katan', 'Cattan', 'Catan', 'Qattan' or 'Qatan'.

In Arabic, 'Kattan' comes from the word 'cotton', although it is also a Hebrew word, meaning 'small'. As a result, I am sometimes asked if I am Jewish. A few years back, a startled Israeli soldier at Qalandia checkpoint, near Ramallah, surprised that I was standing at the front of a long line of Palestinians seeking entry into Jerusalem, told me that Kattan is a Jewish name and asked me what I was doing in the 'territories'. I had no choice but to reply, rather apologetically, 'I'm visiting family. I'm not Jewish', which was met with a measure of disappointment and, I sensed, disapproval. But there have also been some humorous incidents, such as the time when my mother went to collect her little Peugeot from the Hadley Wood Garage in North London after it had been serviced, to be told that 'the Bentley is ready for you madam'. A little astonished and bemused and not wanting to drive off with someone else's car, my mother inquired whether there had been a mistake. 'No mistake madam. You are "Mrs Kattan"?' 'Yes,' my mother replied, 'but I do not own a Bentley.' It transpired that the Bentley was owned by a Jewish family.

I have difficulty answering the question, 'Where are you from?' because my identity is complex. My mother is British, of the Church of England, my father is Palestinian, of the Church of Rome, and I was born in Sudan, a virtual Islamic Republic. I grew up all over the world, except in Palestine. Ever since my father set foot in the British Isles he has become very fond of islands. Vanuatu, the Turks and Caicos Islands and Bermuda have all been our 'home'.

Undoubtedly though, I am Palestinian, in the sense that my father was born in Bethlehem in the British Mandate of Palestine in 1946. His family can trace their ancestry back three hundred years on Church records to Jacob and Elias Kattan. Giries, my great-grandfather, a justice of the peace, was appointed the mayor of Bethlehem by the Turks and the British, and Tewfic, my great uncle, was elected three times the representative of Bethlehem to the Palestinian-Jordanian Parliament. Tewfic was also made a pasha for his services to Jordan by King Abdullah, the grandfather of the late King Hussein. Before he was assassinated, King Abdullah would visit 'the Seil', the family house in Beit Jala, every summer. Legend has it that Col. T. E. Lawrence and General Allenby visited Giries several times when he was the mayor of Bethlehem and would walk up and down the long veranda of his house overlooking the Jericho valley. Victor, my Palestinian grandfather, was so fond of the British Empire in his youth that he decided to name my father and his brothers after the Kings of England. So, in addition to my father William, there are my uncles George, Edward and Henry. In contrast, my grandmother Marguerite was more cosmopolitan than my grandfather and not such an Anglophile. She spoke fluent French and Italian, which she learnt from the Catholic nuns growing up in Bethlehem, in addition to her native Arabic, and she only learnt English later in life.

I view my Palestinian identity not in a cultural, ethnic or religious sense, but 'emotional'. I self-identify with other Palestinians and with the cause, and I avidly follow contemporary political events in Palestine as if I lived there. Today, most Palestinians do not live in Palestine. Indeed, it is not so well-known outside of Palestinian circles just how multicultural the Palestinian diaspora is. Even prior to the *Nakba* there was an exodus of Christian

Palestinians from the Holy Land. This explains why I have family in Chile, France, Honduras, Italy, Jamaica, Jordan, Lebanon, Sudan, the United Kingdom and the United States. Some members of my family even settled in the Russian Empire and had to flee after the Bolshevik Revolution, and two of my elderly family members' earliest memories are of life in a Japanese internment camp in the Philippines. Yet others belonging to the Italian branch of our family have memories of internment in a British camp in the Anglo-Egyptian Sudan.

But Palestine was always their home. It was my grandfather's dream to retire to a house that he had built in Jaffa on fifty *dunums* of land (around twelve acres) planted with orange trees. He spent only one night in the newly built house when hostilities forced him to flee to his family's home in Bethlehem. He would never return to live there, as Israel prevented him from visiting Jaffa and confiscated the property which was turned into a kibbutz. He passed away in 1980, thirteen years before the signing of the Oslo Accords, which relaxed immigration restrictions and would have allowed him to visit his homeland as a tourist. Instead he is buried in the dusty Catholic cemetery in Khartoum where few can visit.

Today, the vast majority of Palestinians in the diaspora cannot return to the land that was once their home except on a tourist visa (assuming they hold the passport of a country that has diplomatic relations with Israel). Even with my British passport, the experience of having to travel through Ben Gurion International Airport always fills me with dread, for I face the prospect of being pulled aside, questioned at length, having my possessions confiscated, being detained and refused entry. But despite these obstacles, I remain undeterred in my desire to be able to freely visit my ancestral homeland. Profound changes have taken place in Palestine since 1948, but the bonds between Palestinians in the diaspora and those who still live there endure.

Tanya Keilani

Tanya Keilani is a New York-based researcher and community organiser. She completed her graduate studies in anthropology at Columbia University, where she surveyed the impact of Israeli policy on Palestinian intimate, communal and familial life. She is the founder of the Love Under Apartheid project.

A Vision Affirmed

Summer holidays in Amman, Jordan, where relatives on both Mama and Baba's side lived, form the first of my memories. I relished in toting my younger brother alongside me as we feasted on sweets and *shawarma* and fed the leftovers to stray cats. In the afternoons we watched bootleg comedies on my cousins' computer while they cracked jokes in Arabic that my diaspora tongue could only pretend to understand. The ladies would gather in the salon, air hot and dry, to catch up on the family gossip. My aunt, known for her sass and her sweetness, would grip my lanky frame and curse me lovingly for my prolonged absence. Though I spent much time grumbling about the tedium of Amman, there was a certain comfort in seeing the way Mama and Khalo (maternal uncle) looked exactly alike and how Baba's brother could make him laugh until sunrise. Still, I knew Amman was not my home, although a passport marked 'The Hashemite Kingdom of Jordan' bore a photo revealing my sheepish, dimpled grin.

Questions of identity emerge in every community that is separated from its origins, but the balance is all the more complex when the community is forcibly expatriated. In contrast to some immigrant groups, members of the Palestinian diaspora are often not voluntarily uprooted. We are drawn together by our lack of certainty and closure. Unable to return to our home-land, we imagine and narrate identity to ourselves, to each other and to those outside of our circuit. We speak our stories on station platforms, in lecture halls and at the supermarket checkout in order to affirm our connection to a home that is not only distant but under threat and in need of preservation. The urgency grows: another day of life in displacement, another year of absurd negotiations, and still, we are out of place.

Unlike many of their siblings who ended up in Amman – some by force, others for lack of options – Mama and Baba never lived in Jordan. I never understood why we possessed those passports, only that it was desperately important to have some kind of document, something that would guarantee us a home, no matter how many times we became displaced. My parents' fears of expulsion were not unfounded. In 1990, home shifted again, and by some providential fate asylum pleas turned us from Gulf War pawns into brisket-loving Texans.

Some things persisted, no matter our location: Baba's syrupy *knafeh*, Mama's city lilt and their collective nostalgia. But the place that cultivated our palates and our colloquialisms was obscure, unfamiliar to me. I knew Palestine only through my elders, and the more time that passed, the more mythical it became. In Jordan, relatives dug up yellowed photos from before our exile: my folks on their wedding day, a family trip to the Dead Sea via Jericho, and Teyta (grandmother) poised, clutching her children to her lap in the 1940s, some years before Mama was born. Portions of my adolescence were consumed with dreaming up conversations with family that remained in Palestine, wondering if we had the same dispositions and if I was too American to ever belong there. There was a constant insecurity.

How do we construct our communities and ourselves across multiple experiences and geographies? How does this variation shape us, and how do we avoid essentialising Palestinian-ness in our mission to protect our history?

As a twenty-something, my ill-coordinated feet fumbled until they mastered choreographed *dabke*. A lifetime of watching wedding parties circle ballrooms, hands clasped together, made this feat all the more glorious. In my childhood, my mother drove me nearly an hour on Sundays to learn Arabic and the Quran in a converted Dallas home garage of an Iraqi woman who scolded me whenever I challenged her. I refused to believe cats didn't end up in heaven, and I was not an exemplary pupil. Regretting poor reading and writing skills in my native language, I have started and stopped relearning Arabic in adulthood, sounding out words of fiction with such painful slowness that I have nearly given up on the idea altogether. At twenty-one I travelled to Palestine for the first time, and without my parents. They were too traumatised by soldiers confiscating baby formula at checkpoints to take me there, but I needed to go. Not to Jordan, not Egypt where Khalto's family lived, nor Germany where we could visit Auntie Imborg and cousin Till.

I found resolve in disentangling the mythical visions of home, but no symbol, no indigenous ornament and no recipe for stuffed grape leaves could emancipate me from the myopic exercise of identity-making. All of these conventions did not make me more Palestinian.

I have spent much of my life tripping over identity's delicate dance; various orientations refuse to completely assimilate me. I would like to say something sensible about Palestinian life in the diaspora. How one senses nothing but rootlessness anywhere and everywhere, or one's memories blur with each news report and we are all a little afraid of forgetting the stories that have been passed on to us. These ideas might produce comfort, but the only thing that rings true is that being Palestinian in the diaspora has no singular meaning.

Who are the Palestinians without *tatreez, sumoud* and *dabke*? What if we cannot identify our village's embroidered handiwork, or our spirits waver and we cannot bear to carry the weight of Palestine on our backs? What if white foreign bodies adapt to our rhythms more gracefully and organically than we do? What if we partner with *ajanib* (foreigner) and produce half-Palestinian babies or none at all? What if we never set foot in Palestine, never know the names of our relatives? Will we remain Palestinian without the symbols and tropes?

Palestine awaits us so long as we exist. Our connection to Palestine cannot be bound or measured. I wonder how many Palestinians and ways of being Palestinian in the diaspora are among us, uncounted. What vision of home includes us all?

Reem Kelani

Singer, musician and broadcaster Reem Kelani was born in Manchester to a father from Ya'bad and a mother from Nazareth. Kelani released Sprinting Gazelle – Palestinian Songs from the Motherland and the Diaspora *in 2006. Her forthcoming projects include a major work on Egyptian composer Sayyid Darwish, a CD on Ibrahim Touqan and a live album.*

Photo: Saeed Taji Farouky

Bridge to Palestine

I often compare notes with my friends about our first moments of consciousness in life. I cannot remember my infant years in Manchester, but I do remember our house in Kuwait, the country where I would spend my formative years.

And it was in Kuwait that I first realised my identity. I was singing Fairuz's ode to Jerusalem, *Zahrat al-Madā'in* (Flower of Cities) at a school concert when the audience burst into tears. As a child of four, I was unable to comprehend that people were crying because of the defeat of 1967 that had left Palestinians feeling dejected and defiant. I burst out crying: 'Mama! They don't like my singing!', and the audience spontaneously reacted with tear-tinged laughter. I knew from that moment on that my sense of being, what I would later know as 'Palestinian', had been formed, and that it would always be associated with sadness, laughter and song.

The second incident took place two years later, when I was watching television with my paternal grandmother, Jamileh, who was visiting from Jenin. Suddenly she started crying and waving her scarf at the television: 'What have we done to deserve this?', referring to the burning of the Aqsa Mosque in Jerusalem in 1969.

Grandmother was addressing the perpetrator – an evangelical Australian who claimed that the burning of the mosque would hasten the 'coming of Christ' – and the occupier that was, and is, Israel.

The third and perhaps most seminal incident took place in Palestine. In

1974 my father took us to visit for the first time. There we were, riding a cranky old bus across a creaking wooden bridge, watching the tiny strip of water that was the River Jordan beneath us. Before the bus set off, a Jordanian officer had asked women wearing 'Palestine map' pendants to remove them. 'The Israelis', the officer explained, 'would otherwise take them away!'

When we arrived on the other side of the river, my mother, who had not seen Palestine since leaving it as a young woman, almost fainted at the sight of an Israeli flag. My father gave her a bottle of juice and sat her down at a bench in the waiting room. On a neighbouring bench was another woman of a similar age. She looked Palestinian, but was speaking Hebrew with one of the soldiers, making an inquiry of some sort.

When a man approached the woman, my mother shouted with subdued joy: 'This is my sister's husband!' It transpired that the woman on the nearby bench was none other than my maternal aunt, In'ām, whom my mother hadn't seen for twenty years.

My uncle drove us on from the crossing point, while my mother and aunt did not stop crying and gossiping all the way. When we arrived in Nazareth and entered my aunt's old house with its gypsum-decorated ceilings, all I could see were weeping faces and rows of relatives hurrying to dig their heads into Mother's shoulders.

On that visit we attended a wedding at a village south of Nazareth called Nein. It was there that I watched old women sing and older men lead the wedding in a group dance. I noted that the bride changed her dress seven times, dancing with shy sensuality and holding a candle in each henna-clad hand. She was beautiful.

From then on, I knew that someday I would reconnect with those songs. My attachment extended to other accompaniments: stuffed pumpkins cooked in tomato sauce; chicken cooked with a million chopped onions and sumac; strong black coffee and silver trays heaped with freshly opened cigarette packets.

I became aware of my being because of these pivotal moments.

I am Palestinian because I sing traditional songs and because I refuse to be neutralised in media broadcasts and music festivals when my music is only played, or I am only invited, if, and only if, there's an Israeli act to justify my being.

I am Palestinian because of everyday words that continue to haunt and beautify my life:

dunum: from the Turkish *dönüm*, a unit of land measurement used in Ottoman times and still in use today. I grew up listening to my father and his generation talk about the *dunums* of land they had struggled to keep because of Israel's usurping of our ancestral land or, worse, because of family inheritance feuds.

el-jiser: one of the bridges which Palestinians have to cross between Jordan and Palestine, and at which they are routinely subjected to humiliating scrutiny by Israeli soldiers.

kushān: a land title deed and another word my father uses constantly. Many of the deeds that belonged to Palestinians are now held in the Ottoman archives in Turkey. Some traditional Palestinian songs even speak of 'hiding the *kushān* in the folds of our exodus'.

lamm el-shamel: a permit that allowed Palestinians with Jordanian passports to visit Palestine. I had one for most of my life, but it somewhat lost its validity with the Oslo 'peace' process.

tanakeh: the tinned container that my mother always looked forward to receiving from our paternal family in Ya'bad. It contained olive oil, olives or sheep's-milk cheese.

taṣrīh: a temporary permit that allowed some Palestinians to visit their homeland. We always felt lucky that we had the much-prized *lamm el-shamel*, but were constantly pained by the difficulties *taṣrīh* holders had to endure.

thob fallāhī: the traditional embroidered Palestinian dress. Until the First Intifada in the eighties, some Palestinian women of a certain class would refer to it as 'peasant' garb, with a derogatory nasal twang of the 'â' syllable of *fallāhī*. After the Intifada, however, most Palestinian women began to wear it as a national symbol and fashion statement.

And so, the more Palestinians are separated from Palestine and from each other, the closer we become; the more we sink into death, the more we are determined to live. It is this uncomfortable yet life-affirming *sumoud* which underlies our and my sense of being.

Basem Khader

Basem Khader was born in Jaffa in 1938. He spent most of his working life with the United Nations, where he was engaged primarily in development and humanitarian programmes in developing countries. As a US citizen, and since his retirement, he was involved in peace and justice activism. He passed away peacefully on 19 July 2014.

Badge of Honour

Within Palestinian society, my identity is established by reference to my religion (Roman Catholic), clan (Du'abis) and place of origin (Zababdeh). In the wider world, the only identity I carry or that matters to me is being Palestinian. It was not always so. As I rose through the ranks of the United Nations, and in my early years in the United States, there was persistent advice to play down my identity, if not suppress it altogether. Indeed, Palestinian friends of mine felt they had to be of Greek origin – after their maternal grandmothers – in order to make it and integrate in an inhospitable environment.

What has being Palestinian meant to me? First and foremost, fighting injustice and helping the underdog, both professionally and personally. In time, I was able to unshackle myself from the political correctness of the day, and expose double standards and the abuse of euphemistic language. This was not always without cost, but sacrifice, loss and struggle are what being a Palestinian is all about.

In the United Nations and other international organisations, staff are normally sponsored by their respective countries, although the theory is that international civil servants, apart from some political appointees, are selected on merit. So a Palestinian without a home country is decidedly at a disadvantage. In my case, I moved from toning down my Palestinian identity to wearing it publicly as a badge of honour, thanks in no small measure to the writings and public appearances of the late Edward Said, who so eloquently captured our predicament. An indication of the hostility of the environment was that even before his illness, he was invited less and less to appear on, or write for, mainstream media.

I applied to become a citizen of my adopted country, the US, after retiring from UN service. When the Immigration Service came to issue my passport, the agent told me they had no country called Palestine, though I was indeed born in Jaffa, Palestine, during the British Mandate. I was furious, and refused to be 'attached' to any other country. Someone at the Service had the brilliant idea of changing my birthplace to Gaza (another badge of honour!). No country was shown, but neither was my identity in any doubt.

My sense of being Palestinian is not about form, but even in my adopted country I oppose any attempt to erase my country or my identity, convenient as that may be to some. As a descendant of peasant stock who have been attached to their land for hundreds of years, I have tried to make up for the loss of that physical attachment with cultural links, like collecting the old folk-loric songs dating back to Ottoman times that my mother, and before her my grandmother, used to sing. Or by gathering traditional Palestinian proverbs, a favourite hobby of my father. Some of the old songs bring tears to my eyes.

A new generation of Palestinian young men and women is preserving identity through film, poetry and political activism, and now that I have more time on my hands I make a point of taking part in events featuring their work and following their progress. I am particularly heartened by the number of women who are carving a name for themselves, an indication, if any was needed, that Palestinian identity will not only be preserved but rejuvenated.

As an 'out of place' Palestinian, I have travelled far and wide in the world trying to do some good, living up to, in some sense, the biblical injunction of being part of 'the salt of the earth'. An appropriate role, one might say, for a person rooted in the Holy Land. Deeply rooted like an ancient olive tree, yet violently uprooted.

As a secular person, I have had little time for religious affiliations. In my adopted country, Christian churches, including my own, have bewilderingly failed to fight injustice, oppose war or help the downtrodden. Having grown up in an Islamic culture, the call of the *muezzin* is as familiar to me as the sound of church bells. By the same token, current Islamophobia is offensive to me, as is the Medieval Inquisition or Tsarist anti-Semitism. As for the religious arguments now used to justify my own dispossession, I take these with a grain of Dead Sea salt and know that history will expose them for the mythical narrative they are.

Lisa Suhair Majaj

Lisa Suhair Majaj is the author of Geographies of Light, *winner of the Del Sol Press Poetry Prize, and of two poetry chapbooks. She is co-editor of three collections of critical essays on non-Western women writers, and has written extensively on Arab-American literature. She lives in Nicosia, Cyprus.*

Homemaking

My house is suffused with the distinctive odours of *molokhiyeh* – its fried garlic, coriander, allspice – invoking Palestinian memories: the cool respite of my aunt's shady Jerusalem garden, a drift of spices leading to a table overladen with succulent dishes. The sensations signal homecoming and return to a place of origin: Palestine.

But Palestine is a homeland in which I have never lived. My father left Palestine as a young man, seeking work and a college education, and like so many Palestinians was not allowed to return. In Iowa he met and married my American mother. They moved to Lebanon, then Jordan, seeking a means of existence and a place to be. My own identity, a complex weave of many strands, was shaped by this diasporic trajectory. Born in the US, I was raised in Jordan, educated in Lebanon and then back to the US. Although I had relatives in Jerusalem and the West Bank – those who weren't dispersed and hadn't lost their residency permits – my own relationship to Palestine was forged through occasional visits to Jerusalem and the confusions of my familial culture. It was forged, too, from Palestinian realities that impinged on my life in direct and indirect ways: from the Irgun bomb that killed my uncle's wife in January 1948 as she waited for a bus at Jerusalem's Jaffa Gate, leaving my two cousins motherless; to the 1967 war that punctuated my six-year-old sky with air-raid sirens; to Jordan's 1970 Black September onslaught against Palestinians, which I lived through for a month before fleeing with my mother and sister to the US; to the 1982 Israeli invasion of Lebanon, from which I escaped on a cargo ship stopped by the Israeli navy and taken to Israel for interrogation; and more. Being Palestinian, I learnt from a young age, means being hammered on an anvil, living a reality in which no dreams are left untroubled.

But being Palestinian is not just a trauma. It is also a birthright. Although I have spent most of my life distanced from its central axis, Palestine has always held me in its force field, its cadences structuring my life's trajectory. Palestine is a million sensations and memories woven together, linking the land and the people: the tart sweetness of Jericho oranges, the ritual of cardamom-scented coffee, the odour of Nabulsi soap. Being Palestinian is not a matter of a passport. If it were, Palestinians, long denied passports, would have become extinct decades ago. It's a matter of existing and remembering, and of asserting one's fundamental *being*, one's birthright as a human.

Yet it is precisely this bass-note of humanity which is so often obscured and denied. Palestinians are, above all, ordinary people seeking ordinary lives. But what does it mean to be Palestinian when Palestine is a place most are forbidden to live in or even enter? When familial land passed down for centuries is confiscated, homes sheltering generations bulldozed, carefully cultivated orchards razed to bare earth? When collective punishment is routine? When bombings flatten apartment blocks, hospitals and schools? When parents are forced to bury their children? When Palestinian identity and right to exist in the world is so bitterly contested that the very colours of the Palestinian flag were for decades forbidden, even in children's drawings? Being Palestinian is waking up to displacement, lunching with diaspora and going to bed with dispossession. Ask any Palestinian who still clutches the iron key to their confiscated front door. It's watching the news and knowing that your own story will not be there, or will not be represented accurately. It's writing letter after letter to presidents and politicians and newspapers, knowing that they will be tossed aside unread. It's realising that no matter how many atrocities your people suffer, the world won't do anything, because Palestinians were born on the wrong page of history.

But being Palestinian also means knowing that no tree is rootless. It's waking up with memory and going to bed with knowledge. It's understanding that even though homelessness is bone deep, home is carried home in one's bones. Being Palestinian is knowing that truth is truth and injustice is injustice. It's insisting that identity cannot be stripped from a person like a residence permit, bulldozed like a house or extinguished through murder.

Being Palestinian means believing that one day the world will come to its senses and acknowledge that Palestinians, too, are human.

And part of being human is the act of homemaking. Exiles know a lot about making the world their home. It's a matter of survival. I've spent a lifetime trying to perfect that exilic art. I fill my home with Palestinian embroidery, Jerusalem pottery, and memories from both parents, trying to weave the spaces I inhabit into a haven of belonging. With Palestinian existence denied and suppressed as both fact and as metaphor, and with Palestine itself so often relegated to memory, perhaps it is no surprise that I linger over the aroma of Palestinian spices. After all, they offer the dream of home, and it is from this dream of simplicity and return that I write my way forward, because being Palestinian means, above all, that we belong on this planet. Notwithstanding the devastations of history, it means holding on to hope. It means believing that one day, being Palestinian will be a metaphor not for tragedy and despair, but for the simplicity of an ordinary life, like spices wafting across a kitchen, promising a future.

Jean Said Makdisi

Jean Said Makdisi was born in Jerusalem but lives in Beirut. She is the author of Beirut Fragments: A War Memoir *(1990) and* Teta, Mother and Me: Three Generations of Arab Women *(2005). She taught English and humanities at the Beirut University College before devoting herself to writing.*

Stranger to my Own Story

I am a Palestinian. I am a Palestinian in the diaspora. I am a Palestinian in the diaspora who does not live, and has never lived, in a refugee camp.

I repeat these phrases over and over, comparing them, trying to distinguish and identify the nuances of meaning in them. How are they different?

One thing is clear. To be a Palestinian of any sort is to be the bearer of a continual, unbroken, violent history of political, social, military and cultural injustice, and to be perpetually obsessed with this historic set of grievances. Being Palestinian is not just a national experience, but a personal, deeply felt consciousness of loss and alienation. That is how I feel it, in my heart, in my gut, in my senses. It is a state of mind, a constant indignation, an intense thirst for justice that does not allow one to rest, to lay down the burden, but to carry it as it grows, day by day, heavier and heavier.

For some people, however, being Palestinian is not merely a state of mind, but a fundamental reality, an inescapable identity forced on them by their being, precisely, Palestinian. Some are second-class citizens in their own land, watching their way of life swallowed up by an alien force. Others have fallen victim, as Palestinians, to poverty and misery, to occupation and bombardment and siege and arrests and killings and land confiscation and houses blown up and orchards bulldozed. In the diaspora, others, with even less choice, are imprisoned outside their land in refugee camps, within borders drawn up by force and governed by cruel bureaucracies that issue (or worse, refuse to issue) official papers without which they cannot live. The presence or absence of these all-important papers can be equally damaging to the bearers (or non-bearers): if they have them, they are identified as Palestinians and therefore subject to all the forms of discrimination which can make their lives miserable. If they do not, woe be upon them!

I am always and constantly aware of the fact that I do not live in these horrific circumstances, that, by accident of birth and personal history, I have been spared them. I feel left out of the very historic drama that most marks me. I am a stranger to my own story, and for this I feel a terrible shame, the shame of failure. This is not self-pity; it is closer to anger at a national leadership that has provided no role for me – and others like me – in the political drama, and at myself for not creating one.

Some Palestinians in the diaspora outside the camps see the dream of recovery as hopelessly unrealistic, unrealisable. They believe all is irretrievably lost and they bitterly dismiss anyone with a more hopeful vision as ridiculously naïve, unwilling or unable to accept that defeat and ignominy is the unalterable destiny of Palestinians. Most people I know, however, believe in the restoration of justice in Palestine as a kind of political Holy Grail, something to be believed in and sought at all costs, to be worked for, even to suffer and die for. Some have taken up arms, while others are drawn to the camps as social workers, volunteers, researchers. Some, like me, deal in Palestinian memory, writing, painting or filmmaking, imposing our story on the cruelly unjust or the placidly indifferent world around us, and crafting memories into a political stand and material for a thousand books. It is difficult to avoid defensive chauvinism when we do these things. I have been as appalled by Palestinian chauvinism as I was by Lebanese during the long Lebanese civil war, which I lived through, raising my children in the violence.

But my obsession with Palestine is not always and necessarily negative. In some ways, being Palestinian outside Palestine is like being young and in love, feeling a passion and a tenderness that never fades even if the beloved departs. One can endlessly feel his presence, no matter how far away he is. His reality, however lost, remains unalterably alive in memory. And similarly, Palestinians outside Palestine cultivate their memories of the place or, if they are too young to remember it, gather memories from family photographs, from the obsessive retelling by older generations – dying out now – of stories from the past, especially descriptions of homes, gardens, farms, city streets, village squares, weddings, songs, dances and schoolrooms which, from being evocations of the past, become, in their new transplanted state, present and living realities. These inherited memories are sown as farmers sow seeds extracted from the previous season's crop, in their own hearts, and in the minds of the following generations, so that they no longer act as memories do, but as real experiences: the experience is the memory, and the memory the experience.

I have often noticed how many of us Palestinians in the diaspora hang maps of Palestine on the walls of our homes. Almost invariably they are pre-1948 maps: the towns and villages maintain their Arabic names and there are no cruel lines dividing the place up. Some people wear gold maps of Palestine on a golden chain around their necks.

Sometimes, often, I wish I could forget Palestine. I wish I would not leap up at every mention of it, at every provocation by those not similarly engaged, at every foolish remark made by the ignorant and the misled, at every media report that covers up the truth instead of exposing it, at every new example of violence and injustice, at every refugee camp bombed, at every killing, every arrest, every act of humiliation, every insult, every house bulldozed, every family dispossessed, every orchard uprooted, every olive tree chopped down, every child terrified, every mother mourning.

Sometimes, often, I do not want to hear about it anymore. Or about the corruption, the lies, the wickedness of those in power everywhere in the world who allow the injustice to continue. Sometimes, like Job's wife, I want to curse god and turn my back on the place.

But I know I cannot. I need to carry the story of a gentle place in the past into a gentle future not mutilated by terror, exhaustion and hatred.

George Makhlouf

George Makhlouf, born in West Jerusalem in 1943, is an Eastern Orthodox priest who was ordained in Jerusalem in 1985 and has served in Ramallah and New York. He received his education in Terra Sancta School in Jerusalem and Collège des Frères in Bethlehem, followed by theological studies in Jerusalem, France and Lebanon. He now lives in Duluth, Georgia, USA.

No Room in my Luggage

Every immigration has a story behind it. In the fall of 1994, I received a message from the Antiochian Orthodox Christian Archdiocese of North America suggesting that I serve in New York state because they needed someone who was bilingual to minister to immigrants whom they called the 'Zero Generation'. I had a good mastery of Arabic and my English was not bad so I thought I could manage, and agreed to come out of concern for our people living in diaspora. I shipped my body to the US, but there was no room for my soul, heart and mind in my luggage. I left them in Palestine where they belong and will stay forever. These I had to leave back home, but other things I needed so much I insisted on bringing them with me: my legacy, my love for my country, my commitment to its cause, nostalgia and good memories of my life in Palestine.

My two sons and my wife (who has since passed away) also came to America. My younger son got a scholarship from Hiram College in Ohio and left six months before the idea of me serving in the Antiochian Archdiocese of North America came to mind. My other son, who was studying biochemistry at Birzeit University, followed with his mother six months after I left. It is much easier for the younger generation to adapt and acquire a new culture than the older generation. My sons were less homesick than their mother and me. Since their early childhood they had focused on education and they studied hard in their new country to become what they wanted to be: a physician and an attorney. My wife and I are proud of what we have given to this country, we have given Palestinian brains. For me, it is worthy of note that after all these years in the US my sons have kept relations with their classmates and friends from Palestine not only back home, but worldwide. They have joined Arabic churches and are friends with young Palestinians and Arab Americans, as well as other Americans from different backgrounds, but mostly with Arabs.

A news reporter once came to our house to interview my wife. On that same day the Israeli Occupation Forces raided the City Hall of Ramallah. To my wife the municipality of Ramallah was her second home, for she had worked for the city for thirty years, since she had left high school. The reporter was stunned to see tears on her cheeks while she watched the news on TV. With the story he published about Palestinians there was a picture of her with tears running down her cheeks while she watched the news on TV. When she passed away, the reporter called me saying he wanted to write an obituary about her life. The first thing he wrote about was the time he came to our house on the day the Israeli army raided the Ramallah City Hall. My wife, who was always surrounded by parishioners who loved and cherished her in New York, used to cry on the dates of religious festivals that we used to celebrate in Ramallah.

Our identity is the awareness of our lost identity. To be a proud Palestinian is much more than being patriotic. It is the struggle to prove who we are and what we are. When we come to the US we meet people who know nothing about this part of the world. Some don't even know the difference between Palestine and Pakistan. When we say, 'I am from Jerusalem', they ask, 'Are you Jewish?' Very few people search to find the truth that they would never get from the media or from the mouths of politicians, for some of whom we are an 'invented people'. Evangelicals are also abusing the Holy Scriptures by using the word of God for political reasons. They confuse the metaphoric, spiritual Israel with the State of Israel as a political entity founded on the Land of Palestine in 1948. These challenges might make us frustrated and hopeless, but there is no room for hopelessness: perseverance is the only way to achieve our goal of freedom and justice.

America is a nation of immigrants, and we are part of this nation. We do not own Palestine yet, but as American citizens we own this country and we call it our country. America is my country and Palestine is my homeland, and for this reason we have to be good citizens and faithful to our country. To be Palestinian American is a responsibility to both our country and our homeland. As citizens who know their full rights, guaranteed by the US Constitution, we can unite and stand up to those who do not recognise our existence as a people. We are not a mistake of history, we are the native indigenous people of the Land of Canaan. Also as Americans, we are contributing to the progress of our country by educating our children so they can go on to serve society. President John F. Kennedy said, 'Ask not what your country can do for you; ask what you can do for your country.' One has to agree. We all have to do something for the progress of our country, but at the same time our country should be appreciative of our contribution and, as part of this country, we have to demand fairness when dealing with our people at home.

Bashir Makhoul

Bashir Makhoul is Pro-Vice Chancellor at Birmingham City University and professor in art and design. He was the former Rector of Winchester School of Art, University of Southampton. He is a practising artist and a writer. His work has been exhibited widely internationally, including Venice Biennial Italy, Hayward Gallery, London and Hermitage, St Petersburg. He is the author of books such as Return in Conflict, Palestinian Video Art *and* The Origin of Palestinian Art.

Labyrinth of Memories

The tang of the *za'tar* my mother makes from wild thyme gathered in the hills of Galilee; the soft touch of the white stone I carved as a boy, from those same hills; the breeze in the ancient olive tree I inherited from my father; the music I used to play at weddings; the rhythm of the *dabke* I so enjoyed during those celebrations; my favourite lines from Mahmoud Darwish; and on and on.

I could offer all these things, remembered so clearly, to describe being Palestinian. But committed to paper, private attachments at once become part of a collective cliché. I could add grimmer realities: humiliations and funerals, the friends who became drug addicts, my brother being tortured. But private grief, too, is all too easily co-opted by a public, political rhetoric.

And there is a sense in which being Palestinian is largely a matter of clichéd, collective rhetoric; a national identity brought to the fore by Zionism, the nationalist ideology par excellence. I have witnessed so many examples of the stupidity, shallowness and brutality of nationalism in Israel that I mistrust any form of nationalism, from any quarter. Its value, of course, is in galvanising resistance – and the terrible injustices committed by Israel must be resisted and righted – but it must always be recognised that nationalism itself is also the source of these injustices.

It is usually place of origin that identifies nationality. But how does one avoid confusing origins with beginnings? I am Palestinian, but on my passport it says I was born in Israel. My life began in Israel, but my origins are elsewhere, and that elsewhere is in the same place. Growing up in Israel meant that simply calling myself Palestinian was a provocation. My national identity was at odds with the state in which I lived and I, like all Palestinian Israelis, was constantly reminded of this. Palestinians in Israel are tolerated. To be tolerated in your own land . . . It is clearly better than trying to survive in Gaza but, although they are not subjected to the same barbarism, they get to see how deeply rooted racism is against Palestinians throughout Israeli society.

For many people in this kind of situation nationalism becomes very attractive, offering collective comfort and security rooted in a romanticised past. But I have no desire to attach myself to some fixed point in time and space with my bag of memories. It's fine to be a bit sentimental about the past, or take comfort from certain kinds of food, or enjoy the subtle complexities of one's own language, but not to cling to it. The security we gain from national identity is illusory. I want my identity always to be open to question, and to present a challenge to the identity of others. Better to think of oneself not as *being* Palestinian but of *becoming* Palestinian.

And so I find it difficult to write about being Palestinian, and I shrink from the corny nostalgia of a nationalistic reverie. Better to keep it to myself. From this position, I find myself as an artist always at a crossroads of unavoidable contradictions: wishing to keep my memories, feelings and views private, yet making art which draws upon my cultural heritage, inevitably exposes these things to the public gaze. My art is a narrative of cultural identity, but a dynamic, emergent cultural identity. I try to reframe the culturally resonant patterns of the past, looking for new patterns for the future. I find patterns in familiar things: the scatter of olive leaves, the bullet-ridden ruins and spilt blood of the old conflict, and fix on their newness and hope. I overlay images of the present on images of the past, not because I want to go back, not because I want to take shelter in the past, but in order to find a trajectory, a forward direction, a sense of emergence and a sense of the future, reclaimed, fresh and exciting. A sense of becoming.

It is easy enough for me, of course, from the security of British citizenship, to maintain such an attitude. For those languishing in refugee camps or trapped under Israeli occupation, a sense of national identity and national solidarity is much more important. These people are being punished for being Palestinian, and for no other reason.

I look forward to the day when Palestinian nationalism is no longer necessary. But this cannot happen until Israelis decide that Zionism is no longer necessary. Palestinians and Israelis already live together on the same land; the problem is that one group is imposing a brutal colonial regime on the other, and it is this that needs to be addressed, not the fulfilment of some imaginary national destiny. It is dangerous to confuse a desire for some mystical homeland to which we will one day return with a desire for justice.

It is not in the near future, but one day there will be a binational state and Palestinians and Israelis will have to live together as equals. I believe that becoming Palestinian not only entails an acceptance of that, but is also a state of mind that will help to bring it about. The ideological basis of Zionism must be relentlessly challenged, not simply countered with more nationalism. The day I am imagining is one when it really doesn't matter what being Palestinian might mean, and when the flimsy security of national identity is superseded by the real security of a passport and the full rights of free citizenship for all who have truly become Palestinian.

Sinan Suleiman Malley

Sinan Suleiman Malley is a fourth-year medical student at the University of Edinburgh. He was born in Edinburgh to Palestinian parents and attended George Heriot's School. Sinan has travelled to several Arab and European countries as well as South Africa.

Palestine the Brave

'So, where are you from?' is a question I have encountered for as long as I can remember. Every so often I invite the individual to have a guess, resulting in a colourful array of responses, some close, others very far off. I suppose it is unfair asking them to somehow deduce that despite my accent varying little from the next Scot waiting in line for his can of 'Irn-Bru', and my surname giving off the scent of a four-leaf clover with its resemblance to the Irish surname 'O'Malley', I am in fact Palestinian. A Scottish Palestinian who is not split between the two poles of this label, but one who celebrates their communion as befits a person whose roots lie in the Holy Land, with all the suffering and misery this 'holiness' has created for us Palestinians.

Why should a person born thousands of miles away from this land inherit this suffering and misery, I often wonder? Is it a matter of destiny? Or is it the bloody-mindedness of my parents who never tired of letting me and my elder brother know we were Palestinian: speaking Arabic in front of our friends; eating Palestinian food (which I now love) when a pizza would have been infinitely preferable; joining demonstrations for all kinds of causes instead of going to the cinema or playing games at home; helping out on fundraising days for the Scottish branch of Medical Aid for Palestinians with people who seemed as ancient as the olive trees of Palestine; watching news that was often painful and depressing; and caring about the suffering of downtrodden people wherever they were, as if being Palestinian was not enough suffering on its own?

How I wish I was born carefree! But would I, in all truth, not want to be Palestinian? The answer is 'no'. Being Palestinian is non-negotiable. I can't tell you why because I don't know why!

Being Palestinian in Scotland involves a lot of toing and froing between here and there to have Palestinian-ness instilled in you. Our summers spent as a family when I was younger involved trips to visit relatives living in Jordan where we would stay at my grandparents' homes. Their exuberant and zesty characters were like no other: heart-warming yet hilarious, and their Palestinian accents and sense of dress were testament to their strong sense of heritage and identity. Having developed a love for both my grandmothers' Palestinian dishes from when I was a child, and a fondness for the warmth and generosity of my aunties, uncles and cousins, I came to understand the strong sense of unity that Palestinian identity brings to the family, a unity that is beautifully displayed when the whole extended family, young and old, congregate around the dinner table in multitude.

Those special occasions instilled in me a love for my mother's Palestinian cooking back in Scotland. As a university student living away from my parents, I have attempted to learn how to make some of those dishes for my friends, though I will need a little more practice if I am to do them justice and give them a true taste of Palestine, not just as a culinary experience but as a cause that transcends the limits of its geography. Palestine as food! Palestine as food for thought! Palestine as a family bond and as a site of friendship!

My visits to Palestine as a child have helped to shape my view on the Israeli–Palestinian conflict as an adult. I remember my second visit in 1998 when I was just six years old very clearly. As we approached the Allenby Bridge crossing to the West Bank from Jordan, I felt a mixture of fear and anger at the prospect of having to cross a military-controlled border, restricting our freedom to simply move in and out of the country we called 'home'. Watching the scene at this crossing, with surly-looking and bored armed men and women watching us, gave me a lasting taste of the realities facing Palestinians living in the occupied territories. As a Palestinian in the diaspora I can avoid this reality but, at an emotional level, I cannot be shielded from it. It is part of what it means to be a member of a people whose most basic rights are questioned, even denied, and it is this which makes you determined to be a Palestinian rather than just happening to be one.

Despite the trip getting off to a less than ideal start in my mind, I thoroughly enjoyed exploring several cities and towns in Palestine, especially

Old Jerusalem. Having grown up in Scotland with pictures of the Old City, seeing it for real was worth a thousand pictures. The shade and light, serenity and human energy, scents and aromas, cacophony of sounds and my father's memory lanes all created a lasting impression on me. Our trips to the Dome of the Rock and the Church of the Holy Sepulchre were especially memorable. The rich architecture of the Church and the impressive golden crown of the Dome stood out when we looked out across the Old City from the top of my father's school. Despite how close the two monuments looked from there, the walk between the two felt like an eternity on an empty stomach. I made it a challenge to try to see above the top of each monument, but I often became distracted by their architectural intricacies, and surprised by how well they had survived the passing of time. Such resilience was reflected in every Palestinian we met, whose faces bore the scars of their painful reality. The result of my challenge was one sore neck, and one child in and from a faraway place inspired to celebrate that resilience in all that matters to him.

Visiting Palestine as a child afforded me the opportunity to taste and experience the culture and beauty of a place that was home. I remember the journeys from Jerusalem to Ramallah that we made almost daily in order to eat Rukab's ice cream, a well-known delicacy of Ramallah. My favourite flavours were mango, strawberry and vanilla. The ice cream is made with gum arabic, which made each lick stretch before my eyes for what seemed like miles. Or our encounter with a waiter at a restaurant in 'Akka who, elated at meeting Scottish Palestinians, gave us a generous portion of falafel on the house, 'the best falafel in the world' we were told. To this day it is the benchmark against which I rate falafel I come across anywhere. The task of finding citrus fruits as sweet as Palestinian oranges is something I am yet to accomplish. I developed a love for satsumas as a child. I remember when my father bought me a bag of them to enjoy on a walk through the Meadows in Edinburgh one day. He recalls walking ahead of me with my brother and soon after turning around to find that I had left a trail of satsuma peel on the ground behind me as far as the eye could see. Every time I walk through the Meadows now I recall the 'satsuma peel trail' and my mind travels thousands of miles away to Palestine.

I visited Jordan for a few days in 2013. One of the highlights of my visit was floating effortlessly in the Dead Sea, covered from head to toe in the mud freshly dug from the sea bed. Watching the sun set over Palestine and seeing the flickering lights of Jericho at night across the Dead Sea allowed me time to reflect upon 'my Palestine'. A Palestine of memories, some inherited and others archived from family visits. A Palestine of commitment to causes that extend beyond Palestine itself to a resistance of occupation and oppression in all its forms and wherever it occurs. A Palestine that doesn't let go. A Palestine glowing with a distant light in the depth of my Scottish winters!

Khalil Marrar

Khalil Marrar is professor of political and justice studies, specialising in the intersection between public policy and foreign affairs. He authored The Arab Lobby and US Foreign Policy *and* Middle East Conflicts: The Basics, *and various articles, chapters and reviews. He has lectured on Arab and Muslim as well as American, comparative, global and Middle East politics, and is a contributor to various media.*

From Ajjur to America: Rootedness in Diaspora

Being Palestinian in diaspora has always been a bittersweet experience. I feel a sweet sense of connection to the pre-*Nakba* Palestine of my parents, who trace their ancestry to the land at least seven hundred years back. Through the memories of my mother, born to a long line of farmers, I imagine the fertile soil out of which almost every growing plant was edible: the delicious oregano, basil and mint, plucked from the land and served with steaming taboon bread made of recently harvested wheat and freshly pressed olive oil; the home-grown figs, oranges, cactus fruit and olives my father had enjoyed since he was a boy; the beauty of the land and sea; the difficult but satisfying work necessitated by everyday survival; the large extended family, all together. Being Palestinian in diaspora means struggling not to forget my family's memories.

Being Palestinian also means inheriting a sense of profound loss. With the *Nakba* came the destruction of Ajjur, my family's thriving village, and with it the end of a way of life. Family ties faded as branches scattered across the Earth. Many simply relocated, within and outside of refugee camps, but some members were lost forever in the struggle for Palestine, such as my uncle who I know only through the portrait hanging above the fireplace in the small Mississippi River town I call home. What it means to be Palestinian in diaspora is therefore different for me than for previous generations of my family. I was not born in Palestine. I did not grow up there. I really don't know 'Palestine', except for what I have seen on occasional visits, such as the heartbreaking ruins of Ajjur contrasted with the ancient beauty of Jerusalem. Being Palestinian for me means carrying the loss of my family, and with it a sense of unrootedness.

Being Palestinian in diaspora means grappling with a loss of control over my own circumstances. It manifests in the preference of closeness over distance; the choice of domestic comforts over adventures abroad; a sense of gratitude for every person, place and organisation that offers refuge. It means a longing for things reminiscent of Palestine, such as *dabke* and falafel, and an identity torn between one place and another, accentuated by deep nostalgia and an inclination towards the familiar. Being Palestinian also includes a bit of the American pioneering spirit – wandering, yet constantly seeking the comforts of home.

And this leads to the bitter part. My existence is both a testament to my family's and my people's survival, yet that fact is too often a problem for others. Because of the charged political context in the US surrounding the Arab–Israeli conflict, honouring my family's history as other immigrants do is sometimes met with suspicion. I feel a sense of hesitation each time a stranger asks, 'Where are you from?'

At the same time, America has offered me a way forward, a synthesis of sorts that allows me the liberty to be grounded in multiple cultures. As a 'Palestinian American' I try to embrace both sides of my identity, the part of Jerusalem hummus and Hebron olives and the part of Chicago hotdogs and New Orleans Bananas Foster. Being Palestinian in diaspora has for me and my family meant aspiring to return to Palestine yet making a home elsewhere, trying to make sense of what could have been and what actually is, and navigating towards a home I have never been to and, because of the conflict, may never reach, in order to comprehend the origins of my identity.

Being Palestinian in diaspora is difficult, if not dangerous. I don't live in the West Bank or Gaza and therefore have no experience of the appalling conditions there, but I too face challenges, the biggest of which is speaking out about the conflict and ways of ending it. Ultimately for me, to be Palestinian in diaspora is hoping for and working towards rootedness based on a sense of connection to two communities. And perhaps also that my efforts might in some small way matter for those who remain, simply, Palestinian.

Dina Matar

Dina Matar is Senior Lecturer in Political Communication at the Centre for Film and Media Studies at the School of Oriental and African Studies (SOAS), University of London. She works on the relationship between culture, communication and politics, with a special focus on Palestine, Lebanon and Syria. She is the author of What it Means to be Palestinian: Stories of Palestinian Peoplehood *(2010) and co-editor of* Narrating Conflict in the Middle East: Discourse, Image and Communication Practices in Palestine and Lebanon *(2013).*

In, but not Of

I had thought writing about 'Being Palestinian' would be easy. I could jot down some thoughts that occupy me much of the time, as a Palestinian and as an academic, and string a few sentences together to provide a narrative that can capture the multiple feelings and experiences that, for me, are all about what it means to be Palestinian in Britain. However, the more I tried to think about this and the more I tried to begin writing down my thoughts, the harder it became to provide a coherent reflection that is both true and meaningful. I could not think where to start, as writing about being Palestinian is not merely about belonging or longing, or home and homeland, nor is it an argument about the uniqueness of the Palestinian experience and story, but rather a complex narrative of multiple experiences, memories, feelings and senses that shift and change according to various situations.

Like thousands of other Palestinians in Britain, my personal experiences are not exceptionally painful. In fact, unlike thousands of other Palestinians, my family and I did not suffer dispossession and the humiliation of being forced out of our home, or the constant fear of being squeezed out or into constantly diminishing spaces of historic Palestine and elsewhere. I moved to Britain at the end of 1988 with my English husband and my son, and have been living in a London suburb ever since, apart from the three years I spent in the United States in the mid-1990s.

In those early days in Britain, my reflections about being a Palestinian did not cause me much anxiety as they were only visible to, and sensed by, me. I did not talk much about my roots or where I came from as I attended to mundane details of everyday life in an active and demanding city. I was busy balancing a hectic career as a journalist and editor with home duties in the 'fixed' and 'stable' territory I found myself immersed in. I don't remember feeling particularly envious or aware of those around me who had lived in the same place all their lives, or those who truly 'belonged', but I sometimes felt the lack of 'fixity' or immersion in a place. Palestine for me was also a shifting space – it did not seem to represent a total image, either in my memories or on those occasions when I would watch a television programme with images from Palestine. It was somehow fragmented, as a memory, accentuated to a certain extent by the fact that I did not visit, finding excuses in a busy schedule and bringing up my son. However, I did maintain a relationship to it through an obsession with news and through calling friends and family to exchange reports, to find out what was missing in the grand narrative of politics and endless talk about what was going to happen next. This practice continues until today.

For various reasons I did not go and visit like many others did following the ill-advised Oslo peace process. I was determined to wait until something more tangible happened on the road to imagined statehood. In 2007, I finally made my first visit home for thirty years and started to go back more regularly, arriving through the River Jordan crossing. I had a good excuse: fieldwork for a book on Palestinian memories and experiences since the 1948 *Nakba*. I met and talked to many different people, old and young, men and women, for hours on end. I was invited to homes, given food and coffee and made to feel I was at home simply because I was prepared to listen.

When the Second Palestinian Intifada broke out in 2000, followed by the September 11 attacks in the US in 2001, the US-led 'war on terror' campaign and the atrocious Israeli incursions into the West Bank, all of which were televised and mediated in diverse ways and forms, I began to feel a sense of disconnect with my surroundings and a certain restlessness that propelled me to become more engaged. I did not have these feelings all the time, but on occasions they were overwhelming enough to make me feel different from everyone else around me and to want to express my 'difference' in diverse ways. I talked to whoever asked me questions, went to protests and began to actively research Palestinian identity in diaspora in Britain and some parts of the Arab world.

Thinking about it now, it is difficult to say precisely whether these feelings were related to the fact that I did not feel England was home, though I was often told I had 'become' English and that I did not 'look' Palestinian, and that I had acquired some aspects of behaviour and modes of speech that were not entirely 'Arab'. I often thought of myself as something of a hybrid migrant that is in, but not of, the situation they find themselves in. It is difficult to say whether these feelings had to do with the realisation that I could not easily explain to 'others' why or how I felt 'different' when, in reality, I do not feel as the 'Other'. But it certainly has something to do with a determination to counter the Israeli narrative that almost always paints you as the 'alien other', and their continuous attempts to deny Palestinians their right to their name: Palestinians. You cannot escape this. And you cannot escape questions about why you are here; why you left your homeland; why the Palestinians did not stay in their homes; why you cannot make peace with the Israelis; why you cannot forget or forgive; why you cannot have peace among yourselves; and why you keep 'causing trouble' wherever you go.

Nabil Matar

Nabil Matar received his BA and MA at the American University of Beirut, and his PhD at the University of Cambridge. He has taught at the University of Jordan, the American University of Beirut and Florida Institute of Technology. Since 2007, he has been Presidential Professor in the English Department at the University of Minnesota.

Lurching at Jericho

Being Palestinian is a pain in the neck.

I

Being a Palestinian means belonging to a land that is in no current world atlas – not even those printed in Palestine.

And so, a Palestinian is an adjective with no referent.

Which is why, being Palestinian defies empiricism.

And the Israelis.

II

Being a Palestinian means loving history because:

Ottoman *defters* and British mandate statistics,

Manger and *Mi'raj*,

Edward Said and Mahmoud Darwish,

all confirm Palestine.

And Palestine glitters in the eyes of a shoe-shining boy in a Lebanon refugee camp: he swears in 2006 that his village is Baysamun – which only survives on page 437 of Walid Khalidi's *All That Remains . . .* of Palestine.

III

Being a Palestinian means being no island all to the self. Where there are peoples recollecting past horrors or keening for submerged villages, the Palestinian pitches his home.

At least I have, adding Palestine to the 500 nations of America, and touching with hesitant fingers the bayonet wounds in the flesh of my Armenian friend's grandfather. I listened to dirges at the foot of the Aswan dam.

To Chaco Canyon and the Nubian Nile, a Palestinian journeys with his portable Palestine,

all the way to the slopes of Ararat.

IV

Being a Palestinian means not figuring out how parents, who went through the terror of the Haganah, could still believe in God.

But they did,

and justified the ways of God to

themselves

(and confused the hell out of me.

How true Philip's ditty, 'They fuck you up, your mum and dad/They may not mean to, but they do').

The markers on their graves read, 'At home with Christ',

among the *shammūtī* orange groves of

Florida.

V

Being a Palestinian means arguing with starry-eyed children.

Why should they not disobey parents or covet their neighbour's bicycle? Their grandparents' house in Nazareth was stolen

by thieves with Bibles.

South of Palestine was when He first pronounced: 'You shall not steal.'

Not implore, beg, beseech, bribe, importune and hug the thieves to please

stop stealing more land and building more colonies.

And claiming falafel as their national dish.

Or hummus.

Or Palestine.

Being Palestinian is a pain in the neck.

'Break it',

as He blows the horn

and lurches at Jericho.

Epiphany 2011

Alaa Milbes

Alaa Milbes was born in Jerusalem and has spent her life between Southern California and Palestine. After receiving her BA from the University of California, Riverside and an MA from Columbia University, she moved back to Palestine to work for the United Nations and is now a college instructor and communications consultant.

Rolling Grape Leaves on a Map of the World

'We're going home next summer.' Home being Palestine, of course. You see, although my parents' families left Palestine before the *Nakba*, they continued to go back, building homes, teaching their children Arabic and ensuring they understood the culture of the country my siblings and I call home. Creating a home, learning the language and understanding our cultural identity are what my parents taught me it means to be a Palestinian. Now, in my mid-twenties, I have a different perspective.

I was born in Jerusalem, raised between Palestine and California, and went to graduate school in New York, then moved back to Palestine and worked in Jerusalem for two years. For me, being Palestinian has meant different things at different stages of my life.

In 2002, at the age of thirteen, my family moved back to California after three years in Palestine. Although the Second Intifada had begun, being Palestinian then did not mean anything to me. It was in those first few weeks of high school, when schools were commemorating the first anniversary of the September 11 attacks, that I began to identify strongly with my Palestinian identity.

As a recently arrived international student, racism from teachers and peers surfaced. Statements like 'I don't know how they do it over there, but here, things are different' made me realise that I indeed was 'different'. In those early teenage years, I knew on a subconscious level what post-colonial studies and Edward Said would give me a vocabulary for years later – that I was 'the

Other'. This self-awareness led me on a long path of club organising, debates and politics.

At the University of California, Riverside (UCR), being Palestinian meant making lifelong friends, some of whom would later become family. Most Palestinian-American students there were of similar backgrounds. Their families were from neighbouring villages and had emigrated to Latin America and then to the United States. In general, the outstanding diversity at UCR meant that my 'Palestinian-ness' was not threatened, and I was relatively comfortable expressing myself. Palestine was always in reach. Many of us had either visited or lived in Palestine and were in the United States for economic reasons. As a young woman still in her teens, these family friends were already part of my Palestine in the US.

It was in New York that I truly started questioning my identity. When people asked where I was from, I was not sure what to say. Should I call myself Palestinian? Arab? Muslim? American? Am I from California or Palestine? I would later start naming both. In New York, being Palestinian meant establishing a close-knit community of young men and women with whom I shared holidays, started a Palestinian *dabke* group and, most importantly, spent hours rolling stuffed grape leaves during the more stressful periods of our lives. Unlike my community at UCR, these Palestinians were refugees whose families had fled to Syria, Lebanon and the Gulf, among other places. It was in New York that I was introduced to the 'other' Palestine, that before then I had only heard stories about from my grandparents, documentaries and history books. It was in New York that I was introduced to rich and poor Palestinians, educated and non-educated, the diplomats and the teachers. In New York, they were my Palestine.

In Lebanon, being Palestinian meant that in the Shatila refugee camp, my outdated *fellahi* (peasant) dialect was a source of happiness to the older generation of Palestinian refugees whose children and grandchildren have ceased to use it. It meant having my favourite meal, *maklooba*, taste and be served the same way in the refugee camp as it was at another friend's house a few miles away in one of the most expensive neighbourhoods in Lebanon. Both families had fled Palestine to Lebanon. One was lucky enough to have had a family member attend school in the United States, obtain a degree and move to the Gulf states for work, while the other was not so lucky and forced to endure life in the cramped refugee camp without education, working long hours in an extremely harsh environment. Both of these families welcomed me into their homes with open arms, one in the guest bedroom in their home in an upscale neighbourhood of Beirut and another in the small yet beautiful living room of their cramped home in Shatila. On my last night there, the Shatila community hosted Palestinian singer Abu Arab. That night, our different upbringings were temporarily forgotten as we sang familiar folk songs like '*Zareef el Tool*' and '*Hadi Ya Bahar Hadi*', about a common topic of loss and exile. Two families, two paths, with one thing in common: a land they have yet to see and are denied due to their Palestinian background. In Lebanon, they were my Palestine.

In modern-day Palestine, being Palestinian means summer trips to our town north of Ramallah, al-Mazrah al-Sharqia, where endless weddings and parties make you forget about the occupation (if temporarily) and fall in love with the other, often forgotten, Palestine. It is that fact that draws people 'home' from hundreds of cities and several countries to reunite, if briefly, for the summer. And despite having left Palestine before their teenage years, many, like my grandfather, have retained relationships with school and neighbourhood friends. Being Palestinian means walking into a market in the village and people recognising me as from '*dar Hijaz*' (the Hijaz family) because I remind them of one of my aunts or uncles. A friend, whose family members are refugees from a village in the Galilee, related a story once about a visit he made to his ancestral village. An older woman who had lived through the *Nakba* told him: 'My son, *al-Nakba* is not the loss of land or property, it is the fact that when I look at your face, I do not know who you or your parents are.' In al-Mazrah, we avoided the dispossession of 1948 as a village occupied in 1967. Still, although the older generations of Al-Mazrah recognise my family by looking at my face, I cannot say the same for them or their children and grandchildren. Today, Al-Mazrah and the stories I have of growing up in this town represent my Palestine.

Being Palestinian is not a place or a thing. It is the relationships that define us as a diaspora community trying to assimilate into the lives that have been forced upon us without forgetting our 'Palestinian-ness'. Palestine is home, whether in Southern California, New York, Jerusalem or Beirut. Palestine lives in us. It is not a border, because if we thought of it as such, then our occupiers will have won.

Fouad Moughrabi

Fouad Moughrabi was born in Ain Karem in 1942. He grew up in Bethlehem and attended the Christian Brothers School (Ecole des Frères). He attended Duke University on a scholarship, where he received his BA and MA. He lived in France for a number of years and finished his doctorate at the University of Grenoble. He taught political science and retired in 2013 as head of the political science department at the University of Tennessee, Chattanooga. He founded the Qattan Center for Educational Research and Development in Ramallah and served as its director for a number of years. He also served as a visiting professor at Birzeit University.

An Act of Resistance

Some years ago as I was about to give a lecture on Palestine at some American university, a curious thought occurred to me: were it not for the Palestine cause, I might have studied something I loved, such as classical guitar, instead of political science. Then I would have travelled about giving concerts to entertain and make people happy instead of talking about the Palestine problem and getting them depressed. I chose to study politics in order to help liberate Palestine. For Palestinians of my generation, Palestine has always been a sentence. Everything in one's life is subjected to the overriding business of defending and promoting the cause of the Palestinian people.

Unlike other sentences that one suffers grudgingly, this one was in fact welcomed gladly. Taking on the challenge gave meaning to one's life. In reality, if Palestine was not a cause, I most probably would have spent my youth fighting against apartheid in South Africa or some other similarly noble cause. That is why I almost instinctively stood for civil rights and against the war in Vietnam during my early student days.

What does it mean to grow up Palestinian?

The very first thing one has to deal with is the sense of radical dislocation and permanent loss. This is as true in the case of 1948 refugees, like me, as it is in the case of others who have remained in their own homes and whose existence is constantly threatened. One goes through life as if on a journey, refusing to settle down in any real sense. Even if one does settle down, one still feels that this is all temporary, that sooner or later one will be forced to move on again. The sense of loss does not relate to material things: toys, one's favourite pillow or other belongings. Neither is it a romantic kind of yearning. It means losing one's bearings and one's spot in the world even though you may have chosen not to live on it for long. But it will always be the spot where you feel natural: the colour and feel of the soil, the olive tree, the fig tree, the wild flowers that burst through the arid landscape in early spring, the old house where you were born and grew up, where you had your first cup of coffee with your mother on the steps in the early morning hours. It is the spot where you will want to be buried when you die because that is where you will enjoy eternal rest. Even after spending more than forty years of my life in the United States, I cannot possibly feel that I will rest in peace if I were buried anywhere on this continent. This is not and can never be my spot on earth.

This is precisely how my mother felt. When she passed away on Signal Mountain, Tennessee, I had to take her back to Jerusalem and bury her in the Islamic cemetery adjoining the Dome of the Rock. And this is also how my late friend and colleague Professor Ibrahim Abu-Lughod felt. When he passed away in Ramallah, a number of us worked very hard to honour his wishes and have him buried in his hometown of Jaffa, right next to his father and one of his brothers in the cemetery by the sea where he used to swim as a young man before 1948.

Because we are always on a journey, we have become a people of many goodbyes. We are always either welcoming or saying farewell to someone, often many times during the year. Over time we learn not to shed a tear as we say goodbye. We do it stoically, with dignity and with full confidence that we will definitely be seeing each other again. We have also become experts at controlling our emotions and our anger. How can we deal with all the sadness that happens around us? The constant and continuous killing and destruction as well as the repeated 'glorious' defeats that we have been suffering since 1948, the year of our first, but by no means our last, or only, *Nakba*.

As a Palestinian, even with an American passport, let alone someone whose passport is issued by the Palestinian Authority, one is always suspect. A long time ago I used to be annoyed at the humiliations at borders and checkpoints until a chance encounter at Allenby Bridge with an old Palestinian man who shared a small cubbyhole with me as we were both being searched by Israeli guards. He told me not to fret or be angry, 'they' do this because they are afraid. All of a sudden I felt some mischievous relief at the notion that 'they' live in a perpetual state of fear and most likely will do so for many years to come. The circle of fear has now expanded to include the United States of America, a great country that has, unfortunately, become 'Israelised' in so many ways.

That is why living and working in America has always felt like living in enemy territory. One is compelled to remind oneself of some important historical facts: for the settler colonialists who carried out a major act of genocide against Native Americans, the suffering of the Palestinians appears almost insignificant. Their natural inclination is to side with other settler colonialists, the bearers of Western civilisation.

Above all, being Palestinian means being engaged in various acts of resistance. Everything you do becomes an act of resistance: what you write, what you buy, with whom you associate and how you behave in daily life. Even the act of lovemaking becomes an act of resistance because in the process you affirm and reaffirm life and define your existence and your identity. I am a human being like the rest. I eat, I laugh, I make love and I dream. My mere existence as a Palestinian is a threat to 'them' and this is, after all, a good thing. Who are they? I won't even bother to make a list because they know who they are and the rest of the world also knows. Do I hate them? No. Because the energy spent on hating them is better spent on something more useful and constructive.

Being Palestinian has also become a metaphor throughout much of the world for the search for justice, not vengeance. This is why people in faraway places respond knowingly when they hear Mahmoud Darwish's poetry, or when they watch Elia Suleiman's wonderful film *All That Remains*. I continue to cling to the hope that America, my reluctantly adopted country, will hopefully someday catch up with the rest of the world.

Michel Moushabeck

Michel S. Moushabeck is a writer, editor, publisher and musician. His books include Kilimanjaro: A Photographic Journey to the Roof of Africa *and* Beyond the Storm: A Gulf Crisis Reader. *He is the founder of Interlink Publishing, a Massachusetts-based independent publishing house. He serves on the board of trustees of The International Prize for Arabic Fiction (IPAF), and is a founding member of Layaali Arabic Music Ensemble. He is the recipient of The Palestinian Heritage Foundation Achievement Award (2011).*

The *Mukhtar* and I: A Day with my Grandfather in the Old City

*I*f *someone in a pub asked me to describe my family's story in one sentence I would say: exile and starting over; exile and starting over; and exile and starting over. I would probably add a clarification that I did not repeat those words three times because I had too many beers. But my family's experience of multiple exiles – from Katamon, to East Jerusalem, to Beirut, to New York – is not unique; it is but one of the many sad episodes of 'being Palestinian'. Our stories of exile, displacement and injustice will live on, as will all our beautiful memories of our homeland. This is one such story I wrote for my Palestinian-American children to share one day with their children and their children's children.*

The morning my grandfather and I took a walk together in the Old City, he turned to me and said: 'Today you get to spend the day helping Sido (grandfather) at the *qahwe* (café).'

The year was 1966 and I was barely eleven years old. We were living in Beirut. Often during the summertime my mother would take me, together with my younger brother and my sister, to visit Tata (grandmother) and Sido in the Old City of Jerusalem. Sido Issa Toubbeh – a stern-looking, *tarboosh*-wearing (fez), *za'oot*-sniffing (snuff), narghile-puffing, mustachioed man – was the *Mukhtar* (literally, 'the chosen'), the head of the Eastern Orthodox Christian Arab community in Jerusalem.

As a young boy, I dreaded staying at my grandparents' residence. I was petrified by the sight of all the ugly, bearded monks with foot-long keys who occupied the Greek Orthodox Convent, where my grandparents lived after their forced exile from their home in Katamon. The intoxicating smell of incense and burning candles, the spooky, narrow, cobblestoned alleyways of the convent grounds, the robed priests roaming around in the dark – all contributed to a feeling of anxiety and discomfort I could do without. But on that morning, which was unlike any other morning, a sense of joy swept over me.

My memories of that day are as vivid and bright as a silver coin in the sun. Sido and I, hand in hand, walked through the streets of Jerusalem, stopping every few paces to greet people he knew and those who knew of him. Along the way we passed the market, a bustling collection of colourful fruit and vegetable vendors. I instantly felt the flow of musical energy emanating from the place and its people. Music was simply all around: from the unforgettable melodic chanting of the *muezzin*'s call to prayer – often juxtaposed against the ringing of church bells – to fruit and vegetable vendors in the market singing the praises of their pickling cucumbers 'as small as babies' fingers' or prickly pears 'so delicious they melt in your mouth'; from the cheerful foot-thumping sounds of children practising *dabke* to the powerful emotional songs of Oum Kalthoum blasting from transistor radios on windowsills. To this day I am still able to close my eyes and transport myself back. I am still able to smell the delicious food sold by street vendors, especially the wonderfully rich and evocative scent of roasted chestnuts and, of course, the sumptuous sweets drenched in *ater* (sugar syrup) sold at Zalatimo's; I am still able to see the old street photographer with the wooden camera whose head often disappeared underneath a black cloth; still able to touch the olive oil soap stacked in long cylindrical towers at the corner store.

But the one thing that intrigued me most of all, the one person who had a profound influence on me, was the juice vendor who walked with his body leaning forward and his Bordeaux fez with the black tassels tipped back. Not only did he carry a big tank filled with *sous*, *jallab* and lemonade on his back as he travelled by foot from neighbourhood to neighbourhood, but he was a percussionist of the highest degree. I was fascinated by how he announced his arrival, and mesmerised by how he played beautiful, intricate rhythmic patterns using brass cups and saucers, to entertain customers and alert them of his presence – rhythms very similar to the ones belly dancers moved their hips to in Beirut restaurants. From that moment on I was hooked. I would sit on the sidewalk with my eyes fixed on the juice vendor's hands so I could learn his art. Back at the house later on, to my grandmother's horror, I would practise the same rhythms using her china, which produced disastrous results and, it goes without saying, a spanking.

Adjacent to Jaffa Gate was my grandfather's long-established café. Known to family and friends as *al-Mahal* (The Place), and to others as *Qahwet al-Mukhtar*, the café was a renowned Jerusalem institution frequented in its heyday by the Palestinian literati, nicknamed *al-sa'aleek* (the vagabonds). Poets, musicians, historians, storytellers, folks who wanted to be seen in their company, young Palestinians who aspired to be like them, or simply those who just wanted to listen to the exchange of ideas taking place, gathered at *Qahwet al-Mukhtar*.

The café was buzzing with people when my grandfather and I arrived from the market. For the next hour or so Sido attended to the business of recording births, deaths and marriages in his oversized leather books, giving advice in-between and stamping official documents that required his seal. When he was done, he signalled to me with his walking stick to follow him to the café's backyard, a large paved area with rows of plants on each side, a round tiled fountain in the middle surrounded by tables and chairs and a massive cage that housed chickens and over a hundred pigeons.

As we sat in the sun and snacked on watermelon and *Nabulsiyyeh* cheese, he told me funny stories and answered the many questions I had stored up over the years. His answers to silly questions like, 'Why do you wear a *tarboosh* (fez)?' and 'What's that stuff you sniff and makes you sneeze all the time?', and more serious ones like, 'Why did you leave Katamon?' and 'Why did you not fight the *Yahood* (the Jews) when they took your home?', kept me enthralled the whole afternoon. He told me about the bombing that demolished the Samiramis hotel down the road from their house in Katamon and how the blast that Menachem Begin masterminded at the King David Hotel, close to my Uncle Michel's office, instilled fear in the community and was the catalyst that drove many Katamonians to flee their homes. I cried when he told me the story of the massacre that took place at the village of Deir Yassin. A quick change of subject to the art of pigeon-flying restored my smile. And before we headed back home, he gave me an impressive demonstration by releasing all the pigeons and showing me how to fly them in a circle and then guide them back to their cage – all with only the help of a black piece of cloth tied to the end of a long stick. What he failed to tell me was that this exercise was done to attract other flying pigeons to the flock and ultimately back to the cage so that Uncle Mitri could later serve them to the customers.

Back at the house that evening, while my grandfather rested his feet on a chair in the living room, Tata asked me to run over to the neighbours to borrow a bowl of rice. 'What's going down at *beit al-Mukhtar* (the *Mukhtar*'s house)?' asked the neighbour. I shrugged. My guess was that he told another in the neighbourhood, and another told another, and in no time more than twenty-five or so family and friends descended on my grandparents' house, which sent my grandmother – and a dozen or so female helpers – scrambling to the kitchen to prepare food for the guests. The feast and the festive atmosphere were like nothing I'd encountered before. Suddenly musical instruments appeared from nowhere, and poetry became the flavour of the day. While the men sang and played music in the living room, the women danced in the kitchen, and the children shuttled back and forth between the two. In-between solo improvisations on the *oud* (a fretless lute), the *qanun* (a zither-like plucked instrument) and the *nay* (a reed flute), that brought sighs of appreciation, the singer sang soulful *mawwals* (vocal improvisations in dialect) and made up new lyrics to familiar tunes. I recognised many of the rhythms from listening to the juice vendor and I was encouraged to join the musicians on the *riqq* (tambourine). The fun was interrupted when Tata ordered everyone to the dining room table. And what a table it was! There were *kefta*s (meatballs) and kebabs, *hashwet jaaj* (chicken with rice and pine nuts) and *koosa mahshi* (stuffed zucchini), and meze plates as far as the eye could see: hummus, *babaghannouj* (eggplant dip), stuffed vine leaves, glistening black olives, braided white cheese, glossy vegetables, plump nuts and lush juicy fruits. It was like magic: where did it all come from? I wondered.

After dinner we all retired to the living room and the music resumed. This time the men and women danced together to the soothing and hypnotic compositions of Zakaria Ahmad and Sayyid Darweesh, Mohammad Abd el-Wahab and Fareed el-Atrash. And I, naturally exhausted by the events of the day, fell asleep on my grandfather's lap.

Early the next morning a crowd of family and friends lined up at the convent entrance to bid us farewell. We got into the *service* (taxi) that drove us to Amman, and from there back home to Beirut. From the car window I waved goodbye to my teary-eyed Tata and Sido and yelled *kalimera* ('good morning' in Greek) to the bearded monk with foot-long keys.

That was the last time I saw my grandparents; the last time I saw Jerusalem.

Ibrahim Muhawi

Ibrahim Muhawi received his PhD in English literature from the University of California (Davis) in 1969. After 1989 his career emphasis gradually shifted to translation studies and Palestinian and Arabic folklore. He retired from teaching in 2005, but remains active as a scholar and translator.

Parsley, *Miryamiyah*, Rosemary and *Za'tar*[1]

My birthdate of 1937 places me in the middle of the Great Rebellion and on the cusp of major historical changes foretold by ominous partition plans that, like secular prophecies, have all come to pass. Having been born during the period of the Mandate, my birth certificate is in three languages. I see this fact as foretelling my multilingual life as translator, folklorist and literary scholar. I also feel, on the understanding that history repeats itself, that it has historical significance, and may even represent a hope for the future of the country after all the changes that have to take place have taken place.

My originary sense of identity springs from my birthplace of Ramallah. Mahmoud Darwish's poem ''anā min hunāk' ('I'm From There') resonates with all Palestinians who live outside the homeland. There, in Ramallah, I smelt the breezes from the Mediterranean and roamed the rock-strewn hills in spring, red with blooming anemones and green with thyme. There I was part of a seamless community in which everyone was related to everyone else either directly or indirectly. There I ate the Palestinian cuisine expertly prepared by my mother – the cuisine that we (men and women alike) carry with us wherever we go and prepare for friends and loved ones. There I attended folk festivals and wedding celebrations that went on for several nights of *dabke* and song under the trees. (I could not have know then that this immersion in the life of the community would later lead to a lifelong engagement with Palestinian culture.) There, as a schoolboy, I sang the national and youth songs *mawṭinī* ('My Homeland') and *naḥnu al-shabāb* ('We the Youth'). And from there I rode the bus to Jerusalem as a boy of ten, standing next to my father, who was a driver on that line. My first experiences of Jerusalem and the landscape of Palestine beyond Ramallah took place in that bus. The moment when the bus reached the end of the line just beyond the Notre Dame Hostel in the Musrara quarter – a mixed Arab and Jewish neighbourhood – was special because the people were different from Ramallah in their speech and the way they dressed and even the way they looked. Special also was the treat at the end of the line – *ka'k u-beiḍ* (sesame-encrusted bun with a hole in the middle like a doughnut and oven-roasted eggs) with salt and *za'tar* (now so well-known it needs no definition). Jerusalem *ka'k* was like no other.

Childhood wasn't all *ka'k u-beiḍ*, however. Concomitantly, present with me at all times in varying degrees of intensity were the events of 1948, not only the loss of the country that haunts many of us in the moments between sleeping and waking, but unforgettable individual experiences, like the stream of hungry and bedraggled people driven out of Ramla and Lydda (the original home of St George) – men, women and children – stumbling into the town helter-skelter looking for a place to escape the horror of the massacre in the Great Mosque; the terrorist bombing of the King David Hotel, which brought Charlie Moghannam (an employee of the Mandate) home in a coffin; the loss of the family livelihood when the Ramallah–Jerusalem line stopped running; the anticipated attack on the town and the preparations for defence on the outskirts; the palpable fear that Ramallah would fall; the actual attack; its outcome in the form of seventeen dead soldiers laid side by side in a school-yard shed; and the relief that people felt afterwards, when it became obvious the attack had failed. I am entangled in this history; if Ramallah had fallen I would still be entangled in it, but it would be a different history.

The loss of Palestine in 1948 turned us into West Bank Jordanians. Though in our hearts Palestine was not dead, in our mouths it tended to be a quasi-forbidden subject. When I left the homeland in 1954 to study electrical engineering in the US, I had a Jordanian passport in my pocket. Many years later, in 1975, when I returned to Jordan to teach English literature at the University of Jordan, I discovered that people referred to us as 'Belgians'.[2] Much later, when I was at the University of Edinburgh, an English friend whom I had known when I was teaching in Tunisia called from London to say hello. The first words out of his mouth were, 'Welcome home, Ibrahim!'

I was touched by the warmth of the sentiment, but could not help feeling amused by the unintended irony.

After the conquest of the rest of the country in 1967, the sealing of its borders against all Palestinians turned me into an exile. I had by then acquired US citizenship, an advanced degree in English literature and a position at a Canadian university, so though I was technically an exile I did not feel like one. However, the point was driven home with brute force between 1977 and 1980 when I was a member of the English Department at Birzeit University and had to leave the country and return on a tourist visa every three months. Applications for family reunion that would have allowed me to regain my birthright and remain in the country fell on the deaf ears of the Israeli Military Governor. Apparently I was destined to live in exile, part of a national diaspora that spans the globe.

The three years at Birzeit brought about my rebirth into a more fully developed sense of national and cultural identity. I wasn't allowed to remain in Palestine, so the solution was to bring it along wherever I went. My focus henceforth would be on Palestine: its literature, culture and folklore. I never felt that my identity was at stake in teaching English literature, much as I loved the subject, as it is in my present work on Palestinian cultural production both written and oral – our collective memory. This is work that brings the beauty and depth of Palestinian culture to anyone who can read English. Our history and our collective memory are so intertwined that loss of one may lead to loss of the other. Palestine teaches us who to be, and how to be.

Notes

1. A reference to the second line of the traditional English ballad, 'Scarborough Fair': 'parsley, sage, rosemary, and thyme'.
2. There are a number of folk etymologies around the term: that Palestinians are not originally from the region, that *beljiki* ('Belgian') is a corruption of 'Bolshevik', or that *beljiki* is derived from the root BLJ, the acronym for *min barra la-juwwa* (from the outside to the inside).

Nadia Naser-Najjab

Nadia Naser-Najjab, PhD in Middle East Studies, is an associate research fellow at the European Centre of Palestine Studies – Institute of Arab and Islamic Studies, University of Exeter. Her research explores Palestine and the Palestine–Israel conflict. She has extensive teaching experience at Birzeit University, Palestine. In 2010 she was awarded the AMIDEAST 'Teaching Excellence Award' that recognises commitment to teaching and non-traditional class methods.

In Search of a Common Language

We travel like other people, but we return to nowhere.
As if travelling
Is the way of the clouds . . . We have a country of words.
Speak speak so I can put my road on the stone of a stone.
We have a country of words. Speak speak so we may know the end of
this travel.

Mahmoud Darwish, 'We Travel Like Other People'

For many Palestinians, national identity has assumed form and meaning in exile. Whether as refugees, political exiles or economic migrants, Palestinians have sought self-definition in isolation from their homeland. In some respects, exclusion confers certain advantages. Freed from a repressive political environment, exiled Palestinians have simultaneously recreated an idealised Palestine within their own minds, and conceived of their homeland as an ensemble of deeply personal attachments and reminiscences. From a Palestinian perspective, subjective experience simultaneously assumes form in relation to a broader political context of occupation, struggle and resistance.

Although I reside in Britain, I remain trapped within reminiscences of home, of the images, places and people that constitute me and provide purpose and meaning to my life. It is a dualistic existence, which elicits the sensation that I simultaneously inhabit two places.

This isn't something that I, or indeed anybody else, can control. National identity can't be escaped, it is ingrained in various levels of being. In a similar vein, Mahmoud Darwish conceived of the 'self [as] full of collective memory'. Although living in Britain has enabled me to develop my sense of a personal identity, my collective identity was always in the background. For Palestinians, it is always in the background, strengthened by the Israeli occupation. In contrast, British people are generally more guided by their sense of personal identity.

Living in Britain has provided me with an opportunity to see both sides, to encounter the positive and negative aspects of individualist and collectivist ways of life. When living in Palestine, I had often dreamt of living as an individual, of loosening the constraints which social life placed upon me. In focusing upon myself, I also dreamt of law and order, a life without checkpoints and a country which wasn't arbitrarily divided into individual parcels of land.

Living in Britain has enabled me to enjoy life as an individual. On many occasions I have chosen not to answer the phone or to open the door, a privilege that is not always available in Palestine. Here I can focus on myself, my needs and my desires. However, when I look at broader British society, I cannot fail to be struck by the costs that come with these benefits: freedom can all too easily become selfishness, individuality can easily transform into narcissism, and the pursuit of self-interest can become an inability to appreciate the needs of others.

Because I come from a different society, with a different way of thinking and acting, I am able to critically reflect upon British society, an option that isn't always available to British people. They cannot see, for instance, that it is unthinkable for a Palestinian to allow an elderly relative to visit a hospital by themselves. They cannot see, precisely because of a cultural specificity which they barely acknowledge, that many of the things they consider important or significant appear utterly insignificant or perverse to outsiders.

I experienced this during the Second Intifada. Although I was surrounded by people who were sympathetic to the Palestinian cause (some of whom were engaged in solidarity work), I felt removed, geographically, from Palestinian society, but I also felt removed in a more political/social sense, from the society which I inhabited. At times this detachment assumed an almost surreal character. During the Second Intifada, when West Bank cities, villages and refugee camps were being subjected to brutal incursions, my discussion with a saleswoman turned to the subject of her dog's hysterectomy. I remember being amazed that people could find time to think about, much less discuss, such things.

Sometimes, in searching for common reference points, I have found Palestinian food to be an especially fruitful point of engagement. I have taken the opportunity to prepare *maqloubeh* (literally 'upside down') for British friends and acquaintances. In preparing the food, I always take the opportunity to explain the exact details: the laying of the meat and the cooking of the vegetables and rice. The appreciative reaction makes me feel proud and gives me a sense that I have shared an important aspect of my culture.

Unfortunately, cultural communication is sometimes an uphill struggle. As elsewhere, the post-9/11 context in the UK has aggravated and opened up new distortions and misrepresentations, where culturally specific idioms and meanings have become lost in translation. As a Palestinian woman in the West, it is not uncommon for it to be assumed that I have somehow been 'saved' from oppression. Some women have even said to me, 'you must be glad to be here'. When I explain and clarify the reality of Palestinian women and the diversity of their situations, people show disbelief. Many shrug and say, 'It's the media.' In the Western imagination, Arab women are frequently reconstituted as victims, as objects of concern who need to be protected from the encroachments of Islam and backward cultural traditions.

I continue to engage these misunderstandings in the hope that it is possible to achieve a common language and to find a form of communication which traverses national and cultural boundaries. As a commitment which is as much personal as it is political, this engagement enables me to see both my host and formative society through new eyes.

Sharif Hikmat Nashashibi

Sharif Hikmat Nashashibi is a British Palestinian journalist and analyst on Arab affairs. He is a regular contributor to numerous Middle Eastern and British media outlets. He is the recipient of an award from the International Media Council 'for both facilitating and producing consistently balanced reporting' on the Middle East.

Fostering Palestine

Trying to encapsulate my identity as a diaspora Palestinian is no easy task, for it permeates every aspect of my life. It is akin to answering the fundamental question: 'Who are you?'

I have never come across a people that embraces its identity with such tenacity. Worn as a badge of honour, it is more than just pride in our culture. It is also borne out of our history of struggle, oppression, survival and success against all odds – the stuff of Hollywood epics. When faced with ethnic cleansing, dispossession, colonisation and occupation, to *be* Palestinian is itself a form of resistance, the most enduring form. However, as the diaspora is almost seventy years old, it has developed multiple identities separate from those inside Palestine. This is not only natural given the period of time, but is also testament to the ability of Palestinians to assimilate and thrive in their host countries (when they are allowed to).

My generation have dual identities: Palestinian, and the countries in which we were born and raised. This leaves me conflicted, for Britain is the only long-term home I have known, yet it is responsible for the creation of my people's plight, and effectively ensures its continuance by supporting Israel. There is no contradiction in having a dual identity, but it can be a double-edged sword. On the one hand, we are a bridge between different peoples, but on the other, it can feel like we do not completely belong to either. In Britain I am seen as an Arab, and in the Arab world I am viewed as British. When I worked as a media consultant for the United Nations Development

Programme (UNDP) in Palestine, I was often called '*al ajnabi*' (the foreigner). At first this upset me, as I felt as Palestinian as those around me. However, I came to accept that in their eyes I *was* different, in the way I spoke, behaved and thought. This was not problematic. Our different backgrounds, experiences and viewpoints made for enlightening conversations. Such exchanges are crucial because of the physical barriers between the diaspora and those under occupation.

Despite such barriers and differences in societal development, there is a disarmingly strong bond between Palestinians worldwide, a unity that transcends politics, religion, borders, time and distance. This manifests itself in a love of the homeland that is as instinctive as loving a parent. Diaspora Palestinians have been forcibly separated, so our feelings towards our homeland are akin to foster children yearning to find their biological parents, their curiosity only growing with time. For me, this moment came when I worked for the UNDP. This gave me the opportunity to really get to know my country and people, with whom I fell in love. I was particularly touched by their friendliness and generosity, despite their difficult circumstances. I also got to know intimately, and experience first-hand, the hardships and injustices I had been campaigning against most of my life. At the age of twenty-seven I had not just found my home, I had found myself.

Ironically, I am not allowed to enter my father's home in Jerusalem, a grand building with a plaque describing its 'liberation' by Jewish forces in 1948 (this 'liberation' meant my father, his parents and siblings becoming refugees in Lebanon). It had until recently been a court, described aptly by my mother – who still has the deeds and key – as 'a place of justice where justice is denied'. However, the last time I saw the house it was a dilapidated seminary for Orthodox Jews. All I could do was look through its broken windows.

In no time I had forgotten my life in London. After my UN contract expired and I returned to Britain, I was miserable for months. To this day, I remember my time there with a unique fondness, a period in my life when I was truly happy. But it is a bittersweet memory, for it is becoming ever-harder for diaspora Palestinians and foreigners to visit Palestine. When I took my brother and then-girlfriend there four years later, in 2008, the place I had told them about was unrecognisable, and the friends I had spoken of so highly had all left. The situation had deteriorated so much that I am reluctant to return. It is difficult to describe the heartache of seeing one's homeland in such a state. I remember sitting at my favourite, now-empty, restaurant with my girlfriend on the last night of our trip, holding back tears.

There are those who claim that the passion felt for Palestine, particularly by those in the diaspora, is a construct of parental indoctrination. This is as preposterous as it is offensive. I did not know I was Palestinian until I was ten years old, when the first uprising against Israeli occupation started in 1987. Until then, I had been told I was British-Jordanian, owing to my dual citizenship. My roots were revealed when I started asking questions about the youths I saw on TV being shot dead for throwing stones. Upset that this information had been hidden from me, my parents said they did not want to politicise me. They did not need to. The conduct of Israeli troops stirred me to research my origins, homeland and people, and champion their cause for freedom and human rights. Given what they were suffering and sacrificing, how could I not? To me, it was never a choice – it was my duty, not just as a Palestinian, but as a human being.

Some say Palestinian children are 'taught to hate'. In truth, what they learn at school or are told by their parents is irrelevant when faced with their brutal reality. My identity was shaped despite my parents, not because of them. Israel often portrays Palestinian nationalism as a threat, but it has contributed greatly to its zeal through repression.

Ironically, many in the diaspora, myself included, have no documentation to show that we are Palestinian, though it is a defining aspect of our identity, and we are unable to vote in elections that shape the future of our homeland.

For many of us too, facing and overcoming prejudice is a sad fact of life. My first such memory is having to rewrite an exam essay at school because my roots were the topic. At my next school, racist abuse against Arab students was commonplace. The day after Iraq surrendered to the Allies in 1991, we were taunted by students in front of a teacher, who did nothing. After graduating, I applied to head the Middle East department at the Royal United Services Institute, a UK government think tank. From his name and accent, the interviewer was clearly Israeli. This did not bother me, but his first question did: 'Have you ever criticised Israel?' Was this a suitable question to define whether someone was fit to head a department whose focus was an entire region? I answered 'Yes', persevered through a very awkward interview, and was not surprised when I was declined. To this day, I regret not taking matters further.

The job I got as a news editor at Dow Jones Newswires was at times no less awkward. I once had a heated argument with the head of the London office, in front of my colleagues, because she instructed us to describe all Palestinian attacks against Israel as 'terrorist'. I objected, saying we either had to define terrorism and use the term, where appropriate, on both sides, or not use it at all. I was then told that Israeli forces do not kill civilians, and that settlers 'just want a quiet life'. She backed down after my fellow editors sided with me. On another occasion, I raised with a superior the issue of the Dow Jones Newswires/Associated Press Jerusalem bureau (the origin of most of the content on the Israeli–Arab conflict) being staffed completely by Israelis, with no Arab presence. I expressed concern that staffing a bureau in charge of covering a conflict with people solely from one side of that conflict could affect objectivity. 'This is a very serious claim you're making,' she said. 'Nonetheless, it's the truth,' I replied. The situation remained unchanged in the three years I worked there.

My identity as a Palestinian in the diaspora has at times changed and evolved as I have grown up, but it has never diminished. I hope this chapter enables my fellow Brits to understand my background, and my fellow Palestinians to relate to it.

Jamal Nassar

Jamal R. Nassar is Dean of the College of Social and Behavioral Sciences at California State University, San Bernardino. Previously, he served as professor and chair at the Department of Politics and Government at Illinois State University. His many publications include Globalization and Terrorism: The Migration of Dreams and Nightmares; Politics and Culture in the Developing World; Intifada: Palestine at the Crossroads; *and many others.*

Seeds of Justice

I had studied English from first grade through high school and I really thought I knew the language until I set foot in JFK Airport. At the entry check, I was met by an African-American border agent who asked questions. I did not understand a word of what he asked. His accent was very different to the British English I had learnt. Shortly after my arrival, I headed to Houston, Texas. There, I was faced with choices: which bathroom do I use, the one labelled 'colored' or the one labelled 'white'? On the bus, I had to decide whether to sit at the front with whites or in the back with darker-skinned people. Given my Palestinian olive skin colour, I always attempted to sit in the middle. It was in Houston in 1966 that I came to the realisation, for the first time, that one of my high school teachers in Palestine was black. My Palestinian culture did not have space for skin colour, but in Houston, skin colour was the constant human demarcation.

Needless to say, I could not take Houston in 1966 so I moved to Detroit. The first summer there was one to remember. The 1967 'Black Riots' engulfed the city and our area went up in flames. Stores were burnt down and my roommates and I were escorted by the National Guard for our protection. That summer also witnessed my homeland going up in flames. The 1967 war destroyed my dreams of return as Israel came to occupy the remainder of Palestine where my family had taken refuge after 1948. With the new occupation I was unable to return and live in my own homeland. I had no

Israeli identity card because I was not there when the occupation took place. I became stateless and the United States became my adopted homeland.

The US was not very friendly to Palestinian Arabs. I was called 'camel jockey' even though the first time I ever rode a camel came decades later in western China. I was assumed to be Muslim even though I am Catholic. Ignorance with regard to my people was rampant even among those who should have known better. In the mid-1990s, a colleague of mine, a professor who teaches comparative politics, asked me when I had converted to Christianity, even though he had known for years that I was born in Jerusalem. All I could do was give him a cold look and ask: 'Why? Was Jesus born in McLean County?' Hollywood stereotypes of my people made life in the US very difficult and forced me and my family to deal with regular harassment. Hollywood had no good Arabs, only greedy oil sheikhs, terrorists and bad guys.

I had to travel the unavoidable path of conflict between my Arab identity and my American one. Often, I felt like the man on the cross, one hand pointing east and the other pointing west. When in the US, I am homesick for Palestine, but when I am in Palestine, I miss my home in the US. Being Palestinian in the diaspora means being a fighter for justice in Palestine, but when you are part of the diaspora in the US, it means going against the mainstream narrative, that of your people's oppressor. Speaking, teaching, writing, organising and demonstrating become a part of your fabric and an unavoidable chapter of your life in the US. The struggle for justice for Palestine simply consumes you wherever you are.

You also learn that injustice abounds all over and your struggle for justice becomes global. Whether it is the rights of minorities, Native Americans, workers or distant people oppressed by the power of your adopted homeland, you become involved, always on the side of the weak. In the process, your American-ness is questioned by those around you because you are never a true American. In reality, you become a citizen of the world, not of the state. Borders feel like barriers to your common humanity. Being Palestinian becomes being global in a world of nations and states. Palestine comes to rest in your heart as a slice of your global being. In the process, you become a traveller and navigator for truth and justice but you rarely find them. Truth becomes invisible in a world of denial, and justice remains hidden behind a cloud of greed.

Of course, deep in my heart I know that denial is temporary and clouds disappear. Truth will eventually prevail and the rays of the sun will expose greed and injustice. It is this knowledge that keeps my heart warm in the midst of every winter storm. My struggle in the American diaspora is not in vain, as I know that the US will eventually awaken and realise its own contribution to injustice in Palestine. Just like my recently planted fig and olive trees in California, Palestinians in the US have planted the seeds of truth and justice in America, and eventually they will grow and be full of fruits.

The fruits of justice in Palestine will benefit not only Palestinians, but Americans as a whole.

Maha Nassar

Maha Nassar, PhD, is an assistant professor in the School of Middle Eastern and North African Studies at the University of Arizona. She is currently writing a book that explores the cultural and intellectual connections between Palestinians in Israel and the Arab world during the 1950s and 1960s.

My Resilient Flag

My flag was not there.

It was 1984, and my fellow fourth graders and I were drawing flags to display at our suburban public school's upcoming 'Heritage Night'. Most of the students traced their lineage back to Europe, so it was easy for them to find and copy their respective flags from the numerous reference books strewn about our classroom. But the flag for Palestine did not appear in any of them. I wondered why I could not find the black, white and green tricolour with the red triangle that I had seen so often in my home and in the homes of friends and relatives.

That was the first time I realised that my parents' country of birth, the one my father and grandfather had described to me with such pride and nostalgia, was simply not recognised in America. I would stare at the 'Flags of the World' section of the *Funk & Wagnalls New Encyclopedia* that sat on our bookshelf at home, wondering why my flag was not listed between those of Pakistan and Panama, where it belonged. One day, when my father came home with a new edition of the encyclopaedia, I grabbed the 'F' volume and opened it to the section I had studied so many times before, hoping *Funk and Wagnalls* had updated its flag entries. 'Pakistan . . . Panama'. I was crestfallen. I started to think, was this flag even real?

The First Intifada brought a measure of reassurance. I watched Palestinian teenagers on the news as they defiantly unfurled huge flags on the streets of the Occupied Territories, their faces obscured by *keffiyehs* as they ducked

Israeli army fire. They confirmed to me that not only was my flag real, but there were Palestinians willing to risk their lives for it. At the same time, I became immersed in Chicago's sprawling Palestinian-American community, where I started to notice the flag all around me: in the mosque, during conferences and on the stages of student *dabke* performances at my Islamic high school. Such events were meant to express solidarity with fellow Palestinians 'back home' (*fi'l-blaad*), but they also allowed me – the child of 1948 refugees who had never set foot in Palestine – to connect to a country I was not able to visit.

While I had grown accustomed to seeing symbols of my heritage on display within the nurturing comfort of my community, they were still largely absent from the wider world. With the signing of the Oslo Accords in 1993, this began to change. The following year, as I perused keychains for sale bearing the flags of the world, I suddenly shrieked with delight. At last! There it was, the flag of Palestine, on display as an equal with the other flags of the world. I immediately bought it and switched all my keys over so I could take my flag with me wherever I went.

But the sense of validation that I had upon seeing my flag recognised was soon tempered. I came to see the flag as a co-opted symbol, drained of its original meaning and significance. The Palestinian Authority used it to mimic the trappings of statehood when no such state was forthcoming. Meanwhile, self-proclaimed 'peaceniks' sported buttons with intertwined Israeli and Palestinian flags fluttering over the words 'Shalom, Salam, Peace', implying parity between the two sides when none existed. Despite endless rounds of official negotiations and despite the growing ubiquity of the flag, there was no discussion of *my* Palestine, of Barbara or Jaffa, my parents' birthplaces from which they were expelled. The flag started to seem like a feel-good symbol, brandished to mask the ongoing subjugation of Palestinians under occupation and to silence the Palestinian refugees. The flag was now a common sight, but somehow I still felt left out.

My estrangement from the flag continued into the 2000s. I knew that no amount of flag-waving could mitigate the horrible loss of life from that cruel decade. I knew that American recognition of our flag would not end the siege of Gaza, or allow the refugees to return, or end the internecine squabbles. When I saw Palestinian delegates waving our flag at the United Nations General Assembly after Palestine was granted the status of 'non-Member Observer State' in 2012, I cynically rolled my eyes.

As a Palestinian child in America, I had longed to see my cultural heritage reflected back to me, to be no different from my friends of German, Cuban or Chinese extraction. But once this recognition came, it did not have the significance I thought it would. And as Palestinians around the world increasingly raised the possibility of a one-state solution to end the conflict, the fate of the Palestinian flag seemed more tenuous than ever. I began to think that perhaps we needed a new symbol for our people, one that had not been co-opted by those seeking a false sense of power or a false sense of peace.

Or maybe not. Like Palestinians all over the world, in 2013 I caught Mohammed Assaf fever. The twenty-three-year-old singer, whose looks and voice bear an uncanny resemblance to those of Egyptian superstar Abdelhalim Hafez, had made the inspiring journey from the Gaza Strip to international stardom when he won the 'Arab Idol' singing competition. Seeing Palestinians jubilantly wave our flag in the streets of Ramallah, Gaza and Nazareth in celebration, and watching as a teary-eyed Mohammed held up our flag in triumph, gave me chills for the first time in years. It reminded me that no matter how scattered Palestinians are around the world, the flag still brings us together.

It turns out my flag is more resilient than I initially thought. Twenty years after I bought the keychain with the Palestinian flag, I still take it with me wherever I go. All four corners of the plastic casing are chipped, but the flag is unmistakably there, peering out through two decades of scuffs and scratches, hoping to see a better future.

'A Scottish Palestinian who is not split between the two poles of this label'. Sinan Suleiman Malley marvels at Edinburgh Castle in formal dress, 2014.

The *Mukhtar*. Michel Moushabeck's late grandfather and former head of the Eastern Orthodox Christian Arab community in Jerusalem.

Issa Mikhail el-Toubbeh, *Mukhtar*, 1882–1973.

A moment of peace. Ibrahim Muhawi relaxing during a camping trip with his wife at the South Fork of the Boise River, Idaho, July 2014.

'Under the shadow of the gunships'. Nadia Naser-Najjab with her two children on the front page of the *Express & Echo* newspaper in Exeter, UK, in October 2000. Nadia was interviewed about living in Exeter while her husband, Walid Najjab (right), was in Ramallah during the Second Palestinian Intifada.

'I am from there and I have memories', a line from Mahmoud Darwish's poem, 'I am from there', on the gravestone of Abbas Shiblak's mother, Zahia Shiblak, in Oxford, UK. Abbas also followed his mother's wish to include the distance between Oxford and Haifa: '3,200 km'.

A gift of Palestine. Suha Shakkour's first piece of Palestinian folk embroidery made for her sister's wedding day. Suha learned embroidery from her mother in Canada on frequent trips to visit from the UK where she lives.

The British Mandate Palestine Passport of Monawar Zeine, the mother of Simine Tepper. The passport was issued to Palestinians during the British Mandate from 1925 to 1948.

Visiting family at Kalandia refugee camp. Jameel Zayed with his brother, Luay Zayed, and their grandmother, Ghalia, during a visit to the West Bank in 1989–90.

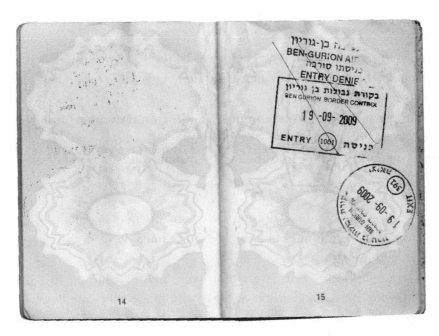

'Entry denied'. The stamp in Jameel Zayed's passport after being refused entry to Israel. Jameel was later banned from visiting Israel for five years without explanation.

Naomi Shihab Nye

Naomi Shihab Nye was born in St Louis, lived in Jerusalem and now lives in San Antonio, Texas. She has written or edited more than thirty books, including Habibi, Sitti's Secrets, 19 Varieties of Gazelle *and* The Turtle of Oman. Tender Spot: Selected Poems *was published in 2008 in the UK.*

Written on his Forehead: My Father, Aziz Shihab

He was Palestine for me, he was the arm stretched across the world remembering and reaching out to homeland.
    Joan Norris

The day before he died, my life-loving dad said, 'It's my time. I'm ready to go!'

He was sitting in a hospital bed, angry to be there. Ironically, after years of heart trouble, diabetes, kidney failure and dialysis, it was a broken arm giving him severe pain at the end.

To our credit, neither my mom nor I said, 'Don't say that.' Instead, 'We love you so much!'

'Sure you do. But won't you still love me when I die?'

He got that right.

The next morning, a nurse outside his room opened her arms wide. I'd spoken to him thirty minutes before. 'He didn't make it.'

She hugged me tightly.

It's a strange phrase. This sweet man who 'made' a life on two sides of the world, who 'made' half my own life – who made everyone laugh, made things up, made things better, made his own kind of mischief and always had keen insights – gone. Or, everywhere.

I'd call that making it, myself.

At eighty, his anthem for suffering became, 'What can we do?' His days had diminished to napping, unhappy little meals, fanatical ice-sucking, difficult attempts to stand or walk, medication, dialysis, late-night classical music on the radio. But he was lucid and never lost his way of shaping a phrase.

He had begun visualising his father, who died in Palestine half a century earlier, and his mother, who lived to be 106. He told an Iraqi friend his mother was calling to him in his dreams.

All his life, he believed one's 'time of departure' is written on one's forehead, a popular Middle Eastern belief. I would argue, what about young people? Accidents that erase large groups at once? How could dying be written on so many foreheads in the same place at the same time?

He never wavered in his belief. Hopefully it gave him comfort.

He was disappointed with such little positive resolution in the Palestinian-Israeli disaster of nearly sixty years. Since losing the family home in 1948, he'd never stopped advocating for justice for his people. He believed Arabs and Jews could have stayed cousins, and not become enemies. If bigger powers had kept their opinions and money out of the story, it might have been solved long ago.

Two days before he died he told me he wanted to get well and volunteer to cheer up hospital patients: 'I know what they feel like.' He told our son he was going to renovate his whole house. He told our mom he was moving to a different city.

Clink of dominoes on a marble-topped table. Tiny cups of steaming tea with mint. *Gate of the Sun* by Lebanese writer Elias Khoury open by his bed. 'Each of our bodies holds the entire history of the human race . . . I'm the living proof. Look at me. Can't you see the pain tearing at me? The pain is everywhere . . .'

When we were children in St Louis, our friends' fathers suffered from migraines and stomach problems, took to their beds after heavy drinking, yelled at their kids, while our healthy, nut-brown dad was outside teaching us to make spinning tops from acorns. He greeted everyone 'My friend!'

To a waitress, 'My friend, do you have a special soup today?'

Now when someone asks, 'How did your father deal with racism as a young immigrant?' I can't remember any. He called everyone 'my friend'.

Our father never practised traditional religion. But he read the Quran and blessed us when we drove off. As an adolescent, he hiked with Christian pilgrims to Bethlehem. He told his devout Muslim mother he did not wish to pray five times a day – no fasting during Ramadan, no Mecca pilgrimage. She said, 'Just love God and respect everyone's traditions.' Before his death, he said, 'If I get well, I'll go visit the new Bahai Temple down the street. Bahais are nice.'

On his last evening we watched a film called *Belonging* by Tariq Nasir. Each member of the Nasir family tells the heartbreaking expulsion story so familiar to Palestinians. My father was deeply quiet watching it. 'We all had the same story.' He wanted to write to Tariq Nasir to thank him.

On his own deathbed, Edward Said is said to have urged us all to work harder for justice for Palestine. How many more things should we each be doing right this minute? Are we up to the job?

All the scurrying around that comes with death. Punctuated by vast silence. His clothes. His phone. I'm saddened by how many medical supplies he had.

We find his first passport, British-Palestine, with a picture of him at nineteen. None of us can recall seeing it before.

The 'Valuable Papers' file is empty. Now I know why people are called 'survivors'. We must survive the rest of our lives without that crucial person in the world.

Under my father's obituary picture in *The Dallas Morning News*, we are startled to see a note that says the Texas flag will be lowered to half-staff in his memory. We drive to the newspaper building. Not exactly half-staff – more like two feet lower than usual. A tiny bit dropped. But it's sweet. He'd make a joke. When have we ever cared about the Texas flag before?

After he dies, I answer the phone at his home. A recorded space-zombie says, 'WE ARE CALLING FOR . . . AZIZ SHIHAB. IF YOU ARE THAT PERSON, PRESS ONE. IF THAT PERSON IS AT HOME AND CAN COME TO THE PHONE, PRESS TWO. IF THAT PERSON IS NOT AT HOME, PRESS THREE.'

I press three and hang up.

My brother says he would have pressed one.

Bashier Oudeh

Bashier Oudeh was born in Qalqilia, and lived in Jerusalem before leaving to study medicine in Cairo. He witnessed the Arab–Israeli wars of 1956, 1967 and 1973. He came to Britain in 1975 and has worked tirelessly to champion Arab and Palestinian causes. He is the Chairman of Palestinians in Scotland, Vice-Chair of Fife Arabic Society, a board member of The Scottish Arab Federation, Director of FRAE Fife and Co-Chair and trustee of Kirkcaldy Islamic Centre.

Aiming High

The spring in Scotland seemed to start suddenly in 2014; two consecutive days with almost three hours of sunshine cheered people up, despite the remaining palpable chill. The traffic in Glasgow was quite reasonable when we arrived at the BBC Scotland building. It was mid-morning on Tuesday, 11 March and we were a little early, giving me and my good friend from Iraq, Adnan Miyasser, time to relax after our long journey. We had been invited to take part in three programmes on BBC World, BBC Scotland and BBC Arabic television with two and a half hours of live broadcasts. The topics? Identity, integration and Scottish independence.

Before we went on air I had a brief conversation with our (British/Lebanese) host, Sam Farah. He disarmingly asked me whether I leave my house in the morning 'British' and come back in the evening 'Arab'? It was a good starting point. To live the life of 'different' people while trying to keep a foothold on your own stolen homeland is a never-ending process. It was not 'leaving your house British and coming home Palestinian', but rather living through the weather, the television news and programmes, doing your night shifts and using the language 24/7. This could easily smother your original identity and culture. For me, however, as a Palestinian, my identity has been protected by belonging to a very special place as well as the ongoing injustice in my homeland.

My Palestinian identity was something I grew into; part of a journey of self-discovery that continues to this very day. The first time I heard anyone calling themselves 'Palestinian' was in Egypt when I met students from Gaza. I was then (and still remain) a Jordanian. I never felt that one cancelled the other; to me they were one and the same. It was after the Israeli aggression in 1967 – the point at which the Palestinian resistance came to symbolise what was noble for the Arab masses – that being Palestinian meant identifying with those carrying the banner for honour and freedom. It was only natural for me as a teenage student to identify with being Palestinian, especially as it reflected my true identity.

Following graduation I had the opportunity to pursue my training in Britain. At the time I made two pledges: having lived through three major wars, with all their death, destruction and displacement, I would not inflict this on anyone, especially with 'peace' as a never-ending mirage. The second pledge was never to go back to the region, except to my beloved Jerusalem, free of occupation (which might sound naïve now, but at the time there was still some hope of a settlement). Jerusalem to me was my real home, anywhere else was just the same: exile.

Living mostly in hospital accommodation with occasional Arab colleagues (mostly Egyptians), my main contact with the Arab world was the short-wave radio and occasional phone calls to family. Getting an Arabic newspaper from London was a big event; it was treasured and passed excitedly between friends. Programmes about 'the Middle East' on British television were rare and deserved a special arrangement to see them in our friends' married quarters, as other people in the common room might prefer watching something different. In Britain you have the benefit of a bird's-eye view of what's taking place in Palestine, as well as experiencing first-hand the reactions of the government and people of a nation that has mostly supported your opponents. Living through this for decades has enabled me to speak to my friends and colleagues as an insider with much more understanding and conviction.

The Israeli occupation of South Lebanon in 1982, and in particular the siege of Beirut and the horrific Sabra and Shatila massacres, marked another huge landmark in the development of my Palestinian identity. Marching with supporters in Edinburgh's Princes Street we stopped at The Mound, a microphone was thrust into my hand and, 'as a Palestinian', I had to address the crowds. It was with a sense of awe that I had to look at the hundreds of people hanging on my every word. For a few seconds I had to take it all in but then it all came out: 'Long live Palestine!' I shouted, and that seemed to be what the crowd wanted to hear. They thundered back: 'Long live Palestine!' Encouraged, I chanted again, and after a third time it seemed that I had their full attention. I told the crowd that the latest atrocity was part of a series of massacres intended to punish the Palestinians for, well, being Palestinians. It is so depressing that after more than three decades the same speech could be given again only with a longer list of atrocities.

At around this time my family's persistence finally paid off and I got married to a Palestinian wife. This guaranteed a balance between my established British/Scottish identity and my developing Palestinian identity. It was almost a novelty to return after work to a 'Palestinian' home, with Palestinian food for dinner and maybe Fairuz or Abdul-Halim singing in the background. Conversing in Arabic was another novelty, having lived for months on end in the past only using the language when I phoned home. Family life opened the doors to other families. As more Arabs (especially from Iraq) were settling locally, we established our own Arab Society. Palestine was always a main part of our public meetings.

After the Israeli war on Gaza in 2008, we tried to campaign and raise awareness through our Arab Society and other local Scottish groups, but it became clear that a Scottish Palestinian society was needed. When Mahmoud Sarsak[1] visited Scotland in May 2013, a few Edinburgh Palestinians joined him for dinner at a Palestinian restaurant. I had to point out the obvious: here we were, Palestinians in Scotland, but without any authentic voice. A few of us took part in activities by one Scottish group or another but we really needed to provide our own perspective on matters pertaining to us. And so it was. Following a few weeks of frantic preparations we held our inaugural meeting on Sunday, 23 June 2013. I was honoured to be elected as Chairman of the new 'Palestinians in Scotland' society.

Being Palestinian to me might have been an accident of birth, but I feel really privileged to have this connection. It is extremely difficult to be denied your birthright, your identity, homeland and culture, and it is even worse to have your country under brutal illegal occupation against all the principles of human rights and United Nations resolutions. Nevertheless, I would not have it any other way. Better still, combining this with my British/Scottish identity complements my life experience perfectly.

I truly am fortunate to be Palestinian.

Note

1. A Palestinian footballer who was imprisoned under 'administrative detention' measures in 2012 and was released only after a prolonged hunger strike.

Yousif Qasmiyeh

Yousif M. Qasmiyeh is a poet, translator and instructor in Arabic at the Language Centre, University of Oxford. His articles have been published in the Journal of Refugee Studies *and in edited collections including* Rescripting Religion in the City: Migration and Religious Identity in the Modern Metropolis *(2013). His poems and translations have appeared in* An-Nahar, Al-Ghawoon, See How I Land *(2009),* Modern Poetry in Translation, The Oxonian Review *and* Critical Quarterly.

My Mother's Heels

'I live in Baddawi Camp[1] in a small house.'

This is what I used to tell foreigners every single time they came to my primary school. At times I used to run after them and repeat these words without waiting for their questions. I have always thought that questions are inherent within answers and that answers very often comprise their questions, questions which no answers can address.

It was in the early morning that the elderly woman would approach taxi drivers and workmen on the edges of my home-camp, begging them to take her to Haifa. I was nearly ten when I had the courage to mention this to my father. I knew that he would know the woman personally, since they shared the same origins.

I wanted to interrogate the 'senility' which, for many Palestinians, has become a conscious and legitimate outcome of the validities as well as the enormities of memory. I wanted to know how and in what form the ability 'to not forget' can transform itself into a constant movement towards the missing origin: Palestine.

My father was unexpectedly patient when he proceeded to tell me about the pain we all carry from the moment of our birth, the same pain that has forged a strong bond with memories whose owners had not been given the time to (re)collect. Our time, he continued, was stuck between there and here. We have not yet had the right moment to process the vastness of losing memories so, in a sense, the refugee camps have acted as transitional places, and at times as a meeting point, which are tinged with an amalgam of benign details: those which were carried from Palestine and those which have grown in the whereabouts of these camps.

The woman's back, her small stature and her striking blue eyes, for me, founded the basic signs of the Palestine that I have never seen – the image that demonstrates the moral and symbolic value of having the right to dream *seriously*, and with strength, amid all this immense destruction – but I continue to imagine through the eyes of my parents and grandparents. For me, Palestine has always been delivered through that which my parents have seen. Even more so, I would say, through my mother's cracked heels as she swept the concrete surfaces in our house in Baddawi Camp, through her regular trips to see my grandparents, uncles and aunts in Nahr Al-Bared Camp,[2] and her visits to the cemetery to bid farewell to the deceased and to restate what it is like to be buried in a place which marks both your death and your fixedness as a dead/living person in your camp.

As somebody who was born and brought up in a refugee camp, I have always felt that my Palestinian-ness is the pretext for understanding the 'Other'; for thinking of those people whose rights have been diminished; for 'dream[ing] while remembering' and 'remember[ing] while dreaming', to paraphrase Bachelard. As I recall, the rare trips outside the camp, mainly to Tripoli, with my mother to have my photo taken for my new 'Identity Card for Palestinian Refugees' always prompted me to think of the photos, badly framed, of family members smiling, or looking stern, somewhere in Palestine.

There is no surer way of retracing the footsteps of my parents than to borrow their eyes to see what they were able to see. Being Palestinian is the only healthy sign in very unhealthy settings. It is embodied in recycled UNRWA (United Nations Relief and Works Agency) books; dried vegetables marking the continuous nature of our presence; donated asbestos roofs; reservoirs; my maternal grandparents; the grandfather who spent over two decades in bed hallucinating about his land in Saffourieh in Palestine; UNRWA distribution centres and schools; bomb shelters; small plants, mainly mint and basil, in empty ghee and dried-milk tins, reminding us of the value of beauty in ugly circumstances; shared walls and windows with good and bad neighbours; ever-expanding thresholds; factions; AK47s; political and military marches;

demonstrations; high blood pressure, diabetes, depression and hope; regular Israeli air raids; explosions; visiting relatives in other camps; place(s) of reference; my parents and siblings and their respective families; definition of that life; definition of this life; identity cards; colours and smells; clothes and sizes; the news, songs, poetry and prose; Lebanese national exams and our imminent exposure; strong, feeble and suppressed dialects; friendships; sound barriers; martyrs and their photographs; sensitivity; prophets; tears; death; funerals and sweets; frail bodies; digging; holding coffins; and running away.

The woman, after various failed attempts to board a car, was collected by a taxi driver who did not know her family, and decided to drive her outside the camp. According to those who found her body in the only park in Tripoli, she looked the same, with her two bags full of clothes. Palestine will never fade away as long as the power of imagination becomes an ever more powerful act. Many will continue to die in the refugee camps, many more will die while attempting to put memories in the right order, but one thing is certain, the palpable and symbolic value of Palestine will continue to be entwined with the ultimate values of humanity and fairness.

'Then I remember; then I find myself again.'[3]

Notes

1. Palestinian refugee camp in North Lebanon, 3 km from the city of Tripoli.
2. Palestinian refugee camp 16 km from the city of Tripoli.
3. Bachelard, *The Flame of a Candle*, Dallas Institute Publications (1988), p. 37.

Loubna Qutami

Loubna Qutami has an MA in ethnic studies at San Francisco State University and is currently a PhD student in ethnic studies at the University of California Riverside. She is the former International General Coordinator of the Palestinian Youth Movement (PYM), and formerly the Executive Director of the Arab Cultural and Community Center (ACCC).

Images from a Shattered Mirror

Like a broken mirror, our movement is in shambles – so distorted that one cannot even identify if and where it exists or how to restore it to its original self. We cannot know which reflections of struggle the mirror has absorbed and which it has returned to the world.

For young Palestinians, the broken mirror reflects the current phase of our struggle for a free Palestine. Our generation are merely fragments of an uneven and flawed piece of dusty, cracked, sharp glass. We are often cut by it. For some, like our brothers and sisters today in Yarmouk Camp in Syria, and Gaza, we die from it. Despite this, we focus on the frame around the mirror and argue about what aesthetic appeals most to the eye. We want to beautify it, to make it worth revival. We become immersed in the creation of the most decadent and lavish gold trimmings to fit the mirror's jagged edges. We argue about which wall deserves to host it. We debate who should have access or be denied this reflection of themselves, and which of the mirror's reflections are the most authentic. That very same mirror that we cannot even recognise ourselves in, that which we are cut by, is the mirror that we cannot seem to let go of.

I was born and raised in the United States. I am the daughter of a Palestinian mother and Jordanian father. I was as young as eight the first time I remember crossing my fingers behind my back during the morning pledge of allegiance to the US flag. I didn't know why I did it. I only knew what my parents' and grandparents' faces looked like each time they watched television and the news covered our part of the world.

It was hard to know what those expressions meant at the time. For as much as we pride Arab 'identity' on narratives of oral history, we forget that memories of the past – particularly from a distance to the homeland – can reproduce a complex level of loss, sadness and powerlessness that our elders refuse to relive. In my early adult life, I came to understand that their accounts reflected a deep longing for the homeland, for the past and the way things used to be. The term 'nostalgia' is said to date back to the seventeenth century when a Swiss physician coined it as a combination of the Greek term '*Nostos*', referring to a return home, and '*Algos*', a painful condition. The more I considered the hardships of my family in exile and the history of colonisation in the Arab world, the more I internalised their nostalgia as my own.

In high school, this feeling became more pervasive throughout the Second Intifada and events following the attacks of 11 September 2001. Here, I was an Arab youth straddling the blurred lines where being Arab began and being 'American' ended. Yet my racialised experience as an Arab in the hostile post-9/11 environment pushed me to the margins. The more I struggled, the stronger I searched for a narrative, history and place of belonging which could account for my feelings of dispossession.

When I began my studies at San Francisco State University, I joined the General Union of Palestinian Students (GUPS), where I cultivated a level of politicisation and community connectedness that filled the gaps of my childhood's racial and political alienation. Throughout these years, *nostalgia* became shaped by the traditions of a romantic Palestinian nationalist culture and past. *Dabke*, music, poetry, slogans of freedom and a study of history amplified this nostalgia. I began to feel that every bone in my body would ache until I made my return to Jaffa, where my grandfather dreamt of returning until his dying day.

In the spring of 2006, I returned to Palestine for the first time. The trip indefinitely altered my understanding of loss, exile and yearning. I was finally 'home' and yet I couldn't feel more estranged. It was nothing like I had imagined. I was an insider, as a '*bint el Shatat*' making her rightful return 'home', yet I fell outside what Palestine had been reduced to. In this colonised and post-Oslo Palestine, there was no place for me and other diasporic Palestinians. Being authentically Palestinian was singularly tied to racialised life or death under occupation. I returned to the US with a deep sadness and guilt as I resumed a privileged, and what I saw as an undeserving, life, while my brothers and sisters in the homeland suffered under occupation. At the same time, the United States felt even less like home than when I had left. The grounds from which home was constructed had been ruptured, paving the way for an epistemological awakening and a (re)inscription of what 'being Palestinian' meant.

In 2007, I attended the Palestinian Youth Network (PYN) conference in Vendôme, France along with one hundred young Palestinians from every corner of the world. We shared deep-seated mutual desires for return and liberation, love of homeland and people, commitment to justice and the conviction to take our rightful place as young people in the struggle. But we saw our geographic, cultural and political fragmentation from one another and our land as insurmountable. We engaged in tumultuous debates about the most appropriate discourses, strategies and readings of history in order to singularise our 'Palestinian identity' as the solution to overcoming our fragmentation. Soon, however, we discovered that our differences were in fact assets to our collective identity. Being Jordanian but from the US did not in any way take away from my 'Palestinian-ness', but in fact informed it. This dynamic space allowed for a reconstruction of 'being Palestinian' on a collective level, from the lens of a new generation. I realised I could not know what 'being Palestinian' meant for me unless I could account for the needs, desires and experiences of my generation in all parts of the world. Through a more thoughtful understanding and cultivation of collective consciousness, 'being Palestinian' asserted power and strength as opposed to loss, pain and alienation.

Following the 2007 conference, I became an avid organiser with the PYN, which later metamorphosed into the Palestinian Youth Movement (PYM). Through my work with the PYM, I realised that nostalgia never did and still doesn't encompass the sentiments of my family, nor does it account for how such sentiments have been transmitted to myself and other youth. The current conditions of our struggle, the suffering of our people, and our alienation and fragmentation, all contribute to the complex relationships those in our generation have to 'being Palestinian'. Yet these conditions also generate passion, conviction, agency, resilience and the determination to overcome. Nostalgia alone reaffirms that the personal stays fragmented from the collective. It serves our deeply emotional relationship to the past and to our homeland while in exile, but only through building collective conscious-ness can nostalgia be uprooted from its lonely, powerless and static place.

'Being Palestinian' is about maintaining resilience, agency and resistance despite the broken mirror that has shattered our dreams of Palestine's liberation. But this broken mirror is not the death of the Palestinian movement. The inability to recognise ourselves in our own struggle is only a deficit if we gaze at the mirror nostalgically. For me, the fact that a mirror still exists is enough to celebrate the steadfastness of our people and history. Collectively (re)constructing this mirror to its whole is what 'being Palestinian' is now all about.

Najat Rahman

Najat Rahman is Associate Professor of Comparative Literature at the University of Montreal. She is author of Literary Disinheritance: The Writing of Home in the Work of Mahmoud Darwish and Assia Djebar *(2008) and co-editor of* Exile's Poet, Mahmoud Darwish: Critical Essays *(2008) and* Humor in Middle Eastern Cinema *(2014).*

Be/longing

Years ago, while visiting Gaza, my sister took me to meet an old man from Jaffa who told us his story. He showed us a large door, not attached to anything now, the only thing he was able to recuperate from his house. The new dwellers had thrown the door out of the main entrance. He carried it back with him to Gaza as the only remnant of his old life; a door cheerful in its colours, but now closed, and when it opens leads to nowhere. And yet the door is an undeniable memory of a severance and perhaps even the promise of an unknown passage.

I left Gaza in 2000 after a brief stay. Days later, I watched my landlady on the news showing the rubble of my apartment building to a cameraman. My apartment in Gaza faced the sea, and opened to the sky, to better receive spectacular sunsets and fallen bombs that I can watch on satellite TV near Hamra Street in Beirut. Stepping out of the door of the building facing Arafat's compound, I would be greeted daily by his guards in Hebrew. In Gaza, my earliest memories of Black September came rushing back. But the guards could not have known that.

Years later in North America, during the Israeli bombardments of Gaza in January 2009, one of the members of a committee I was sitting on indicated that she does not like it when one mentions Palestine without Israel. She had spotted Palestine on a list of Arab countries in an Arabic lecturer's file that was being evaluated. Of course no one else had mentioned Palestine, and her connection to Arabic was far from apparent. Was it even useful to remind her that Israel does not consider itself to be an Arab country? How long must we endure exercises in absurdities? Is being Palestinian a stubborn insistence on meaningfulness in words when lives are devastated in no small measure by senseless history? Does being Palestinian have to do with having to constantly account for oneself, with perpetual but inadequate identification, with reassurances, with invisibility? Why not let us grieve our losses at least for that week when there are no doors out of Gaza?

In Gaza, the struggle for being is stark. Elsewhere in Palestine and in the diaspora, to be Palestinian is to be 'out of place': not supposed to be in Palestine, not supposed to be anywhere. What is a being without a place, a place familiar and unfamiliar, where one desires to return, where one desires to die, even if the reality of that desire recedes? What is a being with a memory challenged? With a story denied? What is a being connected to other beings always at risk, under occupation, under siege? How do we belong, other than to ourselves? And yet we must belong everywhere. To be Palestinian is to encounter a language in contradiction with lived life. It is a record of an experience at odds with the worlds in which I find myself.

Once I returned. An unmarked patrol car stopped me. I think they must have been young men from the town. (In fact they were Israeli soldiers in civilian clothes in a civilian car.) In which language did we communicate? How did we arrive at an understanding from such utter confusion? They wanted to know if I was lost. I was not. 'You should not be here.' Where should I be? They wanted to know where I was going. To my grandmother's house. 'Where does she live?' Up the road. They were confused: 'We thought you were lost.' The mutual claiming and misrecognition was intriguing and bewildering. Mahmoud Darwish's verses, about how we will all resemble each other at night, and how 'time conquers us with memories that do not resemble us', come to mind. Do we still resemble ourselves? And is this still a place where I don't feel lost? This home is before language, before experience. I am attached to this early place, an old stone house near Nablus that looks on to a field of yellow in July, attached to a few cherished beings, to certain memories, to certain words and sounds particularly Palestinian. It is an intimate language of childhood that I rarely speak.

I return to this place from time to time. This homecoming never materialises and never ends, the tolls of which I cannot fully fathom. I have been crossing to a place without a name all my life. It is a place denied *only to us,* and it never stops being threatened with loss. Tangible and present, everywhere else is an emblem of this disconnection.

Palestine is an immense joy and grief, wonder turned into the contingent and the absurd. Palestinians have always wanted to be like other people, but I watch as other people have instead become more like us, scattered, carrying memories of home and of selves at odds with their new places in the world. More than an identity, or an experience, or an inheritance, being Palestinian has become a demand in the face of continued and forceful negation, in the face of violent erasure, a crossing precisely of a voice that has not stopped its telling of a story that has yet to be heard, a door that could open on to an elsewhere.

Mona Hatoum's *Turbulence*[1] recalls the marbles of childhood, an insouciance of play and connection to a place that has since turned to transience and disarray, shared with so many others, a collection of instances of beings. One more loss, one more devastation, and everything is asunder again. When meeting Palestinians today in the diaspora, it is as if we constitute such a collection, with all the signals of a 'coming out'.

Note

1. The 2012 artwork by Mona Hatoum consisting of thousands of marbles laid on the floor in a 4 m x 4 m square.

Hanan Ramahi

Hanan Mustafa Ramahi was born in the diaspora to Palestinian parents. She grew up in America where she received her university education. In 1995 she co-established with her late father a kindergarten through twelfth-grade school in Al-Bireh/Ramallah, Palestine, which she continues to direct. The school was established to serve the educational needs of children of repatriating Palestinian-Americans. She is currently pursuing her doctorate in education in England.

Eating Forbidden Palestine

Being Palestinian in the diaspora is at once a moral cause and a celebration of life.

As a moral cause for me it represents everything that is just, a duty and responsibility unto the wretched of the earth, the disinherited and forgotten. Whether for those in Iraq or Harlem, for victims of domestic violence or child abuse, being Palestinian – particularly in the diaspora – means being at the forefront of any and every fight for life and dignity.

Such moral responsibility for the human race is a heavy toll to bear. This is how I felt at the tender age of seven. Whether or not this is possible for a child, it was for me. I recall it vividly. Yet, as an adult I wonder if such premature awareness is normal. Looking back, it seems an unfair robbery of precious childhood. Such was the effect of being Palestinian in the diaspora on me when I was growing up.

My sense of geography and place were also affected. At the age of nine I was astonished to discover that country borders are manmade. It was my beloved late father who explained to me that two Europeans, an Englishman and a Frenchman, drew lines on the map which decided who would be Palestinian and who would be Jordanian, who would be Lebanese or Syrian. Sykes and Picot became the big bad wolves in my childhood fairy tales. I didn't need imaginary ghouls, modern history had provided me with my own set of real ones.

At school in America when asked where I was from, Palestine would be mistaken for 'Pakistan', and when it was recognised it would often be associated with terrorism. My reaction to this, and the other prejudice I suffered, was to try to stand up for every boy and girl that was bullied, or at least comfort them during their hurt. It was an onerous mission, but it was never a choice. Forsaking an underdog was comparable to denying my Palestinian-ness. It was a betrayal of my identity.

University years included history courses on the African slave trade and the Crusades to the Holy Land, and others on colonial and Native American literature. The natural sciences seemed superfluous, a diversion that I did not have time for. As misery loves company, my studies afforded me a warped sense of comfort in realising that the Palestinians were not the only people who were oppressed in the world and in history. The tragedies of others seemed to assuage a lifetime of dislocation and anguish. It may have been mad, sadistic even, but it was human – the need *not* to feel alone in one's suffering.

But suffering is a strange and complex thing, even nebulous at times. Wisely handled it can foster resilience, which can do wonders for character and soul. This decision, however, must emanate from a deep will to overcome.

In the face of Zionist denial and erasure, being Palestinian in the diaspora has been an insistence on life in all its expressions. It's about my mother finding a fig tree that reminded her of the one in her parents' garden back in Palestine. To her reclaimed tree she would take me after school, where we picked and ate the ripest figs straight off the branches. They were deep purple and the insides were menacingly sweet. The pleasure of tasting them was so private that we had to close our eyes. We were eating the forbidden Palestine. At least my mother was; I would be relishing Palestine through her. It wasn't hard to do. The pleasure she took was contagious. If I hadn't been Palestinian, watching my mother made me want to be. Thirty years later, when I eat a fig I do so on her behalf – a compilation of mother and home-land, self and pleasure, identity and belonging. Such is a fig for a Palestinian in the diaspora.

From my mother, I suckled milk and Palestine.

Then there were the olives. No store-bought ones would do for her. She had to hand-pick and prepare them herself, and from the pits she made rosaries that she gave to friends. The olives had to be stored for weeks before they could be consumed. So I waited and waited ever so patiently, because I could see them through the glass jars as they seasoned, green and succulent.

I would run home from school to have them with fresh homemade bread. I ran home to Palestine.

At home, my mother would be cross-stitching swan and rose figures in blood-red silk thread on to sometimes black, sometimes white fabric. She would embroider each stitch individually, never taking shortcuts like some women did. 'See how each cross bursts with life,' she would say. Her mother's *Roomi*[1] told of where her sixteen-year-old aunt had, while embroidering the *Roomi*, laid down her last thread and passed away from the evil eye.[2] Another chest panel spoke of a cousin who bequeathed her cross-stitches in celebration of a new-born. These were the gowns that we Palestinian women wore on special occasions in the diaspora. These were the stories that covered us. They weighed heavily, they and the silk threads that narrated our lives.

But life is heavy, wherever one may be from. For me, being Palestinian in the diaspora is about being human in the displacement of life. It's about insisting on existence in the face of personal hardship, social challenge and national struggle. It's about people, everywhere.

Notes

1. A highly decorative embroidered gown owned by a select few.
2. A malevolent look for reasons of envy that many cultures believe is able to cause harm or misfortune for the person at whom it is directed.

Omar Ramahi

Omar M. Ramahi was born in Jerusalem, Palestine. He has lived in the diaspora since he was one year old. He completed his university education in mathematics and engineering in the US and he has taught at the University of Maryland and worked in industry for several years. He is a professor at the University of Waterloo in Canada.

Palestinian-Something

Being part-Palestinian implies the fearful, dreaded hyphenated Palestinian-something identity. Perhaps that is exactly who I am: Palestinian-something, but that something is not any other nationality. The 'something' is shaped by every non-Palestinian experience I have had, or by that non-Palestinian part of me, but it does not diminish or take away from the Palestinian side. I hope every Palestinian in the diaspora resists replacing the 'something' by a nation.

Despite the reality of the hyphenated identity for diaspora Palestinians, the Palestinian part of mine is frighteningly overwhelming, powerful, dominant and very loud. That part is yearning for justice, not only for dispossessed Palestinians but for every dispossessed person on our deeply violated planet. I cannot see my love for *knafeh*, hummus, *musakhan* and falafel or my *dabke* expertise as an identifier! I cannot see my thick Arabic accent as having any relevance to my identity! I cannot feel any significant cultural connection to Palestinians inside Palestine or outside, because such a connection is the product of a shared life, which has never happened. Despite being very critical of traditional Palestinian culture and its nuances, sometimes I wish I was a part of it, but I am not and cannot be.

It is all about perception. Being well-fed and well-sheltered throughout my life in the diaspora has made me physically comfortable, and carrying the citizenship of a Western country has made me 'secure', but something has been missing. My connection to Palestine through my parents, grandparents, immediate and distant relatives, has made the Palestinian part of me unlike a Palestinian who has experienced the motherland or has had to flee, or was expelled – such as my father, paternal grandparents, uncles and aunts. The Palestinian side of me has been shaped by carrying the weight of the agony of every Palestinian who was forced into exile. The premature wrinkles in the faces and on the minds of young Palestinian women and men oppressed by the brutality of the Israeli-Zionist colonisation. The fractured bones and skulls of the Palestinian youth of the First and Second Intifadas have left a deep fracture in my psyche, and made me sensitive towards anyone who is brutalised in a struggle for justice. The fear of every Palestinian woman living in what remains of Palestine that her loved ones might be jailed or brutalised by settlers, or the fear that her child might be deprived of his innocence in Israel's open prisons, or that he might be sniped by an Israeli soldier-settler, which happened to my fifteen-year-old distant relative, Wajdi Al-Ramahi, in the Jalazoun refugee camp; all have left me with a deep sense of insecurity that something similar could happen whenever my own kids go to school. Being Palestinian in diaspora has connected me to the simple elements of human insecurity caused by force used brutally and unjustly.

The world watched in horror the massacres of Sabra and Shatila in 1982. For me, the resonance was overwhelming and it solidified an unimaginable spiritual link with a culture of sadness and injustice. I have not had a chance to visit refugee camps much, but my few experiences have brought me to identify strongly with the Palestinian refugees who live half-way around the world from where I have spent most of my life.

On my visit to Palestine in 1985 I experienced first-hand the demolition of three houses in the village of Saffa by the Israeli occupation machine. This was my 'coming of age', the equivalent to an American or Canadian boy going to the proms! I heard the story first-hand from a proud Palestinian woman who told me how her husband had spent thirty years labouring in Brazil to save enough money to build the modest dwelling that would be demolished in a few minutes. A photo I took of that woman standing triumphantly on top of her demolished house has served to anchor my identity deep within the innocence of the Palestinian village, despite never having lived in one.

The experience of recent years has improved my perception of the utility of a Palestinian identity. Seeing a junta regime, reminiscent of the infamous banana republics of Central America, this time, however, in Palestinian garb and minted by the very powers that disposed my forefathers, has come to *refine* the Palestinian in me; a refinement that has helped me see an Israeli oppressor as brutal as a Palestinian one.

At the end of the day, in a twist of fate, being Palestinian in diaspora has helped me transcend narrow and choking nationalism, and helped me achieve, or I should say with a modest tone, thrive with an identity that is dependent and reflective of the measure of justice of its surroundings. Of course, there are many who don't experience injustice first-hand but feel it powerfully. In all honesty, I cannot claim to be one of those privileged, spiritual and extraordinary people. For this, I have an enormous privilege, and for this I can only be thankful to every dispossessed Palestinian, every Palestinian child who was robbed of his innocence and every woman who died infinite deaths waiting for the freedom of her jailed son, for connecting me with the strongest human emotions possible and for sensitising me to human suffering in its deepest forms.

Aftim Saba

Aftim A. Saba is a US-based physician who is currently attempting to write his memoir. He was born in Benghazi, Libya to Palestinian parents. His father is from Lydda and was expelled in 1948. His mother was born in Ramallah.

No Paradise to Recreate

Different diasporas have bestowed on Palestinians certain distinctions, much like the diverse soils and environments impart their 'terroir' qualities to plants and their products. Obviously the loss of Palestine, including its great disruption to Palestinian society, was the starting point of this transformation which has been characterised by unceasing injustice. Being Palestinian has been and continues to be very burdensome, intrusive and a perpetually indignant existence. The distractions from life's hopes, aspirations and everyday joys are frequent. Periodically some serious escalation of aggression hits Palestine or the region, demanding still more attention, rumination and sadness.

I am part of a large minority of Palestinians not born or living under Israel's occupation or in the different refugee camps. I escaped the typical experience of destruction, poverty, jails, physical and psychological trauma, hopelessness and imminent deaths. As Palestinians living in Arab countries, Libya in our case, we were constantly reminded of our exceptional vulnerability to losing our 'privileged' existence. The fear of imprisonment, or expulsion from our homes, classrooms and businesses was ever present and real. In such environments meekness and lying low was *de rigueur*. Every Palestinian lucky enough to be able to travel has unpleasant stories about Arab airports and borders. A friend, born in Yarmuk refugee camp near Damascus, won the 'green card lottery' in 1980 to emigrate to the USA. Feeling sentimental, he wished to visit what he described as the 'great Arab city' of Cairo before leaving the Middle East for good. He was interrogated, subjected to untold insults and ridiculed for attempting, as a Palestinian, to visit Egypt and was not let in. Before putting him on a plane out, the officials confiscated a manuscript he had written over a period of six years and threw it in the wastebasket of the interrogation room. His pleas to give him back his life's work were mocked. He had no other copy and never wrote again. I still mourn his loss.

Witnessing first-hand how Arab populations grappled with and failed in their nation-building projects and instead laid the ground for variants on the police state, encouraged Palestinians to dream how their future nation will be different. My youthful belief was that the 'Palestinian' would emerge out of these crippled nation-building attempts wiser, smarter, democratic and secular – all reasons for Arab regimes and Israel to attack them.

My relationship to Palestine steadily transformed into a more intellectual one, where quests for universal justice and engagement with large ideas have taken precedent over debating the merits of petty 'biblical' rights, completely rejecting absolutist political dogmas, entrenched ideologies or religious discourses. I read Nietzsche and hoped that out of this Arab mess, the uber-Palestinian vanguard would emerge to transform the region, if only they had the opportunity and space. Vanessa Redgrave's and Jean Genet's love and admiration for the Palestinians and their liberation movement were further confirmation. Israel's all-out war on the Palestinians in the 1982 invasion of Lebanon destroyed this dream.

I joined my parents and siblings in California, where they had settled a few years before, in 1983. We were the last of our extended family to emigrate to the US. To be around family and the larger Palestinian community in a free country was revelatory. In the US I could engage, for the first time in my life, in voting and in freedom of speech activities, in sharp contrast to existing on the margins of society, as we had been forced to back in Arab lands. Paradoxically, given my dislike for expressions of nationalism, I began a quest to preserve our elders' memories of Palestine through videotaped interviews. I also began collecting old Palestinian textiles and every official family document with the name Palestine on it that I could lay my hands on. I got to observe my maternal uncle's Quixotian obsession to recreate his Palestinian garden in his little Californian ranch, complete with smuggled cuttings and rootstocks from what remains of Ramallah's orchards. His sense of the loss continued to be unalterable and tragic. I had no paradise to recreate, I am a diaspora kid, but wherever I settle I establish a respectable vegetable and fruit garden. After a recent move to Arizona, it has been a challenge as the terrain and weather are harsher and hotter, yet the savouring of a sweet fig in the cool summer morning is a joy no matter where the picking is.

For Palestinians, however, it is never that simple. I was aware that outside of Israel, the USA is the epicentre of a large anti-Palestinian movement with the explicit aim of implementing, supporting and protecting Israeli government goals. What I was not prepared for was to discover how pervasive the shockingly dishonest and simply mean anti-Palestinian discourse is in the media, academia and in Congress, a discourse that was far more extreme than in Israel. The power and reach of the pro-Israeli lobby exploited the naïveté of the Americans to keep them ignorant and in perpetual fear. It is a veritable 'struggle' to maintain and exercise the devotion, respect and love to a country while, at the same time, living and breathing this absurd situation on a daily basis. I am certainly not naïve about US imperial reach, but the disasters rendered on the Palestinian people specifically, and the rest of the Arab world especially, following the jingoistic and violent military response to the terror attacks of 2001 have been particularly gratuitous and inspired by a well-connected generation of neo-cons. We Americans of Palestinian roots have found ourselves exhausted, alienated and emotionally drained by the inexorable pro-Israeli political machine, controlling the discourse and the stenographers to power.

Had I ended up living in Western Europe it would have been different: less burdensome and far more exciting for me. My obsession with justice for Palestine would have been the same, I suspect, but the discourse would surely have been far more equitable, sophisticated, engaging and worldly.

When our children arrived, we decided early on that it would be good to protect them from Palestine. To prevent (or perhaps delay) the obsession, the incessant feeling of indignation and the endless burden. Simple things mattered. I wanted them to have friendships with other children for who these children are and not for what their parents think about the Palestine issue. Simple measures like these add up if they begin in early childhood, including actively shielding them from news on the Israel-Palestine conflict and the role played by the major Jewish American organisations. I 'protected' them from the histories of their grandparents and from my experience of 'being Palestinian'. We practised this at the risk of ridicule, accusations of self-hate and treason. But when, perhaps, they decide to discover their father's roots and Palestine, they will do it on their own terms and in their own time.

I wish I had had this chance as the world at large is so much richer and more interesting than constantly having to deal, from early childhood onwards, with the collective madness of a powerful and determined enemy.

Karl Sabbagh

Karl Sabbagh is a graduate of King's College, Cambridge, where he studied mathematics and natural sciences. He was a documentary producer and director for many years and is also a writer, with ten published non-fiction books, including Palestine: A Personal History, *describing his father's family's 300-year connection with the country.*

A Mission to Explain

As the son of a Palestinian father and an English mother I was presumably entitled to think of myself as a Palestinian from birth. But I was raised in England, and was a typical English schoolboy for much of my childhood, with only a strange and difficult-to-pronounce name to mark my exotic origins. In fact, I was christened 'Khalil' after my grandfather, but my mother and her family couldn't be expected to get their tongues round the letter 'kha' so I became Karl.

The transforming event – or the first of several – was when I was invited to stay with my father's family in Beirut when I was eighteen. They lived in a suburb of the city, and I spent six weeks staying with them, and became immersed in alien food, strange music and a foreign culture that – I was made to feel – was in some ways my own. It is strange today to realise that the conversations I had with my family about the *Nakba* concerned events that had happened to them only thirteen years beforehand. It was like discussing today the events of 2000, a mere moment away.

When I came back to England I devoured everything I could find about the events that led up to the dispossession of Palestine, including a book by Neville Barbour, called *Nisi Dominus*. It had been on my shelves for several years since I had been given it by Barbour, a friend of my father's, and it had looked so dry and academic that I had never opened it. Now I found it a powerful case against the takeover of Palestine by Zionists, written while the events were still happening and before the catastrophic outcome. It still bears rereading today.

The evidence of the effect these events had on me is in an article I wrote for *Varsity*, the Cambridge University newspaper, when I went to university eighteen months after my first visit to the Middle East. I had discovered in my conversations and reading that at the time Zionist Jews were arguing that they should be given Palestine as their so-called 'National Home', the population was more than 90 per cent Arab. This seemed so astonishing then, and astonishes many people now, that I made it the centrepiece of my article.

For the first of many times in my writing life I discovered that such things should not be said in public. A student friend of mine who later became a Hollywood movie director stormed into my office at the newspaper brandishing the article and denying everything I had written and accusing me – of course – of anti-Semitism. He was Jewish.

A sixteenth-century English author and diplomat, Henry Wotton, described an ambassador as someone who is 'sent to lie abroad for his country'. This is actually a clever play on words, since 'to lie' meant to live or stay somewhere, as well as to tell lies. Nowadays, the double meaning is often missed, but there is one country whose ambassadors and advocates largely fit both senses of the Wotton description – Israel. Palestinians have become inured to the daily torrent of 'lying abroad' from Israel and its politicians about the history and politics of Palestine, designed not just to put Israel in a good light – that is a perfectly honourable task for a diplomat – but to put Israel in a *false* light, conveying an impression of a nation whose claims to Palestine are entirely legitimate, but who are now attacked physically and verbally by people who have no rights to the land.

This betrayal of truth by a powerful state against a powerless people has led me to take pride in my genetic heritage. This is more than merely *support* for the Palestinians. Anyone can be pro-Palestinian, and thank goodness many uncommitted people are. But in addition I take comfort from knowing that I am *a member* of that national group.

It would be wrong to suggest that it is the vilification and denial of their rights that has given Palestinians a sense of identity (although it seems to me that a factor in the maintenance of *Jewish* identity over the years has been persecution and anti-Semitism). There has been a Palestinian national identity for hundreds of years. For example, the Israeli academic Haim Gerber, in *Remembering and Imagining Palestine*, describes a fifteenth-century text by Mujir al-Din al-Hanbali al-Ulaymi which 'is notable for its extensive use of the term "Palestine"'. Gerber goes on, 'The simple fact is that Mujir al-Din calls the country he lives in Palestine (*Filastin*), a term he repeats 22 times.' This contrasts with the frequent Zionist claim that no Palestinian identity could be traced until after the advent of Zionism.

And that national identity is for me a strong reinforcer of *personal* identity. I am proud to belong to a family whose line can be traced back at least 250 years in Palestine. And this is not unusual. Every Palestinian family knows the villages and towns from which its ancestors came, and usually keeps in a drawer a hand-drawn document showing who begat whom over the last seven or eight generations. By contrast, most modern Israelis *can't* trace any connection with Palestine earlier than the arrival of Jews from Europe during or after the Mandate, a couple of generations, and the ones who can, the indigenous Palestinian Jews, are often horrified at the transformation of Palestine caused by the mass immigrations in the first half of the twentieth century.

The clincher for me was when I started going to Israel and Palestine in the 1980s. I remember my first trip, arriving in the early morning at Ben Gurion Airport, renting a car and driving to Jerusalem. As the sun rose, I saw the twinkling lights of Arab towns and villages embedded in the beautiful Palestinian landscape, and as the modern Hebrew motorway signs flashed past I had an almost visceral sense of the injustice embodied in that contrast of ancient and modern. These Palestinians are *my* people, I thought, and I have felt that way ever since.

Najla Said

Najla Said is an actress and writer. As an actress, she has performed Off-Broadway, regionally and internationally, as well as in film and television. In April 2010 she completed an eight-week sold-out Off-Broadway run of her solo show, Palestine. *That same year she was named one of 'Forty Feminists Under Forty' by The Feminist Press. Her memoir,* Looking for Palestine: Growing Up Confused in an Arab American Family, *was published in August 2013. She is a* magna cum laude *graduate of Princeton University. She studied acting in New York.*

A Heavy, Unwieldy Bag

Being Palestinian is complicated.
'Complicated' is the word my therapist, my friends and my mother use to describe me most often, or, more precisely, to explain why I am thirty-nine and unmarried, or why I may not have gotten a particular acting job, or why I got in an argument with someone about something and am possibly seething.

If I try to come up with a metaphor for what it is really like to be Palestinian, or perhaps I should say 'what it is like to be Palestinian in New York City', all I can think of is carrying a really heavy, entirely unwieldy bag. Of groceries, perhaps. Or rocks, maybe.

I think it is a pretty clear metaphor already, but I will elucidate just in case.

So, imagine you have to carry a lot of heavy things from point A to point B, like, as I said, a couple of bags of groceries. Not just a simple day's worth of groceries (a box of cereal, a loaf of bread and a banana), but rather, a large and varied selection of heavy, precariously packaged items (more along the lines of fourteen glass bottles filled with fizzy water, two watermelons, eighteen oranges and five gallons of milk. And some eggs. And two jars of peanut butter – glass jars, I mean).

You already see where I am going with this, yes?

Well then, now you have an idea of what I am trying to say, because that is exactly what it is like to be Palestinian. Especially in America. Especially, especially in New York City, where I have lived my entire life.

You have to carry these bags, and you have no help. But you think if you balance the weight in each hand equally, and you pay particular attention to your posture and alignment, and you walk carefully and precisely, you will be able to get to your point B with some effort, but ultimate success.

And then you start walking. And the bags feel heavier than you thought they would. So you try to reorganise the way you're carrying them, but you have to be careful of the eggs, and the clanking bottles, and your own back. You consider a different hand position, and you try carrying the bags around your shoulders like a purse, but the plastic handles are small and they make your shoulders feel like they're suffocating, and you become convinced that they will break and the groceries will go flying all over the place. So you put the bags down. And breathe.

You remember, suddenly, that you have a pair of gloves with you. You are certain they will help. But then you can only find one of them. And suddenly the five blocks you have to walk seem like five thousand. And you feel a lump in your throat and just want to give up, but you can't. So you take your time, and you adjust, and you stop, and you reorganise, and rebalance and struggle, and you finally make it home.

But you are frustrated and sad and you hate everyone else on the street for having a tiny purse with nothing in it and you wonder what you did to deserve having to carry all this crap.

And then you realise you didn't do anything wrong. You did nothing to deserve it. You're just in an uncomfortable circumstance, and you can't do anything about it.

In real life, these bags manifest as circumstances you have lived through a few too many times. Circumstances like the fear that gripped you every time you were invited to a Bar Mitzvah in junior high school because you were certain that once you got to the synagogue you wouldn't be let in, or you would be told that there had been a mistake, and you weren't actually invited. Or later, when you realise that to almost everyone who is not Palestinian, the definition of a Palestinian is 'a person who hates Jews', and you have to tell every Jewish person you meet that you don't hate them. Because no matter what, they will ask if you do. Before you've even been properly introduced. Even though you hate no one and just desperately want people to like you.

And if you meet a Jewish man who is romantically interested in you, you have to patiently wait out the inevitable 'What would my parents say?!' monologue after your first kiss, and smile sweetly and laugh with them at the circumstance, which they most certainly do not realise is a circumstance you have been in many times before.

Then there are the political arguments, in which you have to breathe through the comments about terrorism and 'those savage people'. Granted, those comments are always followed by 'but not YOU. You're different.' But you know that is coming before it happens. And yet, each time it punches you in the gut, like someone's steel-toed boot kicking and knocking the wind out of you. You have to breathe through that too, and silently pray that the rage you feel boiling in your stomach will not reveal itself by forcing the top of your head to blow off and bang into the ceiling.

But there are good moments, too, and funny, ironic, story-worthy circumstances sometimes. Like when the old lady sitting next to you at your Jewish friend's wedding asks if you are 'Jenny's friend from Jerusalem', and you say 'Yes, actually, I am', knowing full well that I am not who she meant.

And then there is the mezuzah[1] left outside the door of your apartment by earlier tenants. The one you decide to remove, since you are not Jewish. Until you wonder if your neighbours might think you 'anti-Semitic' for doing so, since you're Palestinian. But then, you get your giggles, when six months later Lubavitchers[2] come knocking on your door because of it, and you say to them, 'Oh hi! Yes, I know I have a mezuzah but I am Palestinian! But I didn't remove it because I didn't want anyone to think I hated Jews! Isn't that funny?', and they look at you like you have seventeen heads and take off immediately while you roll on the floor for hours.

Mostly, though, it is when you realise that you know exactly what it is like to be marginalised, left out, disregarded and forgotten, and that you can empathise with pretty much anyone's struggle, that you remember it is really kind of not so bad to be Palestinian. There really is nothing more powerful than the true goose bump-ly feeling of solidarity, of humanity, of love, of empathy, of pure connection.

And so, in the end, I guess being Palestinian might actually be worth its cumbersome, unwieldy, often torturous, weight.

Sometimes.

Notes

1. A wooden case affixed to the doorway of a building containing parchment inscribed with passages from the Torah.
2. Members of an international Hasidic Jewish Movement.

Mohammad Sakhnini

Mohammad Sakhnini is a PhD student in the English Department at the University of Exeter, UK. He is interested in English and comparative literature, and has published articles in academic journals (The Arab World Geographer, Settler Colonial Studies). *Recently he began contributing to the media (*openDemocracy, Your Middle East and The Outpost) *on rethinking the history of the Levant.*

Lost to Geography

What is it like to be Palestinian?

As a diasporic Palestinian, I find it difficult to define my Palestinian identity in the context of geography. How is it that I am Palestinian and yet I have never been to Palestine? I have always trained my mind to accommodate an uneasy relationship between recalling the actual geography of the land and creating an imaginary construct with which one can live as a Palestinian without necessarily seeing or visiting the land.

Since I was a child, I have been performing my Palestinian identity within the context of ideas. Palestine here is not a land, mountain, desert, valley or sea. It is an idea. When I was growing up in Damascus, my parents would always remind me and my siblings that we are Palestinians, that we were driven away from our land, and that we have a lot to do to regain our rights. One thing I was constantly pushed to do was to prove to my schoolmates that a Palestinian is a top student in class. To be Palestinian, my family believed, meant to seek academic achievements.

At university a new understanding of my Palestinian identity emerged. My Palestinian friends were mostly socialists and communists. They believed that to prove one is Palestinian, one has to disregard paternalistic values. There was a joke on campus, which carried a lot of truth in it, that to be Palestinian is to be atheist. This is why it was important for me to smoke and eat in public while most of the people around me were fasting during Ramadan.

I still retained these old nuances when I came to England in 2009. I met many Palestinian students at the university where I studied, but I found their identity as Palestinians different to mine. A number of these friends were born in the West Bank, Gaza or held Israeli passports. They knew the geography of the land. I did not. They spoke Palestinian Arabic. I spoke the Syrian dialect, as they reckoned. Yet there are many common ideas and memories which nearly all Palestinians retain; we were all agreed about this. Still, we conducted all this in Britain, a place which is not only far from Palestine but also a place in which we were all students – or gatherers of ideas.

While living in Britain, I found that my previous conception of what it meant to be Palestinian needed careful management. Before going to Britain, I couldn't escape its history, as the country to which Balfour belonged and its responsibility for handing Palestine over to the Zionists. I still see it in this way, but I was, and still am, fascinated with the kind of support and sympathy the Palestine cause gets from the British people. I spoke to many activists. Many of them expressed guilt about the historical mistakes, as they said, their governments had made. But many also supported the cause of Palestine from a purely humanist perspective. Here I reconceived what it means to be Palestinian: to be a victim of human injustice, not a partisan of nationalist, Arabist or Islamist slogans. Again, regardless of the route I take to define my Palestinian identity, I cannot escape the power of ideas. To tie myself to the geography of the land is something I cannot do.

When the refugee camp where I was born, Yarmouk, recently became targeted by armed militias in Syria, a new aspect of my Palestinian identity emerged. For me, Palestine no longer constitutes the land where my father was born: the green meadows of the Galilee. Rather, I recalled the story of Palestine from my memories of the ordered narrow alleys of the camp, the place which no longer exists. The lost camp is Palestine for me. It is a world of memories which recalls a geography lost to ideas: the UNRWA (United Nations Relief and Works Agency) school, the narrow streets named after our villages in Palestine, the pictures and graffiti which invite the smiles of Palestinian leaders who rarely visit our refugee camp. There is no place called Palestine for me to recall.

I am now living in Britain, and my family live in Syria, the West Bank, Lebanon, Jordan, Nazareth (Israel), Qatar, Belgium and Sweden. I wonder how it is possible to have an affiliation, both direct and indirect, with these different places and still claim to be Palestinian. But living in these different places, with a strong sense of identity, is precisely what it means to be Palestinian. It is not about a geographical spot. It is about establishing highways of feelings, nostalgia and emotions between the global and the local, between the world and Palestine.

Saliba Sarsar

Saliba Sarsar is a professor of political science and Associate Vice President for Global Initiatives at Monmouth University, New Jersey. He specialises in Palestinian–Israeli relations. His most recent edited book, Palestine and the Quest for Peace, *was published in 2009. In 2013, he received ATFP's Award of Academic Excellence.*

Transcending Blind Allegiance

To belong, to be fully in place, is a fundamental human need. Often taken for granted, this need is not as readily fulfilled by those who seek to fit in without restructuring their identity or personality. This has been the life of many who live in the diaspora, including my own.

I have been in the United States since 1974. Although living far from my birthplace sometimes generates feelings of emptiness and guilt, I am strongly connected to my family and friends in Palestine, to my culture and city, with occasional visits to enliven my being, my soul.

Born on the eastern side of Jerusalem in the mid-1950s, I was raised in Palestinian Christian and Muslim cultures and, after the June 1967 war, in Palestinian and Israeli Jewish cultures. Living between cultures in a conflict-ridden environment, while frequently confusing and tough, enabled me to appreciate difference and find common ground between Palestinians and Israelis and among Christians, Muslims and Jews.

This experience served me well as I pursued my university education in the United States. Being away gave me distance from the ups and downs of daily life in Jerusalem and the Occupied Territories, and the space to engage in deep reflection, but whatever transpired back home impacted me profoundly, of course. Like millions of Palestinians and others, I remain challenged, practically and psychologically, by the nature of Palestinian–Israeli relations.

My multicultural and interfaith backgrounds and my specialisation in Middle East studies have given me innumerable opportunities to comment on Arab, Palestinian and Palestinian–Israeli matters. I often feel that I am put in the position of not only defining reality, but also correcting bias, ignorance and stereotyping, on the one hand, and of defending truth while promoting peace and justice, on the other.

Some people meeting me for the first time say: 'You must be from Lebanon?' Although I do not have a Lebanese accent, it seems that people have a fixed idea about what it means to be Lebanese, or 'modern'. Finding instead that I am from Jerusalem, a smile comes to their faces, while asking: 'Our relative X lives in Tel Aviv. Do you know him?' When I do not respond fast enough, they continue with some disappointment: 'Oh, you must be Palestinian! A Muslim? A Christian?' And so the quiz becomes a lesson in history and national identity.

Whenever a crisis occurs anywhere around the Middle East, even if a few hundred miles from Jerusalem, empathetic questions start: 'How is your family?', 'How are your friends?', 'Are they in harm's way?' While very much appreciated, such questions usually show little understanding of basic facts in the Middle East, and Palestinian–Israeli relations in particular.

Whenever a crisis occurs in Jerusalem or its environs, the comments about Palestinians and Muslims consistently become less favourable. Only a handful of people recognise the existence of Palestinian Christians in the Holy Land, as if Jesus was born in Bethlehem, Pennsylvania! The statements are rarely unfavourable to Israel, whether justified or unreasonable, and, if they are, are usually made by someone who possesses anti-Israeli or pro-Arab sentiments, including some Jews who believe that Israel's military occupation of Palestinian lands is both illegal and sinful. However, the idea should not be to find blame or to score points for one side or the other but to transcend blind allegiance when the truth is being sacrificed on the altar of expediency.

When the dastardly acts of 9/11 took place, it is shameful that some in the Middle East celebrated in the streets. Many in the United States and elsewhere rushed to pass judgement on all Muslims and Arabs. Even though I was among the first to speak out against the perpetrators, I was told, 'You know we care about you, please watch your back.' The concern was because of the fear of reprisals by those angered by the 9/11 events.

My need to set the record straight, my steady commitment to humanising politics and my thoughts of home have set me on a personal and professional journey in support of dialogue and peace. This includes researching and teaching on Palestinian–Israeli relations, and speaking at private gatherings and public fora. The question of Palestine tends to find its way into most of my conversations and presentations at various gatherings. The message from the heart is loud and clear: the suffering of innocent civilians on both sides of the Palestinian–Israeli divide and the loss of hope and opportunities for a peaceful resolution and social justice are unacceptable. However, while listeners receive the messenger, few hear the message. It seems that fear of the other, of the unknown, of change, have imprisoned people in a circular trap of claims and counter-claims, convincing or otherwise, with no exit in sight.

What I have learnt in the diaspora is that principle and pragmatism must be balanced in a realistic assessment of what is desirable and what is possible: moderation and compromise are essential for achieving peace. These values await strong voices in Palestine, Israel and elsewhere. Palestinians and Israelis must not fail in their journey. Their children, my children, deserve a better future.

My journey continues . . .

Suha Shakkour

Suha Shakkour is a senior lecturer in human geography at the University of the West of England. She received her BA and MA from the University of Western Ontario and her PhD from the University of St Andrews. She lives in London.

Still a Palestinian

I grew up in Jerusalem, the second of six children, and I lived what I perceived, even then, to be a double life. I went to an American school where I learnt to speak English with a slightly Southern accent, and I could recite the names of the American presidents, all the states and their capitals. Meanwhile, at home, I learnt Arabic, Palestinian history and geography, how to bake bread and make *labaneh*. I spoke English with my siblings, Arabic with my parents, and a mixture of the two with my friends. The double life I lived came naturally and did not seem unusual to me. In fact, even now, recalling my childhood, I consider my memories to be remarkably similar to those of my non-Palestinian friends – though the details differ somewhat. For example, I remember having an assortment of pets: cats and dogs of course, but also chicks from the Old City, ducklings from my aunts and tortoises that had wandered into the garden. I remember picnics and musical afternoons, which turned into musical evenings, with a *kamanja*, *durbakeh* and *oud* played by my uncles and cousins. I remember 'camping', not in the woods, but on rooftops under the stars and grapevines, with my grandmother singing us lullabies and telling us stories.

Later, when I was a teenager, we moved to Canada. Before leaving Jerusalem I was simultaneously excited and apprehensive. Part of me was curious about the 'American life' I had learnt about in school and seen in films and television shows, but the other half worried that I would feel left out. I imagined snowy mountains, rows of trees lining every street, and friendly policemen. And to a certain extent, when we moved, it was as I had expected. It was snowy and beautiful, and in the autumn the leaves really did change colour. I made friends and I was happy, but I missed many things from Jerusalem. While in Canada we had access to everything we could have wanted and we could go wherever we pleased without having to pass through checkpoints, though there were few opportunities to 'be Palestinian'. We still had Palestinian food at home, but the rest of our lives were very much 'Canadian'. In fact, it would be safe to say that for a few years I forgot the double life I had carefully, if subconsciously, cultivated in Jerusalem. I spoke English at home, English at school and English with friends, adjusting my accent so that it matched theirs. In short, I felt that I could 'belong' in Canada's multiculturalism.

It was not until the last year of my undergraduate studies that I began, in a way, to recall and reassert my Palestinian identity. Under the supervision of a sympathetic professor, I explored ideas of home and belonging in my writing and, as a result, in my everyday life. It was, however, only when I moved to Scotland to pursue my PhD that I made my first Palestinian friend since leaving Jerusalem. Together we introduced Palestinian customs and traditions to our friends, taking turns to host 'Palestinian evenings', complete with food, music and stories. In so doing, we created a space in which we could learn to be Scottish and British, while retaining our Palestinian identities. Most importantly, it was in Scotland that I, perhaps for the first time, understood what it was to be a Palestinian in exile. On my frequent trips back to Canada, I would ask my mother to teach me Palestinian folk embroidery. My first piece was a wedding gift for my sister, a tradition that had unfortunately been abandoned by my family some years ago. I also collected all of my mother's recipes, finally measuring the 'handfuls' of flour and rice and 'pinches' of cumin and nutmeg we had all had trouble deciphering.

Today, I work in academia and live in London where, through no effort of my own, it has become 'fashionable' to be Palestinian. I am at once overwhelmed by the solidarity for the Palestinian cause, and wary of becoming too settled. It is, after all, easy to allow oneself to become absorbed into another identity, and the heightened need for acceptance and belonging in exile perhaps makes Palestinians more vulnerable to this. For me, therefore, to be Palestinian is to be able to manage the acquisition of new identities in such a way that other identities are not compromised in the process. More importantly, however, it is being able to accept and even embrace in fellow Palestinians not only our common attachment to Palestine, but also the ways in which our Palestinian-ness has been shaped by our own newly acquired identities.

Abbas Shiblak

Abbas Shiblak is an author and human rights activist. He read law and sociology at the University of Cairo (Egypt) and Kingston University (UK). He worked at the Palestinian Research Centre in Beirut and was Director of the Department of Palestinian Affairs in the League of Arab States. He has been a lecturer at the University of Constantine in Algeria and a visiting fellow at the American University of Cairo (AUC). He is currently a research associate at the Department of International Development, University of Oxford. He has written extensively on issues of forced migration, displacement, statelessness and diaspora.

Homing Instincts

The images I recall of the city where I was born, Haifa, are unclear; I was too young at the time to retain vivid memories. My recollections are a mixture of a small child's hazy first-hand observations. But unlike the obscure nature of many of my memories of that period, our departure remains deeply ingrained in my mind. I remember the day I was bundled into a small black car, together with my parents, two sisters and one of my brothers. The car was an old black Ford, a classic similar to those in 1930s and '40s films. We carried few possessions, but they were enough to fill every nook and cranny of the vehicle. Among those possessions was a Singer sewing machine, which my mother continued to use for several years thereafter, as well as an *oud*, which my parents were very attached to. My mother would often sing the Arabic song so popular at the time, '*Marmar Zamani*', a love song that reflected the bittersweet time of two lovers.

Unlike our extended family and the majority of Haifa's inhabitants who found themselves exiled in neighbouring Lebanon after the city fell into the hands of Zionist militias in April 1948, my parents headed to the West Bank city of Nablus, to which they had a long-standing attachment. They had thought their absence from Haifa would be temporary; they were subsequently proved wrong. Like all Palestinian refugees, my family lost their

home, their citizenship, their way of life and everything they owned. They
became exiled and alien, both in their own country and in their countries of
refuge. For them, as the late Palestinian poet Mahmoud Darwish describes,
'The external world is exile and the internal world is exile.'

I came to the UK early in 1975 to study and work as a freelance journalist
to finance my studies. It was my British passport and my work on issues of
forced migration at the University of Oxford that made it possible for me to
travel to Palestine in 1994. It was a visit charged with emotion and anticipa-
tion. My friend, the late novelist Emile Habibi, was my guide in my birth
city of Haifa where I visited my family's house in Hadara Carmel and those
of relatives in Wadi al Saleeb and Wadi al Nisnas. The houses are made of
stone and surrounded by a number of trees, but they had been left in a state
of neglect and dilapidation. Some were totally or partially destroyed on the
pretext of developing the city and building new roads. Our home was still
in relatively good condition. It is a three-storey building in lower Hadara
Carmel overlooking the bay, and consists of six flats, some of which were
still being rented out to Jewish families. I felt the building still ringing with
the sounds of the day-to-day life and activities of my family members from
the stories I had heard.

Sarah, an old Jewish lady who lived alone on the ground floor, was the
only resident left who knew my family. Emile spoke to her in Hebrew when
she opened the door. She drew a deep breath in surprise and then welcomed
us in. I immediately felt familiar with the place, and the smell of the furniture that had belonged to my parents once, as Sarah told me. Sarah, who
is a Romanian immigrant, behaved as a typical Haifan woman would. She
prepared Arabic coffee and talked continuously in Haifan Arabic dialect,
remembering the old days when she lived under the same roof as my parents.
I listened avidly to her every word. She said, 'This furniture is your parents'. I
took it out of the top flat to take good care of it. It's yours if you wish to take
it . . . Strangers came to inhabit the building after your family left. I don't get
along with them and have little to do with them.' I took some snapshots with
Sarah, who kept insisting that I stay longer.

My father died without being able to see Haifa again and my mother had
refused to travel with me. She said, 'I am frail and might not survive the shock
of seeing strange people taking over our house.' My mother joined my sister
and I to live with us in Britain after having lost three homes in three different
countries, moving involuntarily from one Arab country to another. Time had

stood still for my mother and, like many of her generation, she carried her native Haifa within her wherever she went. Whenever we went to the seaside, she would gaze out with sadness and say, 'No sea is as beautiful as that of Haifa.' My mother passed away in 2007 in Oxford, and I followed her wish to write on her stone the distance between Oxford and Haifa, along with a quote from Darwish: 'I am from there and I have memories.'

While travelling in Palestine, whenever I passed through a city or a village I would recall dear friends in exile, some of whom have passed away, and some of whom are still alive. These exiles have been prevented from seeing their homes and families for decades. Photographs on their walls speak of the dear ones on the other side of the border who cannot be embraced. The human stories created by the diaspora have yet to be told in full by Palestinians.

For the Palestinian exile, the image of the lost homeland is not framed by romantic notions of the past but rather a deep sense of dispossession, fragmentation and marginalisation. Exile for me is what Edward Said once described as 'the unhealable rift forced between a human and a native place . . . its essential sadness can never be surmounted'. Having lived most of my life in exile, I am beginning to feel like a member of a 'floating community', which reminds me of a Palestinian folk tale my mother used to tell me about a 'green bird' in flight that is never able to land in its nest. According to the tale, the 'green bird' is the spirit of a man who was killed by betrayal.

This situation, however, has led me to share common and universal values with friends of various origins and backgrounds. Palestine remains for me a fundamental term of reference that goes well beyond the confines of the land. Palestine represents justice, liberation and the rights of outcasts, the oppressed, refugees, the stateless and the marginalised. Being Palestinian shapes one's life. It means being centred on the cause, or at least linked to it. It is the lens through which I see the world and a paradigm of the morality of individuals and states alike.

Ghadir Siyam

Ghadir Siyam was born in Jerusalem. She has a bachelor's degree in industrial engineering, and is currently a PhD student at Cambridge University. She dedicates her studies and work towards improving the education and training system in Palestine.

Born(e) in the Heart

Palestinian identity has for decades not only been mislaid, but stolen. Beyond that, the common history, culture, language and struggle have created a Palestine with no geographic boundaries. This land is now born(e) within the hearts of Palestinians, many of whom have never lived in Palestine, but will still tell stories and give directions to streets lost on the new maps of history.

Being Palestinian has shaped my life in many ways. I was born in Jerusalem in 1986, and at that time Ramallah, my hometown, was only a couple of minutes' drive away. The few kilometres between Ramallah and Jerusalem were 'renovated' in the late 2000s by the wall that has cut through Palestinian land, dividing families and prohibiting many people, like myself, from ever touching the soil of their homeland. Being Palestinian goes beyond this continuous political struggle. Having lived in a number of countries, such as Canada and the UK, it is the past that I did not live, and the future that I hope to live. My identity has been shaped by the summer vacations I have spent in Palestine, the stories shared by my grandparents, parents, uncles and aunts, and my upbringing.

My summer vacations were spent in the narrow streets of Ramallah. The four-month summer passed like a day or two. At first, an important aspect of my identity was fear – the fear of losing my home and family, just like my classmates in the summer school. The fear has only grown with the checkpoints, invasions and rising death toll. In the summer of 1992, my mother, older sister and I were trapped in a glass toy store with the sounds of bullets ricocheting off the walls, and tear gas filling the air. The shots came in violent pulses, and the silence between us was dead quiet. There were a dozen people in the store, also families, mostly women and children. The men – their husbands and fathers – were the last to come in, having cleared the streets of innocents before ensuring their own safety. I thought we would never make it through alive, and the fact that my mother could not protect us was as unbearable for us as it was for her. A few years later, in 2001, my life was redefined when my cousin, at twenty-five years old, was killed by an Israeli soldier while he was driving to bring medicine for his wife who was pregnant with their first child. Not long afterwards my family saw the funeral of my twenty-three year-old cousin, killed just a few weeks before his wedding. What moved me most were my aunts – the mothers – who stood proud, strong and with patience. This loss has engrained a deeper dimension into our identity and struggle.

Being Palestinian for me is the stories of my grandmother, aunts, uncles and friends. These stories take me back to the dramatic events of the *Nakba* in 1948, the *Naksa* in 1967 and the Palestinian refugee camps. They also take me back to my aunt's wedding, with her traditional red Palestinian dress waiting for the groom to arrive by horse; my grandfather's land filled with olive and fig trees; the family trips to Jaffa and Nazareth years ago; the warm tea after every meal and the family gatherings that one should not miss. I learnt that family, generosity, simplicity, neighbourhood and sharing happiness and sorrow are at the heart of our identity.

My upbringing has played an essential role in forming my Palestinian identity. My father, born and raised in a village in Ramallah, had to leave Palestine in the late '70s because of the war that enslaved his life. My mother's family are refugees of 1948, and later refugees of 1967. In 1967, they lived in a school in Ramallah until they, with the help of neighbours, built their new homes in the West Bank. There was never stability in our lives, we were always moving from one country to the other. However, my parents, through the traditional Palestinian handicrafts and pictures that cover every corner of our 'home', delicious authentic food and storytelling, poetry and singing nights, have indeed made our home a piece of Palestine. My grandmother, who used to spend most of the year at our home in Jordan, used to always wear the beautiful Palestinian traditional dress (*thoub*). I never understood why she was attached to it until after she died, when I realised that the *thoub* was her passport and identity; the way in which the older generation witnessing war would face the world in strong silence, yet saying 'Palestinians DO exist and always WILL'. The *thoub* made her feel secure, honoured and strong. For me, she was Palestine.

Although Palestinians are scattered in countries all over the world, they share one thing: Palestinian identity. So what is it? It is very simple! Palestinian identity is a cocktail which combines a strong belief in our right to live in our land in dignity, with our right to our religion and culture.

Linda Tabar

Linda Tabar is a postdoctoral fellow at the Women and Gender Studies Institute at the University of Toronto. She holds a PhD from the School of Oriental and African Studies (SOAS), University of London. She is currently working on a book titled Palestine and Memories of Dispossession: Native Encounters with Modernity and Imaginaries of Liberation. *Her writings on memory, colonial violence, anti-colonial nationalist agency and the disciplinary power of the aid industry have appeared in various journals and edited volumes.*

Bodily Wounds and the Journey Home

Being Palestinian is a raced, gendered and classed location of enforced 'absence'. My first memories of being a Palestinian child in the diaspora – in a settler colony called Canada, which was built on stolen indigenous land – are of non-recognition. As an Arab girl with dark hair and hair on her arms I was picked on and marked off from the others. I was persistently asked, 'Where are you from?' (meaning 'You're not from here'). Responses varied from misidentification: 'Oh you're from Pakistan?' to outright racism and contempt: 'You're a terrorist', 'You dirty Arabs'. Structures imprint themselves on the minute details of our lives. These encounters were not random. They reflect both the race and class structures within this North American settler society, and the way Zionist settler colonial efforts to distort, and make us invisible and unrecognisable as humans, follow us wherever we go.

For me, being Palestinian is about encountering and resisting the violence of Zionism's ongoing efforts to render us absent in our presence – disappearing natives – whether in *Falastin* or in the diaspora. As a child, you begin to understand that as a Palestinian you are not allowed to discuss what happened to your parents. You are expected to celebrate and legitimise the dispossession of your people, as millions of Palestinian refugees are in camps waiting to return home. You are absent in Western consciousness, and you are expected to remain so.

I grew up listening to soul, R&B, reading about Malcolm X, Black Panthers, Audre Lorde, Angela Davis and the struggles of indigenous people on whose land we are allowed to live. They are heroes for so many of us, and it is from them we learnt to make the connections between overlapping systems of oppression.

Making these connections began at an early age. One of my first memories was of the pain in my mother's eyes as we sat in an airport for hours, my parents interrogated and humiliated by a European Jew because they refused to believe that *Falastin* belonged to these white people. That memory and my father's silence – the things he couldn't say – filled me with a sense that something was wrong, something unspeakable had happened.

When I was twelve years old one of my father's books, by Palestinian historian Sami Hadawi, explained everything my father couldn't say – the role of British imperialism, the Zionist mass expulsions of close to one million Palestinians – in words a twelve-year-old could understand. But it was my grandfather's memories that allowed me to see beyond the repression and the silence of the outside world and learn about *Falastin*. His stories were precious threads that linked me to the details of his life and our history. Like so many of his generation, his memories centred on life before the *Nakba,* the refinery where he worked in Haifa, how it was targeted for resistance and how this resulted in him, like so many others, being forced out of his home. Then the anguish and the silence that engulfed so many.

Yet, being a Palestinian woman would not always be as nurturing as the moments when my grandfather shared his memories with me. I watched my mother working from dawn to cook for her family, then going out to work all day, before coming back home to start the cycle again: mending, cleaning, lovingly telling us everything would be alright. Tired and worn hands, trying to make everything right. How much could one person do? How much could one Palestinian woman's strong back bear?

At university, we Palestinian women, like other women of colour, affirmed that liberation would not be defined in terms of patriarchal colonial ideologies of control; freedom was not dominating women's bodies and lives. Palestinian women's voices were so articulate and often the most defiant in these circles and in demos, yet their rage was not allowed. Anger was reserved for white people and settlers, whether here or in *Falastin,* reserved for the daily violence they enact over our bodies to confirm their domination.

Growing up I became intimately acquainted with another form of violence, one which permeates working-class communities of colour. I was a young child the first time my father broke his back when he was at work moving heavy boxes. Then came the ravages of neoliberalism: greed, forcing people out of work, creating a general state of insecurity, poverty and crushing small businesses. My father became more and more sick, first his heart, then his back again, his spine grew weaker and weaker, crushed under all this weight. A security state, a racist police force and legal system, predatory capitalism and a health care system that gives you the run around and doesn't see people as human. These are the things we encountered as working-class immigrants. We witnessed the devastating nature of this violence. When there is nowhere left for this violence to imprint itself on the outer surface of the body, it turns inward, the violence seeps into the body. It doesn't stop. I think about my grandfather, who slowly lost his sight, and then after my grandmother died, lost his mind. He is still sitting in his house listening to Abdul Wahhab (a famous Egyptian singer), probably wondering if he is home yet. And my own mother, more and more confused, remembering less and less. How many more times will I be able to look into her face and see recognition in her eyes? I think about Malcolm X's own mother, who lost her mind. What greater violence than not knowing whether the next time you call out 'Momma' your mother will recognise you or not? Mahmoud Darwish once wrote, 'Sometimes they arrest you while you are committing a dream.' Sometimes your dreams become as small as the hope that those you love the most will survive, their bodies intact. Will the Zionist settlers who are living in stolen Palestinian homes ever understand the dismemberment they brought on Palestinian lives?

Being a Palestinian means intimately understanding the patriarchal, settler colonial, capitalist and racist forces that trample and repress our lives. Being a Palestinian also means insisting that every native Palestinian's wounded body will go home. In the meantime, it is to fight to make home together – Palestinians and all peoples who resist these oppressive systems – in the ways we recognise, embrace one another, resist and define our future beyond these forces.

Simine Tepper

Simine Bahhage Tepper lives in Boulder, Colorado, with her husband, their two college-age sons and her mother. She holds a BSc degree in mathematics and a MSc in computer science. She was a programmer and project manager for twenty years for three hi-tech companies.

Holding Palestine Close to my Heart

Diaspora. Identity. What do these words mean to me, a person whose circumstances dictated leaving my homeland due to colonisation and occupation? Pondering these words, I am conscious that coming from two Iranian families who emigrated to Haifa, Palestine a few generations prior, I had a different experience growing up than my Arab Palestinian friends whose families were there for centuries, or millennia, and who had made Palestine into the vibrant, beautiful and peaceful country that it was prior to the *Nakba* of 1948.

I left Palestine decades ago to pursue my college studies. The Israeli occupation authorities had slowly strangled my father's business. With no means of income, my parents – with six children to feed and educate – had little choice but to emigrate 'temporarily'. Eventually, I made my way to the US to pursue my graduate studies, and the 'temporary' became permanent.

Being Palestinian in the diaspora, and specifically in the US, is at once a wonderful feeling and sometimes an uneasy one. Wonderful because of the freedom from foreign occupation, from strip-searches, curfews and checkpoints, but also because of the ability to live with dignity, hope and the freedom to plan and pursue one's future. It has afforded me a life of normalcy that I cherish daily. My experience in my adopted country has been a hugely positive one. Americans are welcoming, warm and kind, and I feel that I am part of a loving community.

Living in the diaspora also has its low moments. It can be tinged with sadness. I, and the Palestinians I know, remain acutely aware of the hardships of the people we left behind. We hunger to hear their daily travails, combing through alternative media and communicating with friends and family abroad through social media. Our sense of the daily injustices committed against them is ever present. It spurs us to write articles, talk to people we know and work with human rights organisations to try to correct the barrage of propaganda about our culture, stemming from the orientalist lens of the media.

On the other hand, we also realise that we share a lot with other minority groups that have suffered misconceptions, and oftentimes huge injustices. The degree to which our narrative is actively and vigorously suppressed is extremely demoralising. As the great Palestinian Edward Said wrote, we have no 'permission to narrate'.

The knowledge of our rich history, our civil society, the harmonious and easy living among all religions in the Holy Land – our homeland – prior to its colonisation, its poets, writers, comedians, scientists, doctors, educators, farmers: all give us an anchor from which to protect ourselves from the negative stereotypes that seem to define us in our adopted homeland.

Being Palestinian in the diaspora has its comical moments too. Initially, people I met did not understand where I came from. When I said 'Palestine', they heard 'Pakistan'. When I explained that I grew up on the outskirts of Jerusalem (Shuʻfat) and went to college in Bethlehem, I would immediately be asked whether I spoke Hebrew, which rankled and angered me, because up until 1967 I had not heard a single word of Hebrew, a foreign language that came into our homeland with the occupation. The language of the land was Arabic and had been for centuries.

With time, and as some light started to shine on the real situation in Palestine, the perceptions of some of my fellow US citizens have changed. But over the thirty-plus years I've lived here the narrative has been frustratingly slow to penetrate the psyche of the country. And how could it, when left-wing, centrist and right-wing news outlets are peppered with special-interest pro-Israeli columnists, who hide behind their US citizenship to promote a foreign country's agenda?

As much as I feel integrated and assimilated in America, I wonder when my culture won't be denigrated and I'll be free from receiving, now and again, articles from loving friends with good intentions that applaud 'enlightened' Arabs, Muslims and Middle-Easterners, without understanding that the message they are sending me is that those enlightened ones are the minority from my culture. For Americans, an 'enlightened' Arab is always a Westernised one.

Being Palestinian is having a connection to a precious land and a scattered people that cannot be forgotten. It is understanding the universality of human beings and the humanity in all beings and all cultures. It is yearning to live in a harmonious society. It is loving worldwide food cultures and taking pride in the world's love for the native foods of Palestine and the greater Middle East, though these foods are often misappropriated by Israel. It is the memories of eating street foods such as hot peanuts served in a paper funnel, of hummus and falafel in pita, or *knafeh* and *mtabbaq* made by the famous Zalatimo in the Old City, Jerusalem.

Being Palestinian in the diaspora is yearning for the carefree walks from my home in Shu'fat to the Old City through Damascus Gate, along the cobblestones and ducking into little shops, being proud of the beautiful hand-blown glass art from Al-Khalil (Hebron), and of the hand-made and hand-painted Palestinian pottery.

It is being nostalgic for good times spent with friends of all backgrounds and religions, like our Armenian, Greek and Palestinian Christian and Muslim neighbours who were more like family to us. It is having memories of the smell of jasmine in neighbourhood gardens, the hybrid roses that my father cultivated, the beautiful spring and summer evening breezes in our garden while our fathers played backgammon, our mothers knitted and talked, and we children played, climbing olive and fig trees and jumping over neighbours' fences.

Being Palestinian in the diaspora is having wonderful memories indeed.

Omar Tesdell

Omar Imseeh Tesdell teaches at Birzeit University in Palestine. His academic work explores the relations between environmental problems and sovereignty in the Middle East. He completed his PhD in the Department of Geography, Environment, and Society at the University of Minnesota in 2013.

When All is Not What it Seems

'*Al-isim?*' ('Your name?'), the question is posed. The tickle in my throat arrives.

'Omar,' I say. With a flick of the wrist, my given name, which is common, composed from the root *'ain-waw-ya*, flashes on to paper. '*Wa al 'aylah?*' ('*And the family?*'). It's at this point that I carefully enunciate 'Tess-dal' as hear-able as possible in Arabic. The scribe's hand freezes. No attempt is made to write it down.

'*Esh?*' ('*What?*').

'Really?' I think to myself. I pronounced the name carefully, custom fit for processing by Arabic-speaker ears. My voice raises slightly with irritation: 'Just work with me, I will spell it out for you.' I walk the scribe individually through each syllable: 'T-S-D-L'. It's at this point that the person does one of two things; they either move on with other questions, or, pausing to corroborate my facial features and facility with Arabic with the name I have given them, take it up a notch.

'*Min wayn al-akh?*' ('*Where are you from?*').

Ah yes, the despised question posed to immigrants and in-betweeners the world over. Before, I used to answer such questions with an earnestness any American Midwesterner would appreciate. 'My father is from this place, my mother is from that place and I am their son . . .' and so on. This usually provided for a probing conversation with a stranger whose curiosity had clearly been piqued.

I think the reader can see that I grew to dread these claustrophobic conversations. It was not until watching my more adept sibling handle similar situations that I learnt a few tricks: '*Qissa tawilah*,' I began to answer playfully in my definitively urban Arabic dialect, '*fi gheyr as'ilah?*' ('It's a long story. Do you have other questions?').

Granted, such interactions are produced by innocent curiosity or by an unsurprising Palestinian predilection for family geography. But if we Palestinians have finally come to understand *Shatat*/diaspora as a state of being, in addition to a location, then it does not require a stretch of the imagination to understand that same state of being as multivalent and not predetermined.

My own particular multivalence is tinged with rural life. My upbringing in the rural United States is connected to my academic work on land and environmental issues in Arab countries. Within urban imaginaries both rural America and rural Arabia engender foreboding images of social conservatism. Without a doubt I have experienced this conservatism in both areas.

But rural spaces are not always what they seem. I learnt this on a visit to a town in the West Bank known for maintaining so-called 'traditional' methods of vegetable and small grains farming. Village life in Palestine holds a special place in the Palestinian national narrative as the ostensible repository of the timeless Palestinian link to the land. Think olive trees in a bucolic terraced landscape. Think peasants threshing wheat at the *baydar*, the community threshing ground. These images may have come to mind, especially as I arrived to talk with Um Ahmad. I had been referred to her because she was known in the area for her novel forms of organic and *baladi* farming. Enter timeless peasant Palestinian woman character.

'It is good to finally meet you, Omar,' she said assertively. Absent were the usual formalities and probing questions about where I came from. When we started off walking towards the field she chided me for being late and promptly lit a cigarette. I knew the day of work was off to a good start.

I asked her how long she had been growing wheat this way, something sadly uncommon nowadays in Palestine. 'Since I got back to the *blaad*, my son,' Um Ahmad replied. Thinking she had recently come home from a trip to Jordan, I asked how long she had been gone. 'Oh, I got back from Brazil about fifteen years ago,' she replied nonchalantly. Taken aback, I asked if she had gone to see children who had emigrated there, per a more common scenario.

'No,' she said, 'I lived nearly all my life in Brazil.' It turns out Um Ahmad had married a cousin at a young age and moved back with him to Brazil because nearly all of their extended family was there. In fact, nearly everyone in the village has relatives in Brazil. She was the third generation of her family who had lived in Brazil and established businesses there. Um Ahmad's children were born and raised there. She came back to the village in Palestine where she was born on her Brazilian passport. She stayed 'because she missed the village'. Right, I thought, so she must have learnt about organic farming in Brazil. 'No,' she said, 'I had to learn to farm as an adult. We were in the textile business like most of the other Palestinians there.' Becoming a bit surprised, she asked, 'Are we here to talk about farming?' Embarrassed at my series of presumptive questions, I moved on. It wasn't until my arrival back home that day that I realised Um Ahmad and I never traded probing questions about family pedigree. What accounted for this refreshing absence?

Could this most Palestinian of Palestinian figures, the peasant-farmer, offer a unique view into the hybridity of Palestinian-ness? Some may argue that acknowledging such hybridity dilutes the oneness of the Palestinian cause. However, talking that day with Um Ahmad revealed something quite different. Rather than revealing a weakness, the conversation showed how ordinary Palestinians derive strength precisely by refusing fixed categories of Palestinian-ness. In other words, it was exactly the uneven-ness of our multiple Palestinian selves that gave force and meaning to the complex whole.

This point is not lost on Mahmoud Darwish. In his haunting elegiac conversation with Edward Said, Darwish wrote, '*La u'arrifu nafsi liala udayi'ha*' ('I do not define myself so that I do not lose myself'). Increasingly, I think he may have been on to something.

Lena Khalaf Tuffaha

Lena Khalaf Tuffaha is a Palestinian-American poet born in Seattle to a family from Bethany, Palestine. She first learnt about the beauty and power of language from her beloved grandfather, the late poet Husni Fariz. Her writings have been published in online and print journals in the United States, Egypt and Turkey. She lives with her family in Redmond, Washington.

The Weight of Our Blessings

The experience of being Palestinian-American is one I came to gradually, in adulthood. I grew up in the Arab world and only became aware of my hyphenated self when we moved back to the US midway through high school. I think the experience is best compared to a cup of Turkish coffee: bittersweet, rich and sometimes dark. I carry the images of my homeland with me, and my profound and unwavering love of the land and her people shape so much of the way I see the world. I relish the instant community that Palestinians find with one another, the way we become one another's homeland in exile. That's the sweetness.

The other side of the coin is a form of recurrent survivor's guilt. I often imagine a line of people applying for visas to study abroad in the United States on a summer day in 1967. My father was one of the lucky ones who made it to the US shortly after the war. But I wonder about the others in that visa line. I wonder about the ones who weren't able to become US citizens like he did. Were the people in line that day among the refugees of the 1948 war or the 1967 war? Who among them got married and had families, like my father, whose children survived?

When I was old enough to learn to ride my bicycle, Palestinian children my age in Sabra and the Shatila were massacred. When I was getting ready to graduate from high school, Palestinian teenagers in the West Bank were graduating from the jails of the Israeli occupation during the First Intifada, many of them surviving savage torture and abuse. When I got married and we bought our first home in the United States, land in my father's village in Bethany was confiscated and Palestinian homes in Jerusalem were being demolished to make way for Israeli settlements. The only thing separating me from this life is my passport.

I am thankful for this knowledge, because it frames all of my experiences and reminds me that the barriers we put up between ourselves and others are largely illusory. Papers and borders and other 'official' designations sometimes cloud the truth: we are all human beings on the same journey, together.

In the year 2000 my husband and I were blessed with the birth of our first child. That same month the Second Intifada began and since then hundreds of Palestinian children have been killed in the West Bank and Gaza. Today we are the very lucky parents of three girls. The experience of becoming a mother is transformative, and mine is made even more so by the ongoing events in my homeland. This poem grapples with the fragility and promise of life as I experience it.

After Birth

For my girls

On 29 September 2000, nineteen days after my first daughter was born, the Second Intifada began. Since then, thousands of Palestinians have been killed.

> In thin light of early morning
> we lean into one another
> your tiny head under my chin,
> pink fingers clutching my thumb,
> your heart beating furiously against mine.
>
> I awake to the intoxicating fragrance of your new life.
> No words ever learnt prepare me for the magic of this scent,
> no summer jasmine so strong, no rose so captivating.
> Pristine, delicate as bird's first flight
> spring flower at the moment of blossoming.
>
> Dull pain of the home you made inside of me lingers.
> Heady mix of joy and fear pulsing through my veins
> startling me out of much needed sleep.

At night, while I nursed you, I watched
the little boy in Gaza
crouch behind his helpless father in the rain of bullets.
Sure as the raindrops find their way into the earth
bullets found their way into his skin,
tearing a path through his limbs,
to his heart,
taking his young life.
His father's head rolled to the side
their frames shrank even more
against the wall.

His father would live.
I can't decide which was worse,
sight of the child killed in cold blood
or the wounded father
pleading,
his body not bulletproof.

Watching with you
I am ashamed of this world.
Your father and I readied it as best we could –
the room painted, the crib assembled,
clothes washed, linens pressed.
I took my vitamins, went to check-ups regularly,
sang to you, spoke to you,
we loved one another
and embraced the world
but this world is a frail and shattered place.

What will the father tell the mother
of the little boy in Gaza
who died in terror against the wall?
What can he say to the woman who grew those precious limbs
that heart
inside of her for months?
Can a wound so deep ever heal?

I cling to the dull ache
receding day by day.
I summon the magnificent force that brought you
outside of me
and into the world.
The moment before when I couldn't bear it
and the moment after when I did,
when I came to life with you,
your heart beating furiously against mine.

I want to promise always to shelter you,
be bulletproof against hatred.
Instead, I keep the now dull ache, the miracle of your life
aflame in my memory, in the face of each death.
I wear it as a shield against hatred,
wrap my finger around yours
and walk with you.

Nadia Yaqub

Nadia Yaqub (PhD, Near Eastern Studies, University of California, Berkeley) is associate professor of Arabic language and culture at the University of North Carolina, Chapel Hill. She is the author of Pens, Swords, and the Springs of Art: the Oral Poetry Dueling of Palestinians in the Galilee *(2006) and numerous articles on Arab and Palestinian literature and film. She is currently writing a book on Palestinian cinema.*

A Sometime Palestinian

It has been some time now since I have told anyone that I am Palestinian. I am frequently asked about my background, especially when travelling in the Arab world. 'My father is Palestinian,' I usually answer. Depending on the circumstances I might add, 'And my mother is American.'

Why this hesitation to claim a Palestinian identity for myself? In part it arises from my not having lived any of the quintessential Palestinian experiences. Historically, being Palestinian has meant an intimate association with loss. A Palestinian is someone who had been dispossessed, who lives as a minority in her own land, under foreign military occupation, as a refugee, or at the very least in involuntary exile. I have not shared these experiences. Born in the United States, I grew up in the relative security of the American expatriate community in Beirut, Lebanon. Since 1976 I have made my home in the United States. My children were born and raised here. I own a home here. I vote here, and I have always travelled on a US passport.

My own distance from Palestinian loss was made tangible to me during a conference on popular culture I attended in Morocco in 2007 where I presented a paper on Palestinian film. My Moroccan colleagues were very kind, but I quickly became uncomfortable with the reverence with which I was treated whenever my Palestinian roots were mentioned. Eyes would soften with concern as these scholars fervently expressed their distress over the suffering Palestinians had endured and admiration for their steadfast resistance to occupation and violence. During breaks between academic sessions, colleagues clustered around me to be photographed with 'the Palestinian woman'. While I appreciated these attempts to connect with me through expressions of political solidarity, I felt like a fraud, for I, personally, had not shared in the experiences that gave rise to their sympathy and respect.

But, truth to tell, there are many Palestinians like me. We are comfortable economically. We tend to be well-educated, often multilingual and cosmopolitan. Many of us live between the West and the Arab world, and there is considerable fluidity and variation in the degree to which we have one foot in each world. We may feel Palestinian in some circumstances, but American, European or Jordanian in others. Most importantly, we enjoy full citizenship in another country, a status that allows us to choose just how 'Palestinian' we want to be. One might call us 'sometime Palestinians'.

It is that element of choice that, paradoxically, both protects me from the quintessential Palestinian experiences of loss and dispossession and allows me to engage critically and productively with the idea of Palestinian identity. Even if I were to move to a refugee camp or Palestinian town under occupation, my background, citizenship and personal connections would render my experiences there fundamentally different from those of Palestinians whose circumstances deny them similar choices. I would always have the option of leaving, of resuming in one form or another the privileged life I enjoy now. At the same time, choice offers me the luxury of defining for myself what being a Palestinian will be. The fact that 'Palestinian' blood runs through my veins is an accident of birth – if my parents had been Bosnian, Eritrean or Guatemalan I may well have engaged with a different set of contemporary political struggles. However, that I am not *personally* constrained by the injustices that have created and sustained the Palestinian question allows me to think deeply and radically about what being Palestinian can mean. Being Palestinian can be both greater and smaller than a national or ethnic identity. It can encompass an intellectual and cultural between-ness that inoculates me against being unthinkingly American. At the same time, its association with a particular history of injustice at the hands of an exclusionary ethno-religious nationalist movement helps me to look at history and the contemporary world in human, rather than national, terms. Ironically then, for me, being Palestinian is not about belonging to a community. It is not about sharing a language or a set of customs and beliefs. It is not about a shared history, but about striving to divorce communal bonds, beautiful and necessary though they may be, from individual rights and politics.

What does this mean for my relationship with a broader community of Palestinians, both those living in the difficult conditions usually associated with the Palestinian experience, and those, like me, who have been granted other options? It means that while I do not often feel that I belong to a Palestinian community, I nonetheless care deeply about Palestinian history and current events, avidly follow Palestinian literature, art and film, and dream of a future in which being Palestinian is no longer synonymous with dispossession and struggle.

Munther Younes

Munther Younes is Reis Senior Lecturer in Arabic Language and Linguistics and Director of the Arabic Program at Cornell University. He earned a BA in English from the University of Jordan in 1974 and a PhD in linguistics from the University of Texas at Austin in 1982.

Entry Denied

When I meet my fellow Arabs at professional conferences or in taxicabs in New York City, we talk about life in America, our families, our work and the corruption and incompetence of the Arab governments which forced us into exile. Then we go our separate ways.

When I meet my fellow Palestinians, we ask one another about our hometowns and villages and we criticise the corruption of one side of the Palestinian leadership and the extremism of the other and lament the absence of a third reasonable alternative. Then we move on to the conflict with Israel, sit down and start talking. We talk about the last time we were allowed into our homes, the next time we will be allowed to see our families, the theft of our water by Israeli settlers, the curfews, the checkpoints, the siege, the latest Israeli assault and the next one.

It is no exaggeration to say that discussing any aspect of Palestinian life in modern times without reference to Israel may be impossible. How many Palestinians have not been killed, injured, imprisoned, dispossessed, humiliated, forbidden to travel, forced into exile, or some combination of these as a result of the creation of the State of Israel or as a result of Israel's actions? None. Every Palestinian has been touched by the *Nakba* of 1948 or its aftermath. The *Nakba* meant no less than the destruction of a whole society, which has ever since been denied the opportunity to rebuild itself. The lives of its victims are dominated by its consequences and their worldview has largely been shaped by it.

Although I have not been directly affected by Israel's violence (no one in my immediate family has been killed by Israeli bullets), not a single day of my life passes without some reminder of the destruction of my society and the resulting loss of the country I would have called my own. In my early childhood, we were not allowed to graze our scrawny cows on the hills north of the village because the border with Israel cut through them, and we would risk being shot. Most people of my father's generation were reduced to sub-sistence farming in dry, rocky plots of land or to smuggling cheap goods to Israeli Arabs at the risk of losing their lives, while many left their families and sought work far from home.

1967 saw the loss of the rest of Palestine and direct Israeli control of all of it. Now not only was our movement to the north of the village restricted; it became restricted in all directions. The occupier decreed that our freedom of movement could only be obtained outside our homeland. While I was not made a refugee by force, like hundreds of thousands of my fellow country-men, I became a refugee by choice. I chose to live in exile rather than under military occupation with its violence, humiliation and overall inhumanity.

I left the West Bank in 1970 to go to college. The Israeli occupation authori-ties issued me a permit with the condition that I could not go back before six months had passed, but if I stayed outside the West Bank for over a year I would lose my residency rights. When I returned in the summer of 1971 all representatives of the occupation – the soldiers, customs officers, intelligence agents – made it clear that I was not welcome in my homeland. The long lines, multiple searches, humiliations, long hours of interrogation and simply the looks and the language of the occupiers all conveyed the message.

The same message was conveyed to me thirty-seven years later when I tried to return to my village.

Having obtained American citizenship, I assumed I would fly into Tel Aviv and be driven to my village forty miles away. When I arrived at Ben Gurion Airport after an eighteen-hour trip I was told that since I was legally still a resident of the West Bank, I could only enter through the King Hussein Bridge between Jordan and Israel. I had the option of flying to Jordan or going back to the United States. I did not want to fly to Jordan so I chose to return to the United States.

The next Continental flight back to Newark Liberty Airport was scheduled to depart in thirteen hours. I told the young policewoman accompanying me and watching my every move that I would like to wait at the airport. She said that I would be taken to a building where I would be able to take a shower and have lunch. So I was driven in a minivan to a decrepit building far from the airport, told to surrender my belongings and shoved into a room with seven men who appeared to be from African and South Asian countries. The door was locked from the outside. When I protested that I was an American citizen, the guard answered sarcastically, 'So you think you are special, huh?' I was told that I had to wait until my plane departed in the evening, but I could ask to be let out once every three hours to smoke a cigarette. I never left the room because I did not smoke.

As the time of my flight back approached, I got nervous that they would forget about me. But half an hour before departure time, a policeman came into the room and told me to get ready. I was given back my belongings, except my passport, and shoved into the back seat of a minivan. A sour-looking woman with a pistol at her side sat in front of me and kept talking to the driver and swearing at Arabs in a very angry tone. As the minivan moved in the dark alleys on the way to the airport, I felt like I could die at any moment. That woman, who seemed to hate Arabs, could have easily shot me with her pistol and claimed that I had provoked her. As at checkpoints, or in any situation where the occupied meets the occupier face-to-face, the mere existence of a Palestinian can provoke many Israelis. No one would have questioned that angry woman's right to defend herself, and I would have simply been another dead Palestinian.

Jameel Zayed

Jameel Zayed was born in Cardiff, Wales. He obtained his undergraduate degree and PhD in chemistry from the universities of Cardiff (2007) and Cambridge (2012), and he is currently a postdoctoral scientist in stem cell biology at Massachusetts Institute of Technology. As a student, he led the Middle East Society, and has written on international resource security.

Barricaded

What makes me Palestinian? Being born in Britain with mixed heritage, I was raised without Arabic and without a specific political or religious bias. So where did my identity come from? My experiences travelling to Palestine have forged a synthetic identity. In short, I am Palestinian because there is a need, in today's world, for Palestinian identity to be alive and resilient.

I have been travelling to Palestine to see my family since childhood. My family live in Kalandia refugee camp, which lies on the main road between Jerusalem and Ramallah and has, since the year 2000, seen the gradual growth of what is now referred to by the Israeli army as the 'Kalandia Terminal': an eight-metre-high concrete wall, a twelve-metre-high control tower and concrete barricades, along with remote-controlled metal turnstiles to control pedestrian passage. Upon arrival at Tel Aviv's Ben Gurion Airport, I am placed in a quarantine room with other Palestinians and other suspected 'security threats'. Here I wait for eight hours, without my luggage or passport, and with no access to food. I am taken for numerous interrogations, strip-frisks and baggage searches, met by condescending Israeli security personnel who act as if my very existence is an inconvenience. I have come to understand this as routine conduct, tolerable despite being a British citizen who only takes short trips to Palestine every few years. Such is the learnt helplessness associated with constant subjugation.

In September 2009, things changed when I was told after nine hours of waiting at Ben Gurion that I had been denied entry. Police then took me to a detention facility where I sat in a cell for another nine hours before being escorted on to a waiting flight to be taken back to the UK. After months of tussling with the arrogance of the Israeli embassy, who shrugged it off as nothing to do with them, I was informed that I was not permitted to enter Israel again until 2015. Banned for five years? For what reason was I denied the right to see my family and ageing grandparents? I still wait, with no legitimate explanation other than the standard 'security reasons'. In Israel, I am just another Palestinian. This is in stark contrast to my upbringing in the UK, where, growing up as a European-looking child, culturally integrated and with a pronounceable name, I never felt that I was any different to my peers.

So how do I perceive myself when I am in the UK? Am I different? On this note, I will tell another story that preceded the ordeal at Ben Gurion Airport, one that I remained silent about for a whole year. In September 2008, I was one year into my PhD at Cambridge. It was an early Tuesday morning when I received a heavy knock on the door of my dormitory room. Two plain-clothes police officers asked to be let in, and when they sat down relayed to me an accusation that I was involved in 'Islamic terrorism'. How does one respond to an accusation so completely out of the blue? I was not politically or religiously active at the time, and told them as such. It was forty minutes of me defending myself against a preposterous accusation, thrown at me without any evidence for the claim. In the end they left thanking me for my time, with no charge being made. Until now I do not know what prompted this visit, but I suspect it relates to the UK's surveillance of Muslim and Arab students across the UK. I came out about it only after the Ben Gurion incident, when I thought the two events might have been related . . . I will never know!

When I relayed these stories to an American colleague, he replied, 'Wow, these things don't happen to white people.' So am I just an average Briton? I fit mainly in three categories: Western, Arab and Muslim. So am I fully Western? In general, yes, but I am made to feel the baggage that comes with being a Muslim in post-9/11 Western society. I am clearly perceived by some officials somewhere as a potential terrorist threat. Of course, my relations with the Muslim and Arab world give me a bridge through which to see things from their side, a view that is not often accessible to everyone in the West. But I consider myself lucky to be able to enjoy political freedoms in the West, not enjoyed by many across the globe. I am free to develop and fulfil my aspirations. However, as an Arab Muslim I do not sit comfortably watching the news and the frankly racist propaganda that depicts Muslims and Arabs as terrorists, while the people of Palestine, Iraq and Afghanistan suffer under neo-imperialism.

A phrase I hear Palestinians use a lot is 'We the Palestinians'. Who are my 'we'? I use it in the context of 'we in the West', 'we the Muslims' and 'we the Palestinians/Arabs'. Language reflects a lot of the complex identity of the individual. I find myself both foreign and native at the same time. Is this uncomfortable? I don't think so. In fact, being part of the Palestinian diaspora enables me to traverse the cultural cage that many find themselves in.

I will remain Palestinian as long as resistance to Israeli occupation is required, but otherwise my yearning is to see a world full of world citizens where peace ensues.

Glossary

Assaf, Mohammed – the Palestinian winner of the second *Arab Idol* competition in 2013. Mohammed is from the Gaza Strip and was celebrated for his performance of classic Arab and Palestinian songs.

Awda (al) – 'the Return'. It is used to refer to the 'Right of Return' of Palestinian refugees to homes and lands that were destroyed or confiscated in 1948.

Balfour, Arthur – author of the Balfour Declaration (2 November 1917) on behalf of the British government, which promised a 'Jewish homeland in Palestine'.

bint el Shatat – a Palestinian woman who is born and grows up outside of Palestine.

Birzeit University – a leading university in Palestine. It is located in the town of Birzeit, close to Ramallah.

blaad (el) – 'the land'. It is used informally in different spellings by Palestinians to refer to the 'homeland'.

Black September – the Jordanian civil war, which began in September 1970 and ended in July 1971.

dabke – a ceremonial dance at weddings and other occasions, popular among Palestinians.

dakhel (al) – 'the inside'. It is used by Palestinians to refer to the lands lost to Israel in 1948.

Darwish, Mahmoud – celebrated Palestinian poet and activist who was born in 1941 and died in 2008. He published over thirty volumes of poetry and eight books, and is regarded by many as the 'voice of Palestine'.

defter – a tax and land register in the Ottoman Empire.

durbakeh – a small, portable hand drum.

Fairuz – a Lebanese singer born in 1934 who became well known in the late 1950s throughout the Arab world and whose songs remain popular today. Her full name is Nouhad Wadi' Haddad.

Falastin – Palestine.

fedayeen – members of Palestinian guerrilla organisations. Etymologically, the term means 'to sacrifice oneself for the homeland'.

fellahi – peasant.

First Intifada, the – an uprising by Palestinians against Israeli occupation that began in December 1987 and ended with the Madrid Conference in 1991.

Hadar – a central commercial neighbourhood in Haifa.

Handala – a boy depicted in the cartoons of Naji Salim al-Ali who stands witness to often tragic events and policies in Palestine, Israel and the wider Arab world. Handala is a symbol of Palestinian defiance and, outside of Palestine, a broader commitment to humanitarianism.

ithan – also spelt *adhān*. This is the call to prayer for Muslims.

jaha – a group of notable men.

jallab – a syrup made from carob, dates, grape molasses and rose water.

jiddo – grandfather.

Kalthoum, Oum – a famous Egyptian singer, songwriter and actress who was born between 1898 and 1904 and died in February 1975. She performed on stages across Europe and the Arab world from the 1920s to the early 1970s.

kamanja – a spike fiddle popular in Arab and Persian music.

keffiyeh – also known as a *hatta* scarf. It is a traditional chequered head-dress worn across the Arab world. Since the 1960s, the black-and-white *keffiyeh* scarf has become synonymous with Palestinian nationalism.

khalto – auntie (on the mother's side).

knafeh – cheese pastry soaked in a sweet syrup and associated with the Palestinian city of Nablus.

labaneh – water-strained yoghurt made into balls and preserved in olive oil.

malfouf – rolls of cabbage filled with ground meat and rice.

manna – food provided to the Israelites by God during their travels in the desert.

mansaf – lamb cooked in a fermented yoghurt sauce and served with rice.

maqloubeh, maklooba* or *makloubet – literally means 'upside down'. It is a dish made in one pot, with fried aubergine (*beitenjan*), rice and meat.

mi'raj – the ascension of Prophet Muhammad to heaven.

molokhiyeh – jute leaves cooked with meat and served with rice.

mtabbaq – folded dough filled with white cheese and drizzled with sugar syrup.

muezzin – the person responsible for reciting and leading the call to prayer.

mujaddara – a mix of fried onions, lentils and rice.

musakhan – roasted chicken baked with onions, sumac, allspice, saffron and fried pine nuts, and served with taboon bread (traditional Palestinian bread).

Nabulsi – items or people from the city of Nablus in the West Bank.

Nakba – 'Catastrophe'. It is used by Palestinians to refer to the conflict in 1948 which saw the defeat of the Palestinian and Arab armies and the creation of the State of Israel. The *Nakba* led to more than 750,000 Palestinians becoming refugees.

Naksa – 'Setback'. The Arab defeat in the Six-Day War in 1967.

oud – a pear-shaped lute.

Palestinian Liberation Organisation (PLO) – it was founded in 1964 and is recognised internationally as the representative of the Palestinian people. It was led by Yasser Arafat from 1969 until his death in 2004, and is currently led by Mahmoud Abbas.

Picot, Françoise Georges – a French diplomat who signed the Sykes–Picot Agreement.

qahwah – coffee or café.

Said, Edward – Palestinian-American intellectual who was born in Jerusalem, Palestine in 1935 and died in 2003. He was an influential literary theorist and public intellectual who is best known for his 1978 book *Orientalism*.

Second Intifada, the – a Palestinian uprising that began in September 2000 when the Prime Minister of Israel, Ariel Sharon, visited Haram Al-Sharif where the Dome of the Rock stands in Jerusalem. Its ending is unclear, but considered by some to conclude with the 2005 Sharm el-Sheikh Summit.

shammūtī – also known as 'Jaffa orange'. It refers to a particular type of orange that began to be cultivated widely in the Jaffa region in the mid-nineteenth century.

Shatat – literally means 'Dispersal'. It is used by Palestinians to refer to the state of being in exile from Palestine.

shawarma – meat on a spit which is rotated next to a grill and 'shaved' to be consumed.

sido – grandfather.

sous – a liquorice-flavoured drink.

sumac – a spice used in Palestinian cooking with chicken, fish, salad dressings and raw onion.

sumoud – 'steadfastness'. It has been used by Palestinians since the Six-Day War in 1967 to refer to keeping firm in the face of oppression and continuing to resist occupation.

sura – a chapter of the Quran.

Sykes, Sir Mark – British Conservative MP who signed the Sykes–Picot Agreement.

Sykes–Picot Agreement – a secret agreement in 1915–16 between the British and French governments outlining their spheres of influence in the Arab provinces of the Ottoman Empire should the Ottoman Empire be defeated in World War I.

tabbouleh – a fresh salad made from finely chopped parsley, tomato, mint and onion, and seasoned with olive oil, lemon juice and salt.

tablah – a goblet-shaped drum.

tatreez – traditional Palestinian women's cross-stitch embroidery.

teyta or ***tata*** – grandmother.

thob or ***thoub*** – a woman's ankle-length robe.

zaffeh – a wedding procession.

zaghareed – Palestinian women ululating, typically at wedding parties or celebratory national occasions.

zait – olive oil.

zajal – popular oral poetry.

za'tar – wild thyme.